Pope Francis

Pope Francis

*A Voice for Mercy, Justice, Love,
and Care for the Earth*

Edited by
Barbara E. Wall and Massimo Faggioli

ORBIS BOOKS
Maryknoll, New York 10545

Founded in 1970, Orbis Books endeavors to publish works that enlighten the mind, nourish the spirit, and challenge the conscience. The books published reflect the views of their authors and do not represent the official position of the Maryknoll Society. To learn more about Maryknoll and Orbis Books, please visit our website at www.maryknollsociety.org.

Versions of the following articles, which were published in the *Journal of Catholic Social Thought*, have been reprinted here with permission:
Eberl, Jason T. "A Bioethical Vision," 16, no. 2 (Summer 2019): 279–93.
Massaro, Thomas J., SJ. "'He Drinks from His Own Wells': The Jesuit Roots of the Ethical Teachings of Pope Francis," 15, no. 2 (Summer 2018): 353–73.
Mescher, Marcus. "Mercy: The Crux of Pope Francis's Moral Imagination," 16, no. 2 (Summer 2019): 253–77.
Ngolele, Christophère, SJ. "African Wisdom in Dialogue with *Laudato si'*: An Environmental Ethics Based on the Paradigm of Recognition and Sacred Care," 16, no. 1 (Winter 2019): 5–19.
Selak, Annie. "Missing Voices in *Amoris laetitia*: An Examination of Law, Narrative, and Possibilities for Inclusion in Roman Catholic Church Teaching," 16, no. 1 (Winter 2019): 83–102.
Sniegocki, John. "Alternative Economic Visions," 16, no. 2 (Summer 2019): 209–23.

Manufactured in the United States of America

Manuscript editing and typesetting by The HK Scriptorium, Inc.

Library of Congress Cataloging-in-Publication Data

Names: Wall, Barbara Eileen, 1943- editor.
Title: Pope Francis : a voice for mercy, justice, love, and care for the Earth / edited by Barbara E. Wall and Massimo Faggioli.
Description: Maryknoll : Orbis Books, 2019. | In April 2018, experts from around the world gathered at Villanova University for an unprecedented historical and theological analysis of Francis's papacy. This volume collects sixteen of the best talks from that conference. | Includes bibliographical references and index.
Identifiers: LCCN 2019020132 (print) | ISBN 9781626983496 (print)
Subjects: LCSH: Francis, Pope, 1936—Congresses,
Classification: LCC BX1378.7 .P654 2019 (print) | LCC BX1378.7 (ebook) | DDC 282.092—dc23
LC record available at https://lccn.loc.gov/2019020132
LC ebook record available at https://lccn.loc.gov/2019980998

In memory of our beloved families:
Christine and Thomas Wall, Joan Wall Fealy,
Otello and Milena Iacometti,
Gaetano and Nives Faggioli

Contents

Abbreviations

AG	*Ad gentes* (To the Nations). Vatican Council II, Decree on the Church's Missionary Activity, 1965.
AL	*Amoris laetitia* (The Joy of Love). Pope Francis, apostolic exhortation addressing the pastoral care of families, March 19, 2016, following the synods on the family held in 2014 and 2015.
CA	*Centesimus annus* (The Hundredth Year). Pope John Paul II, encyclical, 1991.
CST	Catholic Social Teaching (Catholic social thinking; Catholic social thought)
CV	*Caritas in veritate* (Charity in Truth). Pope Benedict XVI, social encyclical, June 29, 2009.
DH	*Dignitatis humanae* (On the Dignity of the Human Person). Vatican Council II, Declaration on Religious Freedom, 1965.
DV	*Dei verbum* (Word of God). Vatican Council II, Dogmatic Constitution on Divine Revelation, 1965.
EG	*Evangelii gaudium* (The Joy of the Gospel). Pope Francis, apostolic exhortation on church's mission of evangelization in the modern world, November 24, 2013.
EV	*Evangelium vitae* (The Gospel of Life). Pope John Paul II, encyclical, March 25, 1995.
FC	*Familiaris consortio* (The Fellowship of the Family). Pope John Paul II, postsynodal apostolic exhortation, November 22, 1981.
GE	*Gaudete et exsultate* (Rejoice and Be Glad). Pope Francis, apostolic exhortation on the universal call to holiness, April 9, 2018.
GS	*Gaudium et spes* (Joy and Hope). Vatican Council II, Pastoral Constitution on the Church in the Modern World, 1965.
LE	*Laborem exercens* (Through Work). Pope John Paul II, social encyclical, September 14, 1981.

LG   *Lumen gentium* (Light of the Nations). Vatican Council
          II, Dogmatic Constitution on the Church, 1964.
LS   *Laudato si'* (Praise Be to You). Pope Francis, encyclical
          on care for our common home, May 24, 2015.
MM   *Mater et magistra* (Mother and Teacher). Pope John
          XXIII, encyclical on Christianity and social progress,
          May 15, 1961.
MV   *Misericordiae vultus* (The Face of Mercy). Pope Francis,
          bull of indiction, April 11, 2015.
OA   *Octogesima adveniens* (The Eightieth Anniversary). Pope
          Paul VI, apostolic letter to Cardinal Maurice Roy, May
          14, 1971.
PP   *Populorum progressio* (The Development of Peoples).
          Pope Paul VI, encyclical, March 26, 1967.
PT   *Pacem in terris* (Peace on Earth). Pope John XXIII,
          encyclical, April 11, 1963.
RN   *Rerum novarum* (Of the New Things). Pope Leo XIII,
          social encyclical, May 15, 1891.
SC   *Sacrosanctum concilium* (Sacred Council). Vatican Coun-
          cil II, Constitution on the Sacred Liturgy, 1963.
Sp. Ex.   *Spiritual Exercises of St. Ignatius of Loyola*
SRS   *Sollicitudo rei socialis* (Social Concern). Pope John Paul
          II, encyclical, December 30, 1987.
UR   *Unitatis redintegratio* (Restoration of Unity). Vatican
          Council II, Decree on Ecumenism, 1964.

Introduction

Massimo Faggioli and Barbara E. Wall

Any discussion of a pope cannot be separated from the historical context in which the discussion takes place, especially when it happens during the pontificate of the pope being discussed. Therefore, to make clear the intent and the result of this book, we must locate the project in the time and place of its conception.

This book is the result of the efforts of a group of scholars who gathered at Villanova University, near Philadelphia, for the conference titled "Pope Francis, a Voice Crying Out in the World: Mercy, Justice, Love, and Care for the Earth" (April 13–15, 2018). The decision by Villanova's Office for Mission and Ministry and Institute for Catholic Social Thought to host an international scholarly conference on Pope Francis was made in the fall semester of 2016. In the chronology of Francis's pontificate, 2016 plays a significant role for several reasons, but two, in particular.

First, 2016 was the year of the publication of the postsynodal exhortation *Amoris laetitia* (dated March 19 but released April 8), which followed the synod of bishops that Francis called in October 2013 and that would have the unprecedented characteristic of being held in two different sessions (October 2014 and October 2015) on the same theme: "The Pastoral Challenges of the Family in the Context of Evangelization." The promulgation of *Amoris laetitia* was also the most important example of the reception of Francis's pontificate in the United States and in U.S. Catholicism—a reception that was shaped more by domestic ecclesiastical-political concerns for the consequences of that teaching than by the teaching itself in the context of the pontificate.

Therefore, both the conference held at Villanova in 2018 and this book must be viewed through the hermeneutical lens of the periodization of Francis's pontificate, with these pivotal synodal events.

Arguably, the 2014 and 2015 synods of bishops on family and marriage, as well as the publication and reception of *Amoris laetitia*, represent a key moment in Francis's pontificate. The postsynodal exhortation also cemented a particular relationship between the pontificate and the United States Conference of Catholic Bishops, which had signaled early on its refusal (despite notable exceptions of individual ordinaries and their local churches) to become a vehicle for the reception of this act of the papal magisterium. In particular, the need for a more theological study of Pope Francis's theology emerged around the reception of *Amoris laetitia*.

Second, behind Villanova's decision to hold the conference is the "political" impact of Francis's pontificate at the national and global levels. After the publication of *Amoris laetitia*, the pontificate entered a second period. It must be seen in the context of the accelerating disruption of the international order—from Brexit (June 2016) to the rise and the election of Donald Trump to the presidency of the United States (November 2016), to limit ourselves to the North Atlantic Hemisphere. In the fall of 2016, a little more than one year after the successful visit of Francis to the United States in September 2015, it became clear that his pontificate would navigate much more agitated waters.

The transatlantic relations between the Vatican and Washington were destined to inaugurate a new period, without historical precedent, in terms of tensions and oppositions between the teaching of the 266th bishop of Rome and the 45th president of the United States on a wide range of issues: from the environment to immigration; from the relations between religion and politics to the posture vis-à-vis global Islam. Between 2016 and 2018, therefore, Pope Francis represented a particular moment in the Catholic Church's effort to address the crisis of globalization, and his pontificate was perceived in the United States in the context of a new and unpredictable political season that was not without long-term religious, theological, and ecclesial consequences.

These two orders of reasons—the need for a deeper, intra-ecclesial look at the theology of Francis in the awareness of the attempts to characterize the pontificate in ideological and partisan terms, and the necessity to study Francis's call for a new engagement between the church and the world in a moment of disruption of globalization and of the international order—helped frame the focus of the conference and, therefore, of this book. Faithful to the Augustinian and Catholic identity of Villanova University, the conference was imagined as a contribution to the national and international discussions on the pontificate of the first non-European and non-Mediterranean pope in church history. But it was also a contribution to the Catholic mission of the university and to the life of the diocesan church in Philadelphia, the Catholic Church in the United States, and the Order of St. Augustine.

The chapters in this volume locate the pontificate of Pope Francis within the tradition of his predecessors and the retrieval of Vatican II in response to the major issues and crises of the world—a response grounded in the gospel and actions of Jesus Christ. The early chapters point to an ecclesiology of Pope Francis that, in the words of Cardinal Joseph Tobin, "is the Church emerging from a self-imposed ghetto, abandoning the fortress and entering the disarray of the world, driven by a divinely inspired solidarity with all of humanity and filled in its depths with empathy for the travails of every human being." Vatican II presented a church with a prophetic mission and the call to holiness through engagement with the world.

In "Reconciling Doctrine, Theology, Spirituality, and Pastorality," John O'Malley provides a firsthand glimpse of the energy of Vatican II in the history of the church. The word *pastoral* was used throughout the documents of the council. As O'Malley notes, Pope John XXIII set this new, pastoral tone when he "directed the fathers of the council to address the problems facing the church by 'making use of the medicine of mercy rather than severity . . . demonstrating the validity of the Church's teachings rather than by condemnations.'" Pope Francis, according to O'Malley, has retrieved the pastoral commitment of Vatican II and continues to renew this commitment in word and deed.

The Second Vatican Council provided the historical context for the pontificate of Pope Francis. Massimo Faggioli's "Pope Francis's Interpretation of Vatican II" stresses the "recovery of a Catholic universality that is free from Latin universalism and not about a cultural resistance to modernity and postmodernity." We also see in Pope Francis a retrieval of the emphasis on the poor and the "preferential option for the poor," which is consistent with Vatican II and the tradition of CST.

Francis has called the church to address the realities of forced migration and the rights of immigrants. In the words of Anna Rowlands, "The re-emergence of a pastoral ministry of the borderlands has been a crucial focus for the theo-political ministry of Francis."

Francis has been called the "pope of gestures." According to Cardinal Óscar Maradiaga, Pope Francis's life has always been rooted in the spirituality and popular religious devotions of the Argentinian church. In addition, Pope Francis is about spiritual reform, just as St. Francis was in the thirteenth century. According to Antonio Spadaro, "The pontificate of Francis is a pontificate of spiritual discernment. He is guiding the church through the *Spiritual Exercises*." There is also the thread of "Christian humanism" that, according to Thomas Massaro, emphasizes "the flexible open-endedness of 'finding God in all things,' and fervent dedication to the 'service of faith and the promotion of justice.'"

The primacy of mercy is central in the thought and actions of Pope Francis. Marcus Mescher refers to "Francis's pedagogy of mercy"— mercy that is essential for healing wounds and mediating justice. Austen Ivereigh takes up the issue of a "people-of-God" ecclesiology that incarnates mercy and calls for conversion in "our ways of praying, of managing power and money, of exercising authority, and how we relate to each other and to our world." Agbonkhianmeghe Orobator reflects on how Pope Francis is perceived in Africa. Francis's ecclesiology is not self-referential but an "outward-looking ecclesiology." He commends Pope Francis's leadership style, which calls people to action that transforms the Christian church into a church that pursues mercy, justice, love, and care for the earth.

Christophère Ngolele addresses the complexity of the ecological crisis and calls on the rich cultural traditions of many peoples, especially the African wisdom tradition. The latter stands as an appropriate partner to *Laudato si'* because it is, Ngolele says, "an environmental ethics that is based on recognition and sacred care." The paradigm shift that occurs in *Laudato si'* is consistent with the thinking of recent popes on ecological concerns, which evinces a turn from attitudes of dominion to a more receptive, open attitude to the sacredness and dignity of all creation.

In the chapter "The Concept of Nature from *Rerum novarum* to *Laudato si',*" Barbara Wall continues the process of locating *Laudato si'* within the tradition of CST and uses the principle of the common good as an operative principle for the transformation of humankind's relationship with creation and the continued growth and fruition of the common good.

Margaret Archer responds to Pope Francis's call to reach out and assist those in need of housing and hospitality. We find much inspiration and admiration in the decision to form a charity for resettlement of families, which, legally, socially, and culturally, had many hurdles to overcome. This chapter highlights the importance of what a community can do together to respond to Francis's call.

In a pontificate concerned with the lived experience of the people in all walks of life, in all cultures, and from the peripheries, such as people who are poor and without power, we might benefit from the inclusion of narratives from the lived experience of people who feel left out of the discourse. Annie Selak suggests that there are missing voices in *Amoris laetitia*, and that all could benefit from the "role of narrative and experience in American case law," which provides "an example of a system that straddles universal and particular demands, all while grounded in lived experience."

John Sniegocki provides an explanation of Pope Francis's views on possible economic alternatives that reflect the principles of CST.

Lastly, Jason Eberl emphasizes Pope Francis's impact on many crises in bioethics, stating, "Although we have emphasized the continuity of Pope Francis's bioethical teachings with his predecessors, he has advocated for and exemplified an apparent shift in the church's approach to bioethical issues, changing the tone from mere condemnation to an emphasis on mercy and joy."

There are several people we need to recognize for their support and help in bringing this project to completion. Archbishop Christophe Pierre, the apostolic nuncio to the United States, attended the conference held at Villanova and was an important part of the conversations. Father Peter Donohue, OSA, supported this event and assisted us with hospitality. Erin Buckley, Marcella Bray, Jared May, and Suzanne Wentzel helped in many ways to make everything possible. Father Arthur Purcaro, OSA, translated Cardinal Maradiaga's manuscript. We are also grateful for the fine editorial support provided by Jill O'Brien and Paul McMahon at Orbis Books, especially for their critical eyes and resourcefulness, which were much appreciated.

March 13, 2019
Sixth anniversary of the election of Pope Francis

I

Flight or Field Hospital?

Joseph W. Cardinal Tobin, CSsR

When Cardinal Jorge Bergoglio addressed the College of Cardinals on the eve of the conclave of 2013, he did not hide his anxiety for the church, nor did he deny the thorny issues that troubled the People of God. He did not see the answer as turning inward in self-examination or, worse, self-preservation. Shortly after the conclave, a Cuban Catholic magazine quoted the archbishop of Havana, Cardinal Jaime Ortega, as saying that, hours before his election, the future pope told his fellow cardinals that the church must turn away from self-absorption and "theological narcissism." Instead, Cardinal Bergoglio proposed an embrace of others and invited the church to focus its energies on the "peripheries," which we have come to understand as not only a geographic reference but also an allusion to those who feel marginalized or have been treated as peripheral—the poor, the damaged, and the unbelieving.

Hopefully, this modest contribution prepares the way for the following chapters by demonstrating that Pope Francis's call for engagement with the world—especially in its messiness—is rooted in the Second Vatican Council and featured in the pontificate of the immediate predecessors of our Holy Father, especially Pope St. John Paul II.

In the five years since his election, Francis has consistently invited the church to look outward. At the same time, however, calls have intensified for Christians to accept that this nation and much of the world are hostile to the gospel. As the trappings of a cultural veneer that formerly supported Christianity fall away, some declare that true disciples will necessarily be fewer in number and must withdraw from the world in order to witness effectively to the world.

Set aside for the moment the exhilarating vision of Francis and ask honestly: Do we need a smaller, purer church? In the last several decades, Catholics have joined other Christians in describing the church in the United States as suffering from large numbers of its members who are indifferent, unengaged, dissenting, and even hostile to orthodoxy and orthopraxis. These critics seem to suggest that we need to whittle down our numbers from the current seventy million to perhaps twenty million. Possibly, however, even that number will be excessive and would inevitably include some slackers. Therefore, we might have to narrow our expectation to an assembly of two million true believers. However, even that risks tolerating tepidity, so we ought to reduce our prognosis to two thousand, and then ultimately, to just you and me—and honestly, I am not very sure about you!

This call for a smaller, purer church could be an expression of the individualism that permeates our culture. In the history of the church—even from ancient times—there have been individuals and movements that have tried to define and delimit what it means to be a Catholic Christian. Nevertheless, the universal church has always repudiated such attempts. It is only the Lord who ultimately judges who belongs or does not belong. He does so with the patience of the farmer in the parable who allows the wheat and the weeds to grow together until the harvest (cf. Matt 13:24–30).

The other side of this individualism is the proposal that true Christians band together in small enclaves and establish ourselves almost like fortresses that will safeguard the treasure of Christian tradition in its purest form against the corrosive intrusion of a corrupt society. But ever since St. Paul's speech in the Areopagus, when he cited the poets of ancient Greece to persuade the Athenians of his message concerning the true God, Christians have engaged with the larger world— not always consistently, not always critically, sometimes opposed by higher authorities, sometimes by the sheer force of circumstances.

This engagement often produced surprising benefits for the church. During World War II, Roman Catholic priests and Protestant ministers in Europe frequently were imprisoned together in the same barracks. They could not help but talk with one another and learn more about their respective traditions. These conversations fostered a positive ecumenical climate after the war and contributed to greater openness on the part of the Catholic Church to the ecumenical movement. This was, of course, only one element in an incredible constellation of factors that led to the Second Vatican Council—a constellation so varied and yet so singular in its outcome of the calling of a council that we increasingly recognize it as the work of God.

The council compels us to reject any search for a purer, smaller church based on individualistic criteria or for constructing a citadel to keep out the world. At the very beginning of the Dogmatic Constitution on the Church, *Lumen gentium*, the bishops define the church as "a sign and instrument . . . of communion with God and of the unity of the human race."[1] The church has a responsibility for and a mission to the entire human race.

The church has much in common already with all baptized Christians, but also "those who have not yet accepted the Gospel are related to the people of God in various ways."[2] The church ignores no one. At the same time, the church is composed of sinful members; hence, the council frequently calls for a renewal of hearts and structures. In this sense, a purer church, yes; a smaller church, no. The way of the church is not condescension, but the humility that befits a pilgrim people.

Various documents of the council provide a foundation and guidelines for the church's relationships with other Christians and religions. However, the church's relationship to the larger world is affirmed dramatically by the decree *Ad gentes* on the Missionary Activity of the Church: "The Church on earth is by its very nature missionary since, according to the plan of the Father, it has its origin in the mission of the Son and the Holy Spirit."[3] The church has no other option but to turn outward.

This turning outward extends to the human condition in its heights and depths. *Gaudium et spes*, the Pastoral Constitution on the Church in the Modern World, begins with these stirring words:

> The joys and hopes, the grief and anguish of the people of our time, especially of those who are poor or afflicted, are the joys and hopes, the grief and anguish of the followers of Christ as well.[4]

This is the church emerging from a self-imposed ghetto, abandoning the fortress and entering the disarray of the world, driven by a divinely inspired solidarity with all of humanity and filled in its depths with empathy for the travails of every human being.

Gaudium et spes recognizes the achievements of the modern world but also its many ambiguities. The pastoral constitution seeks to contribute to the entire range of human effort and to the resolution of

---

1. *LG* 1.
2. *LG* 16.
3. *AG* 2.
4. *GS* 1.

the many challenges facing humanity. Underlying this is the church's belief "that through each of its members and its community as a whole it can help make the human family and its history still more human."[5] At the same time, the church "profits from the experience of past ages, from the progress of the sciences, and from the riches in various cultures, through which greater light is thrown on human nature and new avenues to truth are opened up."[6]

Very few doubt that Vatican II's mandate for the church's engagement with the world constitutes one of the many paradigm shifts that have marked the history of the church. As with all paradigm shifts, especially after some ecumenical councils, the vision provoked controversy. In 1971, Pope St. Paul VI convoked a synod of bishops on the issues of justice in the world and the ministerial priesthood. The bishops produced two documents on these issues that were approved by the Holy Father. In the document on justice, the bishops wrote:

> Action on behalf of justice and participation in the transformation of the world appear to us as a constitutive dimension of the preaching of the Gospel, or, in other words, of the Church's mission for the redemption of the human race and its liberation from every oppressive situation.[7]

The bishops are affirming that there can be no true evangelization without action for justice. A case can be made for saying that this statement is a teaching of the ordinary magisterium, since it was made by a synod of bishops with the approval of the pope. Even if it were neglected by subsequent documents from the Holy See, it is doubtful that its validity can be questioned.

Pope St. John Paul II continued the church's engagement with the world, which was not a surprise since he was a major contributor to *Gaudium et spes*. The principle of solidarity was significant in his teaching. At his homily in Yankee Stadium on October 2, 1979, during his first visit to the United States, he commented on the parable of the rich man and Lazarus and exclaimed passionately: "We cannot stand idly by . . . if, in any place, the Lazarus of the twentieth century stands at our door."[8]

In his apostolic exhortation "Reconciliation and Penance," he states

---

5. *GS* 40.
6. *GS* 44.
7. Synod of bishops, *Justice in the World* (November 30, 1971), no. 6.
8. John Paul II, homily at Yankee Stadium, October 2, 1979, http://w2.vatican. va.

that social sins are the result of many personal sins, among which are "the sins of those who are in a position to avoid, eliminate or at least limit certain social evils, but who fail to do so out of laziness, fear or the conspiracy of silence, through secret complicity or indifference."[9] Silence in the face of social evils should be a subject for examination of conscience not only by individual members of the church but also by collegial bodies.

It becomes clear that Pope Francis's engagement with the world—especially in its messiness—is rooted in Vatican II and exemplified in the pontificate of Pope St. John Paul II. Note two other features of his papacy that also resonate in the ministry of Pope Francis. First, in his many visits to almost every region of the world, John Paul II made the church visible by the crowds he drew as well as the various liturgical and nonliturgical celebrations over which he presided. The catholicity of the church emerged in a dramatic collage of developed and developing nations, with an immense variety of languages and cultures representing so many diverse races and ethnicities, all of whom could recognize something of themselves in familiar elements such as song, dance, and clothing incorporated into the celebrations. Pope Francis has continued the tradition of travel but places greater emphasis on visiting the margins. He has made the church visible among those who are most abandoned, most forgotten, most in need.

The second point of convergence can be seen in John Paul II's removal from the 1983 Code of Canon Law of the possibility in the 1917 Code that divorced and civilly remarried Catholics be excommunicated. Earlier, in his apostolic exhortation *Familiaris consortio* (1981) he urged "pastors and the whole community of the faithful to help the divorced . . . to make sure that they do not consider themselves as separated from the Church, for as baptized persons they can, and indeed must, share in her life."[10]

According to John Paul II, they should be encouraged "to attend the Sacrifice of the Mass . . . to contribute to works of charity and to community efforts in favor of justice, to bring up their children in the Christian faith, to cultivate the spirit and practice of penance."[11]

He says that the church must "show herself a merciful Mother, and thus sustain them in faith and hope."[12] Has Pope Francis gone very far from these words in *Amoris laetitia*? Without entering that controversy,

---

9. John Paul II, apostolic exhortation, *Reconciliation and Penance*, December 2, 1984, no. 16, http://w2.vatican.va.

10. *FC* 84.

11. Ibid.

12. Ibid.

here we can say that both popes are united in their care for wounded members of the church.

In convoking an ecumenical council, Pope St. John XXIII, who, by the way, would have known very well what a field hospital was, hoped that a council would lead to a more positive proclamation of Catholic teaching in the context of a very troubled world. This, too, was a form of engagement with the world. Such engagement is very evident in the teaching of Pope Benedict XVI. Particularly relevant was his emphasis on keeping faith and reason in reciprocal relationship. Faith without reason can lead to extremism, and reason without faith can lead to an oppressive relativism.

His first encyclical, *Deus caritas est*, was a powerful plea not only to the church but also to a skeptical world to recognize the beauty and immensity of God's unconditional love for each human being. In a very dramatic passage, he writes, "God's love for his people is so great that it turns God against himself, his love against his justice."[13] No great leap is required to move from this to Pope Francis's constant proclamation of God's untiring mercy.

Some proponents of a smaller, purer church have tried to enlist Joseph Ratzinger as an ally. However, in a study of Ratzinger's theology, Christopher Ruddy, professor of ecclesiology at the Catholic University of America, has shown that, while Ratzinger together with other theologians recognizes that the church may become numerically smaller, "the few are the starting point from which God seeks to save the many." Ratzinger's conception of the church "envisions a humble, diaconal, and other-centered community."[14] No circling of wagons, no fortress here.

Pope Francis's engagement with the world and his urging the church to do the same is the most recent phase of a trajectory that can be traced initially to Vatican II. A further illustration of this connection is his encyclical *Laudato si'*. While ecological concerns have been on the agenda of the Holy See for a number of years, by dedicating an encyclical to these concerns Pope Francis has not only elevated them to a priority in the church's mission to the world but has also established common ground with the many individuals and organizations who share these same concerns. The church in recent decades has been marginalized by many for what they see as a preoccupation with

---

13. Benedict XVI, encyclical, *Deus caritas est*, December 25, 2005, no. 10, http://w2.vatican.va.

14. Christopher Ruddy, "'For the Many': The Vicarious Representative Heart of Joseph Ratzinger's Theology," *Theological Studies* 75 (September 2014): 582.

sexual ethics. The church cannot reverse itself on its sexual ethics, but Pope Francis has shown that there are other issues on which the church and world can work together. This, too, is a step along the path that found eloquent expression at Vatican II.

This trajectory, however, must be traced even further back—to Moses and the burning bush. God has "observed the misery of my people. . . . I know their sufferings" (Exod 3:7), and so God commands Moses to lead his people out of Egypt. When Moses asks for God's name, he replies, "I am who I am" (Exod 3:14). This is the fundamental revelation of God's mystery that has guided Jewish and Christian faith and prayer through millennia. However, note that this revelation is intrinsically bound to his will for the liberation of his people. God cannot be understood apart from his will for the integral salvation of human beings. Note also that Moses is to tell the king of Egypt that he must let the people go so that in the wilderness they "may sacrifice to the Lord, our God" (Exod 3:18). God's revelation of his name leads to authentic worship.

The true God, true worship, and true care for the afflicted—these are so interrelated that they cannot be separated. To offer true worship to the true God means commitment to true care for others. Liturgy is not a refuge but a launch into the chaos of the human condition. True care for the afflicted is not simply social work or action for justice but the zealous restoration of broken hearts and broken bodies to the fullness of human dignity and participation in communities of friendship and faith.

The acme in the trajectory from the encounter with the burning bush to a church of mercy and compassion is Jesus himself. When he was asked by the disciples of John the Baptist whether or not he was the Messiah, he responded:

> Go and tell John what you have seen and heard: the blind receive their sight, the lame walk, the lepers are cleansed, the deaf hear, the dead are raised, the poor have good news brought to them. (Luke 7:22)

Jesus thus identifies himself through the care he gives to others.

His followers through the centuries have pursued that same trajectory. Benedictine monasteries provided shelter, healing, and education to the larger world. The mendicant orders of the thirteenth century walked amid the marginalized people. In the centuries that followed, as one historian wrote:

The great inventive achievement in connection with the Christian religion at the close of the sixteenth century and during the first half of the seventeenth consisted in combining the ardor of religious sentiment and the determination to bring the practice of Christian morality into the temporal world with the spread of a new tenderness and a new gentleness in human relations.[15]

Such "new tenderness" was brilliantly practiced by saints such as Francis de Sales, Vincent de Paul, and Jane de Chantal.

Another important phase in the trajectory rooted in the burning bush was the church's declaration of its preferential option for the poor in the second half of the twentieth century. This is not a one-sided choice that envisions the poor simply as passive beneficiaries of philanthropy. This option makes space not only for the active involvement of the poor in the correction of social injustice and creation of just structures, but also for their voices to be heard by the world and the church. For the poor bear witness to faith, courage, perseverance, hospitality, solidarity, and creativity amid great vulnerability and often dehumanizing conditions.

In a world of comfort and convenience, it is not easy for us to allow the poor to enter into our lives because they remind us of the vulnerability that ultimately every human being must confront. That may be why it is difficult even for Christians to accept Christ crucified. It is much easier to welcome Christ the good shepherd, the gentle healer, the wise teacher. Nevertheless, Christ crucified is the poorest of the children of the human race, confronting us with the stark reality that all of us must be despoiled of everything in order to gain abundance of life.

Pope Francis has allowed the voice of the poor to be heard in today's world. He has gone out to the margins—even before his election—and brought back to the center of the church their cry for justice and their yearning for fullness of life. He has also allowed their faith and love to be seen by the community of church and world.

He appeals to the conscience of all of us to engage in profound self-examination and discernment regarding the direction we want to take as individuals and communities in responding to the cry of the poor, to the structures of sin that envelop us, to the ideologies that warp our thinking, and to every conflict that divides us. I am not sure whether the pope likes to offer toasts, but I suspect that he would make his own

---

15. John U. Nef, *Cultural Foundations of Industrial Civilization* (Cambridge: Cambridge University Press, 1958), 91.

the famous salute of Cardinal Newman, "I shall drink to the pope, if you please, still, to conscience first, and to the pope afterwards." It was, after all, Newman's conscience that prodded him in a long and unrelenting search for truth that led him to recognize the Roman Catholic Church as the church that in its fundamental structures, including the papacy, came from Christ. Today, Pope Francis prods our consciences to foster within our hearts and communities the spirit of mercy, empathy, compassion, and commitment to go out to the margins.

As he reminds us often, however, going to the margins can be messy. Field hospitals are by definition messy. The journey to the margins will prove too daunting for many, and they will prefer to remain within comfortable borders. God's mercy embraces them. The church might indeed become smaller. But there will also be the adventurers, as there have been since the beginning, who perhaps timidly at first, but then boldly, driven by the gospel and their conscience, will go to the margins—maybe close by, maybe far away—and engage themselves in the struggle for justice, for equality, for the recognition of the infinite dignity of every human being, and for peace. The church might indeed become purer.

2

Reconciling Doctrine, Theology, Spirituality, and Pastorality

John O'Malley, SJ

From 1963 until 1965, I was in Rome writing my dissertation on a sixteenth-century reformer, Egidio da Viterbo, prior general of the Augustinian order. I was present in Rome, therefore, for the second and third periods of Vatican II. My fascination with the council began then and has never left me. In the decades that have transpired since the council, I have become ever more aware of the coherency, richness, and the radical ramifications of the council.

The council made us rethink verities that, at the time and even later, seemed immune to rethinking. Most recently, it has made me rethink and radically change my understanding of several of the most basic categories in our vocabulary—doctrine, theology, spirituality, and pastorality. The council dissolved the boundaries separating them and restored to them a coherence among themselves that they lost in the thirteenth century.

In that century, when Christian teachers moved their enterprise from the pulpit to university classrooms, they unwittingly constructed those boundaries. The scholastic enterprise was one of the most stunning achievements of Western culture, but, as is often lamented, it had the unfortunate consequence of radically intellectualizing our faith and of abandoning meditation on the sacred page for debate about it. In so doing, it built walls separating realities that belong together. The walls became instantiated in the four categories of doctrine, theology, spirituality, and pastorality. It took Vatican II to break down the walls and put the pieces together again.

The coherence among those categories that the council reinstated is a single but extremely important instance of the profound coherence of the entire corpus of the official documents of Vatican II. It began with Pope John's allocution opening the council, followed by the "Message to the World" the council issued in its first days, and concluding with *Gaudium et spes,* "The Pastoral Constitution on the Church in the Modern World." We need, therefore, to break ourselves of the habit of looking at that corpus as a collection of discrete documents and, instead, approach the documents as a single corpus, coherent and focused, despite its complexity, inconsistencies, and many particularities.

Vatican II is unique among councils in many ways, and its coherence is one of them. Another is the prominence in it of the word pastoral. In that regard, two instances are striking. The first occurs in Pope John XXIII's allocution, when he told the prelates in the basilica that the council was to have a predominantly pastoral character.[1] The second is the designation of pastoral for one of the council's four constitutions.

By designating the council as predominantly pastoral, Pope John seemed to imply that at least some former councils were not predominantly pastoral. If not pastoral, what were they? Then and now the answer would certainly be that they were predominantly doctrinal. It would seem, therefore, that the pope made a distinction between doctrinal and pastoral.

Even if he did, in that same allocution, he assigned the council a doctrinal character. He said that the world expected from the council "a step forward toward doctrinal penetration." He went on, "and a formation of consciences in faithful and perfect conformity to authentic doctrine."[2] He thus seemed to link a pastoral concern (formation of consciences) with doctrine. The waters, you will notice, are already getting muddy.

The council designated *Gaudium et spes* a "Pastoral Constitution," a designation altogether new in the vocabulary of councils. By so designating it, Vatican II in emphatic fashion set it off from the two constitutions expressly labeled dogmatic—the constitutions on revelation and on the church. *Sacrosanctum concilium* was, however, simply the "Constitution on the Sacred Liturgy"—neither pastoral nor dogmatic—which, when pitted against the other three, raises further questions about the designations pastoral and dogmatic.

Only in the spring of 1965, as the council was entering its final phase, did the coordinating commission assign the title pastoral to

---

1. Pope John XXIII, "*Gaudet mater ecclesia,*" in *Acta synodalia sacrosancti concilii Vaticani II,* 32 vols. (Vatican City: Typis Polyglottis Vaticani, 1970–1999), 1.1, 172.
2. Ibid.

Gaudium et spes. I have not been able to find any discussion of why it did so, but I assume it was because Part Two of the constitution was entitled "Some More Urgent Problems." In that part, the council supposedly descended from timeless doctrine to the contingency of reality—descended to the so-called signs of the times. Was that, maybe, the reasoning? If so, it would conform to the way "doctrinal" and "pastoral" were generally understood at the time. The irony, of course, is that Part Two was rich in teachings. In any case, from that time forward, the document was a pastoral constitution, even though when it first came into being in the early months of 1963, it bore the title simply of Schema 17 and then later of Schema 13.

On October 20, 1962, shortly after the council opened, it issued its glorious but sadly neglected "Message to the World."[3] In so doing, it laid the groundwork for something along the lines of Schema 17, but, as is well known, the more pointed origin was the famous speech of Cardinal Léon-Joseph Suenens on December 4, 1962.[4] Suenens called for the council to take the church as its central focus in the double aspect of its inner life (*ad intra*) and in its external manifestations (*ad extra*). Schema 17, the later *Gaudium et spes,* was meant to be the expression of the latter aspect, which, as Suenens called for it, did not connote a document any more or less pastoral than the former aspect.

Many previous ecumenical councils employed two categories of decrees, one more obviously pertaining to doctrine, for example, confessions of faith, the other more obviously to aspects of ecclesiastical discipline. In the history of the councils, this distinction does not hold with perfect consistency, but in the Council of Trent it received the form with which the prelates at Vatican II were most familiar. The Council of Trent expressly divided its decrees into two categories, those pertaining to doctrine and those pertaining to reform or, more specifically, to discipline.[5] The reform decrees were generally formulated in canons, which ended with penalties for nonobservance. The doctrinal decrees, however, had two parts, the first of which was several paragraphs of instruction and the second a series of canons, each of which culminated in a sentence of excommunication (anathema) for anybody saying, teaching, or preaching contrary to the canon.

The council thus made a distinction between doctrinal and pastoral decrees, but if we examine the substance of the decrees, we see that the distinction is too facile. The instructional portion of the doctrinal

3. Ibid., 230–32.

4. Ibid., 1.4, 222–27.

5. See John W. O'Malley, *Trent: What Happened at the Council* (Cambridge, MA: Harvard University Press, 2013), 81–83.

decrees—the so-called chapters—were created to make the decrees pastorally pertinent. Since both the doctrinal and the reform decrees ended in punishment for nonobservance, both were in that regard disciplinary decrees. Moreover, some decrees of Trent that the council dealt with expressly as disciplinary decrees were in fact doctrinal in content, such as the decree affirming the validity of the veneration of the saints.[6]

Only if we step back for a moment and look at the origins of this phenomenon can we more readily understand what was going on. In so doing, we are retracing ground with which we are familiar, but the retracing is pertinent here. We begin at the beginning. As councils began to develop in the Hellenistic world of the second century, they as a matter of course adopted procedural models current in the Roman Empire, most especially in the Roman senate. Although the so-called Council of Jerusalem described in chapter fifteen of the Acts of the Apostles remained the scriptural justification for councils, the Roman legislative and judicial procedures determined what councils did and how they did it. The senate made laws, to which were attached penalties for nonobservance. Also on occasion, the senate acted as a court of criminal justice by rendering verdicts in high-level cases concerning crimes committed against the state.

The assimilation of the senate form culminated and received paradigmatic form with the Council of Nicaea in 325 CE. The role of Emperor Constantine, who was present at it, strengthened the analogy between council and senate. The emperor convoked the council. He in large measure set the agenda, which was resolution of the doctrinal controversy ignited by Arius, and he determined that the council should meet in the imperial palace under his watchful eye. He was, in effect, honorary president of the council.

The emperor convoked the council as a first step in restoring public order in the empire, which had been badly disrupted by the Arian controversy, especially in the East. Even so, he allowed the bishops direct control of the meeting. If the emperor's goal was restoration of public order in the empire, the bishops' goal was restoration of doctrinal order in the church. The bishops' goal was, therefore, largely coterminous with the emperor's.

The council heard the case against Arius and found him guilty of propagating heresy. It pronounced anathemas against his impious opinions.[7] In subsequent centuries, councils continued to act as courts of criminal justice, as is most notoriously obvious in the Council of

---

6. See Norman Tanner, ed., *Decrees of the Ecumenical Councils*, 2 vols. (Washington, DC: Georgetown University Press, 1990), 2.774–76.

7. Ibid., 1.16–19.

Constance in the fifteenth century. The council not only pronounced the verdict of guilty against Jan Hus but then handed him over to the secular arm to be burned at the stake.

Although the bishops at Nicaea took the case against Arius as their major business, they used the occasion to deal with other matters as well. They made laws prescribing or proscribing certain behaviors, with penalties attached for nonobservance. They, for instance, levied penalties against clerics who castrated themselves.[8] The prelates at Nicaea and at most subsequent councils formulated such laws in canons. Canons are short ordinances prescribing or proscribing certain behaviors.

Nicaea established the pattern for future councils, which in most instances formulated even their doctrinal decrees in canons, that is, as laws. As laws, the doctrinal decrees dealt with observable behavior, not with motivation or conscience. The formula became standard: "If anyone should say or should teach or should propagate such and such, let him be anathema." Not "If anyone should believe or think such and such." Believing and thinking are not observable behaviors.

Councils thus came to be meetings of a certain kind. They were essentially legislative and judicial meetings, and their function was to promote and ensure good public order in the church in both doctrine and discipline. Councils most frequently, most consistently, and most characteristically employed canons to accomplish that goal. The Council of Trent, for instance, issued over 250 doctrinal and disciplinary canons. Even with a drastically reduced agenda, Vatican Council I issued twenty-one canons. Vatican II issued not a single canon, the first clue that something of high importance was taking place.

In his extraordinary address opening the council, Pope Saint John XXIII directed the fathers of the council to address the problems facing the church "by making use of the medicine of mercy rather than severity . . . demonstrating the validity of the church's teachings rather than by condemnations." The fathers, without forgetting the prophetic mission of the church, should show the church to be "the loving mother of all, benign, patient, full of mercy and goodness."[9]

With those simple words, the pope liberated the council from the legislative-judicial model and set in motion a process that led the council to abandon the most characteristic functions councils had performed up to that time, that is, consolidating public order in the church and insulating the church from external contamination. He gave the council freedom to do something new, which led to the coun-

---

8. Ibid., 1.6.
9. *Acta synodalia sacrosancti concilii Vaticani II*, 1.1, 172 and 173.

cil assuming a function for itself other than ensuring public order in the church. It led to a new definition of a council.

The bishops at the council heard the pope's directive to avoid condemnations, and they wanted to comply. To say something positive rather than negative means praising it rather than criticizing or condemning it. Praise, therefore, became the major rhetorical form the council adopted, and praise language is utterly different from the language of laws and judicial verdicts of guilt and innocence.

Vatican II, like all the councils before it, can be defined as a meeting, principally of bishops gathered in Christ's name to make decisions binding on the church. That is how Vatican II is continuous with previous councils. Vatican II is discontinuous, however, in that the decisions consisted largely in articulating values, norms, and ideals to guide persons—popes, bishops, priests, laity, and non-Catholics—in their choices and modes of life. The decisions were, thus, not intent on punishing misbehavior but on providing encouragement and guidance for persons' best instincts and aspirations. Rather than being intent on isolating the church from contamination, they extended a hand in friendship to the Other and viewed the Other more as a source of enrichment than as a threat to the church's purity. The decisions of Vatican II pertained, we can say, to the pursuit of holiness. We are getting close to an appreciation of the coherence of the council's corpus.

If the council was free to do something different, what did it do? It followed Pope John's directive and tried to "take a step forward toward doctrinal penetrations." More specifically, it explored the church's identity, recalled and developed the church's most precious values, and proclaimed to the world the church's sublime vision for humanity. That is what the council set out to do, and that is what it accomplished. That is very different from reestablishing proper public order in the church. That was a revolution in the history of councils. The council forged for itself a new function and a new goal.

Vatican II, I repeat, took as its task an exploration of the church's identity in all its facets, a development and incisive articulation of the church's most precious values, and a resounding proclamation of the church's sublime vision for humanity. From its first moment until its last, that is what Vatican II was doing. If that is what it was doing, that defines what it is. We have, then, with Vatican II, a new definition of council. Once we understand that, we are in a position to see how wonderfully coherent the council was.

The form of discourse that Vatican II adopted was the vehicle by which the new goal was accomplished. Despite the council's extraordinary complexity, the praise-form imbued the council with a simplicity and coherence no previous council had known. Every document of Vatican II relates to the others, a phenomenon promoted and revealed in the remarkable intertextuality of the council's decrees. The documents allude to one another, and they gain momentum from one another. No document stands on its own. For instance, as Massimo Faggioli has shown so conclusively, *Sacrosanctum concilium,* the first document the council approved, contains basic principles that animated all the documents that followed.[10]

If we examine those principles, we see that reconciliation emerges as a fundamental Christian value that becomes the council's leitmotif. When on January 25, 1959, John XXIII announced his intention of convoking a council, he indicated reconciliation with other Christian bodies as a motive for convoking it.[11] When he defined the church as "the loving mother of all, benign, patient, full of goodness and mercy," he ended that sentence with the words "toward all those separated from her." *Unitatis redintegratio,* the decree on ecumenism, was the result.

When John insisted with Cardinal Bea that the Secretariat for Christian Unity produce a statement on the Jews, he implicitly set the council on a wider course of reconciliation, which had enormous implications. *Nostra aetate,* "The Declaration on Non-Christian Religions," imposed on Catholics a startlingly new and utterly unprecedented task—to be agents of reconciliation among different religious confessions, a job description that the popes took to heart and that Pope France is fulfilling in dramatic fashion. *Nostra aetate* thus gave Christian spirituality a new specification.

But reconciliation was profoundly operative in the council in less obvious ways. *Sacrosanctum concilium,* for instance, reconciled the church with non-Western cultures. *Lumen gentium* reconciled the college of bishops with the papacy, a relationship fractured since the Council of Constance. *Dei verbum* reconciled exegetes with modern methods. In a giant leap. *Gaudium et spes* reconciled the church with the modern world and with all persons of good will. And so it went with many other reconciliations.

But beyond particular reconciliations lay a reconciliation of doctrine, theology, spirituality, and pastorality. The council recast the

---

10. See Massimo Faggioli, *True Reform: Liturgy and Ecclesiology in Sacrosanctum Concilium* (Collegeville, MN: Liturgical Press, 2012).

11. *Acta et documenta concilii oecumenici Vaticani II apparendo, series prima (Prepreparatoria),* 12 vols., plus index et appendixes (Vatican City: Typis Polyglottis Vaticani, 1960–1961), 1.6.

relationship among them and showed how permeable were their boundaries. They were no longer free-standing silos.

Let us consider first the reconciliation between doctrine and pastorality. We take it as axiomatic that Vatican II was a pastoral council. Thus it was denominated by John XXIII himself. The pope certainly did not mean that by "pastoral" the council was second-rate, yet in the 1960s and even afterward some drew that conclusion. For such people, the designation pastoral implied that the council's decrees were less substantial and therefore more contingent and more subject to revision or even dismissal than those of the supposedly great dogmatic councils of the past, such as the Council of Trent.

But, if we judge a council's dignity and *gravitas* by the number and importance of its doctrinal affirmations, does not Vatican II qualify as a council of supreme doctrinal importance? True, Vatican II did not define a single doctrine, but, if we look at council language, did the Council of Trent define any? I do not find the word in the council's documents. What Trent did was excommunicate persons who behaved in certain ways concerning doctrine. For instance, it excommunicated thirty-three such persons in its decree on justification alone—it is a little hard to swallow the fact that each of those excommunications constituted a truth of divine and apostolic faith, a truth worthy of a place in the creed. Therefore, the fact that Vatican II did not define any doctrines is not proof that it was not doctrinal or that it was doctrinally lightweight. The council did not define any doctrines because, among other reasons, it adopted a mode of discourse different from that operative in councils that produced definitions, most notably Vatican I.

Not defining does not necessarily mean that the council's more important teachings are less binding or less central to the Christian religion, solemnly approved as they were by far the largest and most representative gathering of prelates in the entire history of the Christian church and then solemnly ratified by the supreme pontiff, Paul VI. We must, moreover, take note, as noted earlier, that *Lumen gentium* and *Dei verbum* are expressly designated as "Dogmatic Constitutions." If we, in fact, count the number and weigh the importance of the teachings of Vatican Council II, the council emerges not as council lite but as the very opposite.

Here are some of those teachings, listed in no particular order, but certainly toward the top is the council's teaching that what God revealed in Jesus Christ was a person (*DV* 1). I do not find that teaching insubstantial. In the same *Dei verbum*, the council taught that the

Bible is truly inerrant but only in what "serves to make the people of God live their lives in holiness and increase their faith" (*DV* 8). In other words, revelation consists in what "serves to make the people of God live their lives in holiness and increase their faith." It is difficult to imagine a truth more basic to understanding all other Christian truths than that one. The repercussions of that often overlooked teaching are profound and significantly reshape how we henceforth must think about the relationship between doctrine and spirituality, and therefore between theology and spirituality.

The teaching highlights and bestows great gravity on another of the council's most characteristic teachings, repeated again and again after it first appeared in *Lumen gentium*, where we learn that the purpose of the church is to promote the holiness of its members (*LG* 39–42). Holiness became a pervasive theme of the council, which, sad to say, is often overlooked by commentators. That the church is about holiness is a truth that is absolutely central to Christianity, and one that, from the first days of the church, appeared in countless texts dealing with our faith. No previous council, however, took the trouble to tell us that, largely because the legislative-judicial model would not let it emerge. Vatican II solemnly ratified it and put it in the forefront of what we believe as Christians. Whatever God revealed, he revealed for the sake of holiness. Christian truth is spiritual truth. You will agree, I assume, that this is not a trivial teaching.

Thus, the council did more than simply produce an abstract answer to the question of the inerrancy of the Bible. It provided yet another impulse establishing the council's coherence. If, through the lens of holiness, we look at the council's official documents beginning with John's allocution and the "Message to the World," we see them anew, and we see how one relates to the others to produce not only a profile of the ideal Christian in today's world but also a program for attaining that ideal. The Middle Ages described Christian doctrine as the *ars vivendi et moriendi*—as the art of Christian living and dying. Making that description of doctrine actual again was the most profound purpose of the council. This was not a small accomplishment.

Besides putting holiness on the council's agenda in a full chapter, *Lumen gentium* taught that the church is constituted by the people in it, so that "the people of God" is a valid, crucially important, and traditional expression of the reality of the church (*LG* 9–17). This is another teaching that has momentous repercussions. Since the People of God are everywhere on the earth, the council therefore taught that the church is at home in every culture and needs to incarnate itself in each of them. Because the council also taught that the liturgy was an act of the whole community in worship and was therefore essentially a participatory action, the liturgy itself had to admit into it symbols and customs from every culture (*SC* 37–39).

Lex orandi, lex credendi—the norm for worship is the norm for belief. The council, therefore, taught that, while the structure of the church is hierarchical, it is also collegial, that is, participatory, as is the liturgy. Or, perhaps more pertinent, *lex orandi, lex vivendi*—the norm for prayer is the norm for how we live and act. In particular, *Lumen gentium* taught the traditional but formerly unexpressed doctrine that bishops, when acting as a body with and under the Roman pontiff, have responsibility not only for their own dioceses but for the church at large (*LG* 18–29). It taught that just as the Roman pontiff has, therefore, a collegial relationship with the other bishops, bishops have a collegial relationship with their priests, and priests with their flocks (*LG* 16, 27).

Vatican II taught that while the church has the heavy responsibility of proclaiming the gospel to the world, it also has the responsibility of exerting itself for the well-being of the world as such, that is, to exert itself for the well-being of the so-called temporal order—to be concerned about social justice, about the heinousness of stockpiling nuclear weapons and the incomparable destructiveness of nuclear war, about the blessings of peace and about the advance of every aspect of human culture (*Gaudium et spes* Part II). It taught that it is incumbent upon Catholics to work with others, even with nonbelievers, in pursuing such goals. At the same time, it taught that this was not a one-way street, but that, just as the church benefited the world, the world benefited the church—an obvious and empirical fact that had never been acknowledged before. The church must listen to the world and learn from it—a remarkable and utterly unprecedented teaching (*GS* 44). In that regard, it taught that, although proclamation of the gospel was the privileged form of Christian discourse, dialogue also was a legitimate form and in some instances a more appropriate one (*UR* 4).

In the temporal order, the council taught the right and duty of persons to follow their consciences in their choice of religion (*Dignitatis humanae*), and, more generally, it taught in some of its most moving words the ancient truth of the dignity of conscience, "that most secret core and the sanctuary of the human person, where they are alone with God, whose voice echoes in their depths" (*GS* 16).

For the first time in history, the council taught that marriage was a partnership in love (*GS* 48). It explicitly taught that grace and the

Holy Spirit were operative outside the visible confines of the Catholic Church and that, therefore, salvation was possible outside those confines (*UR* 3).

These and other teachings of the council are not trivial. They are not of secondary importance. They are not, of course, at the same constitutive level as the dogmas of the Trinity and the Incarnation, but they are nonetheless of the utmost importance as practical consequences of those dogmas for our lives as Christians. If we understand them in that sense, they become pastoral teachings. Many of them occur, in fact, in *Gaudium et spes,* the "pastoral" constitution.

"Pastoral teachings?" As opposed to what? What is the alternative to pastoral teachings? Is it "doctrinal teachings," which is a tautology? Dogmatic teachings is also a tautology. Is it "academic teachings"? Did God reveal academic teachings or academic truths just to satisfy our curiosity? I find it impossible to name an alternative to pastoral teachings, especially if we agree with *Dei verbum* that God revealed "what serves to make the people of God live their lives in holiness and increase their faith." Does this not mean that by definition all truly Christian truths are pastoral truths? Are we not then saying that Vatican II is a pastoral council because of what it teaches? Are we not saying that Vatican II is a pastoral council because it is a doctrinal council? I think we are.

When *Dei verbum* determined that Christian truth was truth that helped persons live their lives in holiness, it dismantled whatever might have been valid in the distinction between a doctrinal and a pastoral council. We can justly distinguish between pastoral theology and certain pastoral skills, such as counseling and preaching. But we can no longer distinguish between pastoral theology and, well, "real" theology.

The council dismantled whatever might have been valid in the distinction between theology and spirituality. We can justly distinguish between spiritual theology and certain practices that help us deepen our relationship to God, such as methods of prayer and the use of bodily penances. But we can no longer distinguish between real theology and spiritual theology. Nor can we distinguish between spiritual theology and pastoral theology. Like Joshua at the Battle of Jericho, Vatican II blew down the walls that kept them all apart.

The coherence that the council reestablished had one extraordinarily significant doctrinal consequence that the council signaled when it proclaimed, "The joys and hopes, the grief and anguish of the peoples of our times, especially those who are poor or afflicted, are the joys and hopes, the grief and anguish of the followers of Christ as well" (*GS* 1). Thus, in the opening line of *Gaudium et spes*, the council sounded the leitmotif of the document and, indeed, the leitmotif of the council itself. With that line, the council was not mouthing a pious platitude but proclaiming a truth central to our faith and thus central to its spirituality and pastorality.

In so doing, Vatican II rescued the social teaching of the church from its exile as a minor, one-credit course in the philosophy programs of seminaries and elevated it to a central element in Christian teaching and, therefore, in Christian spirituality and morality. The council made clear that concern for the so-called temporal order was not a sideline of the church's mission but at its very core, because the church is "the loving mother of all, benign, patient, full of mercy and goodness." Consequently, the council taught in the most prominent way possible that "the joys and hopes, the grief and anguish of the people of our time are the joys and hopes, the grief and anguish of the followers of Christ."

"Pope Francis, a Voice Crying Out in the World: Mercy, Justice, Love, and Care for the Earth" was the title of our conference at Villanova University. The current Roman pontiff is a complex man, not easily analyzed. Nonetheless, we can discern at least three formative influences on him. First, the Global South, which has different experiences and different priorities than the North, especially the North Atlantic. Second, his formation and experience as a Jesuit. I find it easy to detect Jesuit influences on him. When he described himself as a sinner, for instance, he was quoting Decree 2 of the Jesuits' 32nd General Congregation, a congregation that both he and I attended and at which that definition was burned into our souls.

Finally, Vatican II. Francis is the first pope in a half-century not to have participated in the council. In my eyes, that is an advantage, because unlike his immediate predecessors he is not still fighting on some deep psychological level the battles of the council. He somehow early on came to understand the council in a clear-eyed fashion, and he attained, in my opinion, a remarkably comprehensive and authentic grasp of it. It is clear to all, I believe, that Pope Francis's blueprint for the initiatives of his pontificate has been from the very first moment the teachings of Vatican II. In his initiatives, he has been putting the council's message into practice by word and deed.

Both his friends and his foes describe those initiatives as pastoral. The latter often describe them as "only pastoral," and in the same breath reassure us that they are not doctrinal. To his foes, Francis is pope-lite, even though he is doing a great deal of harm.

Let me ask a question: When several years ago, Francis brought back with him to the Vatican twelve Muslim refugees, was he only being pastoral? Was he doing nothing more than performing a compassionate act in the hope that others, especially governments, would be inspired to go and do likewise? Or was he not proclaiming by a deed more powerful than any words could possibly express a doctrine, a spiritual and pastoral doctrine, a doctrine so central to being a Christian that Saint Matthew tells us our very salvation depends on it? "I was a stranger, and you took me in."

3

Pope Francis's Interpretation and Reception of Vatican II

Massimo Faggioli

The conclave of March 2013 took place in a very particular period in the history of the reception of the Second Vatican Council: after the pontificate of Benedict XVI, whose overarching message was clearly about the intention to revisit the Second Vatican Council and its reception and application in the life of the church. In this sense, the election of the successor of Benedict XVI was not just the election of the new bishop of Rome, but it was also framed in the context of the debate on Vatican II. In that debate, Benedict XVI had played a very visible role, because the debate had been prompted by him at the beginning of his pontificate with the famous speech to the Roman Curia of December 22, 2005, on the "two hermeneutics." That speech, one of the most important of his pontificate, was also meant to be the response to the two most important works on Vatican II published in the previous decade: the five-volume *History of Vatican II*, directed by the John XXIII Foundation for Religious Studies in Bologna, and the five-volume *Kommentar* on the documents of Vatican II, conceived in Tübingen, in the department of Catholic theology, where, fifty years earlier, a young Joseph Ratzinger had been hired on the recommendation of Hans Küng.[1]

---

1. See Giuseppe Alberigo, ed., *Storia del concilio Vaticano II*, 5 vols. (Bologna: Il Mulino; Leuven: Peeters, 1995–2001), published in English as *History of Vatican II*, ed. Joseph Komonchak (Maryknoll, NY: Orbis Books, 1995–2006); Peter Hünermann and Bernd Jochen Hilberath, eds., *Herders theologischer Kommentar zum Zweiten Vatikanischen Konzil*, 5 vols. (Freiburg i.B.: Herder, 2004–2005). Benedict XVI's implicit but clear criticism of the five-volume *Kommentar* in the speech of December 22, 2005, has been confirmed by Peter Hünermann himself: "*In*

The pontificate of Benedict XVI represented a culmination of a trend inaugurated before his election. Already toward the end of the pontificate of John Paul II, that is, in the early 2000s, one could see signs of a "policy review" of the Roman Curia about the interpretation and reception of Vatican II—the most consequential being the instructions of the Congregation for Divine Worship, *Liturgiam authenticam* (March 28, 2001) (which inspired and caused a new trend in the translation of liturgical texts, whose fruits are very well known in the English-speaking world) and *Redemptionis sacramentum* (April 23, 2004), about liturgical abuses.[2] This trend became even stronger with the election of Benedict XVI. From 2005 onward, Benedict XVI's interpretation of Vatican II was summarized by commentators on the one side as a polarity between "continuity and reform" and on the other as "discontinuity and rupture." This simplistic caricature of the hermeneutical complexity of Vatican II penetrated and shaped the language of the discourse of the Catholic Church on Vatican II, especially at the level of theological studies and seminaries but also in the theological orientation of bishops and cardinals.

The argument of "continuity with the tradition of the council," which had been presented at the beginning of Benedict XVI's speech as an argument against the Lefebvrian thesis of Vatican II as a rupture with Catholic tradition, soon showed the real objectives of many interpreters of that speech and, in some instances, of Benedict XVI himself.[3]

This is a key element for understanding how Francis's theology interacted with the theological culture identified with the papacy in 2013, and it helps to explain the reception of Francis in the global church today. Pope Francis inaugurated a new phase in the reception of Vatican II, partly due to the disappearance of traditionalist issues from his

---

der Freiheit des Geistes leben": Peter Hünermann im Gespräch, ed. Margit Eckholt and Regina Heyder (Ostfildern: Matthias-Grünewald, 2010).

2. See Massimo Faggioli, "The Liturgical Reform from 1963 until Today . . . and Beyond," *Toronto Journal of Theology* 32, no. 2 (2016): 201–17.

3. See, for example, the lack of clarity in the *motu proprio Summorum pontificum* (July 7, 2007) about the implications of the liberalization of the pre-Vatican II liturgy for the interpretation of Vatican II. In the letter accompanying the *motu proprio*, with the same date of July 7, 2007, Benedict XVI wrote: "In the first place, there is the fear that the document detracts from the authority of the Second Vatican Council, one of whose essential decisions — the liturgical reform — is being called into question. This fear is unfounded." Moreover, Benedict expressed the wish that "the two Forms of the usage of the Roman Rite can be mutually enriching." On both accounts, the reality since the publication of *Summorum pontificum* has been very different from the one Benedict XVI stated in 2007.

agenda, which affected his handling of liturgical and other matters.[4] The pontificates of the popes elected since 1939 have all been defined (in different measures) by the historical-theological debate related to councils—from Pius XII, who decided not to reconvene Vatican I in 1948–1949, to John Paul II, the last pope who had been a member and a key figure of Vatican II and, at the same time, a stabilizer of the council in the post–Vatican II period, to Benedict XVI, one of the most influential theologians at Vatican II.[5] Pope Francis, ordained a priest in 1969, does not belong in this line of popes involved in Vatican II. Francis also differs from his predecessors in that his is the specific heritage of the Catholic Church in Latin America and the legacy of Vatican II for Latin American Catholicism throughout these last fifty years.

Clearly, the Argentine Jesuit Bergoglio perceives Vatican II as a matter that should not be reinterpreted or restricted but implemented and expanded.[6]

There was also something very visible from the very beginning of his pontificate. In the words addressed to the people in Saint Peter's Square after the election, on the evening of March 13, 2013, Francis presented himself as the "bishop of Rome": the binomial "bishop and people," crucial to Francis's ecclesiology, signified from the beginning an emphasis on the ecclesiology of the local church and on the diocese of Rome as a local church.

Francis's quotations of Vatican II have been rarer than those of his predecessors, but they have always been carefully chosen to mark particularly important moments during his pontificate. Remarkably, his first quotation of Vatican II during his pontificate was one week after his election, March 20, 2013. At a meeting with the fraternal delegates from other churches and religions, Francis mentioned for the first time the Second Vatican Council and in particular the declaration *Nostra aetate* (October 28, 1965), on non-Christian religions.

---

4. See, for example, Francis's speech to Italian liturgists gathered for the 68th National Liturgical Week, August 24, 2017, on the irreversibility and ongoing process of the liturgical reform of Vatican II: http://w2.vatican.va. About this see also Cesare Giraudo, SJ, "La riforma liturgica a 50 anni dal Vaticano II. 'Parlare di "riforma della riforma" è un errore,'" *La Civiltà Cattolica*, December 10, 2016, 432–45.

5. See Enrico Galavotti, "Il concilio di papa Francesco," in *Il conclave e papa Francesco: Il primo anno di pontificato*, ed. Alberto Melloni (Rome: Istituto della Enciclopedia Italiana, 2014), 35–69; Enrico Galavotti, "Jorge Mario Bergoglio e il concilio Vaticano II: fonte e metodo," *Rivista di teologia dell'evangelizzazione* 22, no. 43 (2018): 61–88.

6. About this, see Massimo Faggioli, *Pope Francis: Tradition in Transition* (Mahwah, NJ: Paulist Press, 2015).

At the beginning of Francis's pontificate, the influence of Vatican II was more mediated and nontextual than explicit in programmatic texts, more a matter of implementation than of interpretation.

The history of Francis's pontificate makes it impossible to assess Francis's relationship with Vatican II simply from the textual references to the council in the texts of his teaching. Pope Francis's reception of Vatican II cannot be measured in terms of the number of times he quotes from council documents. As a matter of fact, Francis does not quote Vatican II more frequently than his predecessors. His modality of reception of Vatican II is a complex mix of both the *reception of the documents* of the council and *of the act* of the council.

A SPIRITUAL RECEPTION

The two ecclesiological constitutions, *Lumen gentium* and *Gaudium et spes*, are the most important textual references to Vatican II in Pope Francis's teaching: it can be said that Francis's reception of Vatican II is ecclesiological in the sense of a missionary reform of the church. There is also an ecclesiological intention in the selection of sources in Francis's teachings: in the 217 endnotes of *Evangelii gaudium* there are only seven quotations from documents issued by the Roman Curia (four from the *Compendium of the Social Doctrine of the Church* by the Pontifical Council for Justice and Peace and three from the Congregation for the Doctrine of the Faith, all from the instruction *Libertatis nuntio*, on the theology of liberation, 1984), fifteen quotations from Vatican II, and twenty-three from documents of national or continental bishops' conferences.

Francis's response is, above all, a spiritual-theological reception of Vatican II.[7] We can see that from his reception of *Lumen gentium*.

Lumen gentium: *Papal Teaching and the Church*

The conciliar constitution on the church, *Lumen gentium* (November 21, 1964), plays a special role in the relationship between Francis and Vatican II. Pope Francis's apostolic exhortation *Evangelii gaudium*, which is akin to a programmatic document for Pope Francis's pontificate, quotes the documents of Vatican II twenty times, and the most quoted is the constitution on the church, *Lumen gentium*.

Lumen gentium 12, specifically, is significant. In *Evangelii gaudium*, it

---

7. For the distinction between *kerygmatic, theological*, and *spiritual* reception of a council, see Alois Grillmeier, "The Reception of Chalcedon in the Roman Catholic Church," *Ecumenical Review* 22 (1970): 383–411.

is clearly his intent to rephrase the infallibility of the magisterium as based on the infallibility of the People of God:

> In all the baptized, from first to last, the sanctifying power of the Spirit is at work, impelling us to evangelization. The people of God is holy thanks to this anointing, which makes it infallible *in credendo*. This means that it does not err in faith, even though it may not find words to explain that faith. (*EG* 119)

This passage about the *sensus fidei* is even more remarkable because this is the only passage of the exhortation that talks about infallibility, and it does that in terms of infallibility *in credendo* of the People of God.

Francis's choice is clear in favor of an ecclesiology of the people as missionary people that is more accentuated in *EG* than in Vatican II itself (*LG* 17 and *AG* 5–6). This is also an ecclesiology that has in mind a practical restructuring of ordained ministry in the church, beginning with the bishops: the bishop "will sometimes go *before his people*, pointing the way and keeping their hope vibrant. At other times, he will simply be *in their midst* with his unassuming and merciful presence. At yet other times, he will have to *walk after them*, helping those who lag behind and—above all—allowing the flock to strike out on new paths" (*EG* 31).

The local level is emphasized not only with regard to relations between the bishop and the people, but also in the way *Evangelii gaudium* operates theologically. The sources of the exhortation—coming from documents approved by national and continental bishops' conferences much more abundantly than in previous papal teachings—presupposes a *communio ecclesiae* (the communion of the local churches with Rome), not absorbing totally the *communio ecclesiarum* (the communion of the local churches between themselves).[8]

The connection between reform ecclesiology and local ecclesiology leads in *EG* to a paragraph on the reform of the Petrine ministry, which Pope Francis connects to the "conversion of the papacy." Francis admits that little progress has been made since Vatican II and since John Paul II's encyclical on ecumenism, *Ut unum sint* (1995):

> Pope John Paul II asked for help in finding "a way of exercising the primacy which, while in no way renouncing what is essential

---

8. This is one of the "building sites" left unfinished by Vatican II; see Hervé Legrand, "Communio ecclesiae, communio ecclesiarum, collegium episcoporum," in *La riforma e le riforme nella chiesa*, ed. Antonio Spadaro and Carlos Maria Galli (Brescia: Queriniana, 2016), 159–88.

to its mission, is nonetheless open to a new situation" [*Ut unum sint*, par. 95]. We have made little progress in this regard. The papacy and the central structures of the universal Church also need to hear the call to pastoral conversion. (*EG* 32)

Evangelii gaudium is not the only major teaching of Francis that draws from Vatican II. The encyclical *Laudato si'* does not quote *Lumen gentium* but contains indirectly a reception of the ecumenical ecclesiology of Vatican II, expressed also in *Lumen gentium*, with its inter-Christian appeal and sources.

In the postsynodal exhortation *Amoris laetitia* (March 19, 2016) Francis makes progress regarding the reception of the ecclesiology of *Lumen gentium*. From the very beginning of the exhortation, Francis reframes the relationship between the papacy and the teaching of the church:

> I would make it clear that not all discussions of doctrinal, moral or pastoral issues need to be settled by interventions of the magisterium. Unity of teaching and practice is certainly necessary in the Church, but this does not preclude various ways of interpreting some aspects of that teaching or drawing certain consequences from it. (*AL* 3)

This is by far the most important ecclesiological development in a papal document issued after the very eventful, two-year and two-session bishops' synod (2014 and 2015) on family and marriage.

Gaudium et spes: *Recontextualization of the Catholic Church*

The reception of *Gaudium et spes* in Francis's pontificate presents a remarkable reversal of fortune for the last document of Vatican II, the pastoral constitution, from the pontificate of Benedict XVI, who quoted *Gaudium et spes*, but often in a critical way.[9] Francis's theological thrust is about the recovery of a Catholic universality that is free from Latin universalism and not about a cultural resistance to modernity and postmodernity.

---

9. On Joseph Ratzinger's approach to *Gaudium et spes*, see his introduction, in the series of his complete works, to the first of the two volumes dedicated to Vatican II: "Vorwort," in *Zur Lehre des Zweiten Vatikanischen Konzils: Formulierung – Vermittlung – Deutung* (Joseph Ratzinger Gesammelte Schriften 7/1; Freiburg i.B.: Herder, 2012), 5–9, esp. 6–7. See Carlos Schickendantz, "¿Una transformación metodológica inadvertida? La novedad introducida por *Gaudium et Spes* en los escritos de Joseph Ratzinger," *Teología y Vida* 57, no. 1 (2016): 9–37.

The legacy of *Gaudium et spes* is evident in paragraphs 222 and 233, where we have a condensed summary of the worldview of Vatican II in four axioms: "Time is greater than space"; "unity prevails over conflict"; "realities are more important than ideas"; and "the whole is greater than the part."[10] Francis writes, "Giving priority to time means being concerned about initiating processes rather than possessing spaces" (*EG* 223)—a reception of the new awareness expressed by Vatican II about historicity. Then in *EG* 233—"Realities are greater than ideas. This principle has to do with incarnation of the word and its being put into practice"—this is closest to the core of *Gaudium et spes*'s existential-ontological thesis: also in the realm of concrete spiritual decisions, the particular and individual element cannot, despite the real validity of general principles, be simply-drawn general principles. "Time is greater than space" embodies the shift from a purely metaphysical approach to God's revelation to a more tangible "history of salvation." "Realities are more important than ideas" embodies the shift from the deductive to the inductive method.

Francis's pontificate deals with this shift most specifically in his remarkable description of the church as a polyhedron:

> Here our model is not the sphere, which is no greater than its parts, where every point is equidistant from the center, and there are no differences between them. Instead, it is the polyhedron, which reflects the convergence of all its parts, each of which preserves its distinctiveness. Pastoral and political activity alike seek to gather in this polyhedron the best of each. There is a place for the poor and their culture, their aspirations and their potential. Even people who can be considered dubious on account of their errors have something to offer which must not be overlooked. It is the convergence of peoples who, within the universal order, maintain their own individuality; it is the sum total of persons within a society which pursues the common good, which truly has a place for everyone. (*EG* 236)

The universality Francis has in mind means a big-tent church open to the world and against the temptations of creating a smaller, purer church made of smaller communities—with some remarkable consequences for the link, often made by the papal magisterium in the post–Vatican II period, between the council and the flourishing of

---

10. See Drew Christiansen, SJ, "The Church Encounters the World," *America*, January 6–13, 2014, 20–21.

postconciliar lay Catholic movements.[11] But what is especially typical of Francis's reception of Vatican II is not only this anti-elitism but also the retrieval of the almost forgotten emphasis on the poor and the "preferential option for the poor," which finds its source in Vatican II (*LG* 8, *GS* 1, *AG* 3).

The conciliar ecclesiology of the relationship between the church and the world, rooted in *Gaudium et spes*, is expanded on in *EG* 114: "Jesus did not tell the apostles to form an exclusive and elite group." Also, the discussion in *EG* 115 about Christian faith and the plurality of cultures demonstrates a full and unembarrassed reception of the pastoral constitution of Vatican II by Pope Francis.[12]

The encyclical *Laudato si'* draws from *Gaudium et spes*, although, typical of Francis, its text is not overloaded with conciliar quotations, which are mostly mediated through the use of postconciliar teaching—especially that of Paul VI and the national and continental bishops' conferences.[13] It is remarkable that all quotations from Vatican II in *Laudato si'* are from *Gaudium et spes*.

Gaudium et spes also plays a more prominent role in the exhortation *Amoris laetitia* than in other major documents issued by Francis. In *Amoris laetitia*, Francis quotes *Evangelii gaudium* (ten times), the constitution *Gaudium et spes* of Vatican II (nineteen times), and John Paul II's exhortation *Familiaris consortio* (1981) (twenty-six times). As in his previous documents, in *Amoris laetitia*, Francis cites often from documents of national bishops' conferences (Spain, Korea, Argentina, Mexico, Colombia, Chile, Australia, CELAM, Italy, and Kenya), and, in this particular case, very often from the catechesis of John Paul II. But *Gaudium et spes* plays a pivotal role for the exhortation, as it did during the entire synodal process of the bishops' synod of October 2014 and October 2015. *Amoris laetitia* draws from *Gaudium et spes* for the paragraphs of the pastoral constitution on family and marriage,[14] and also from *GS* 22 on "Christ the new Adam" (cf. *AL* 77–78), *GS* 16 on conscience, and *GS* 17 on freedom and human dignity.

---

11. For more on Francis and the new Catholic movements, see Massimo Faggioli, *The Rising Laity: Ecclesial Movements since Vatican II* (Mahwah, NJ: Paulist Press, 2016), 131–53.

12. It is not an accident that in the footnote to *GS* 36 there is an indirect reference to the case of Galileo Galilei when the text talks about the compatibility of faith and science. The reference in the footnote of *Gaudium et spes* is to the book by Pio Paschini, *Vita e opere di Galileo Galilei*, 2 vols. (Vatican City: Pontificia Accademia delle Scienze, 1964). See Alberto Melloni, "Galileo al Vaticano II. Storia d'una citazione e della sua ombra," *Cristianesimo nella storia* 31, no. 1 (2010): 131–64.

13. Like, for example, the quotation from *PP* (1967) in *LS* 127.

14. *GS* 48–50 in *AL* 80, 125, 126, 134, 142, 154, 166, 172, 178, 222, 298, and 315.

Sacrosanctum concilium: *Liturgy and Ecclesiology*

The reception of the liturgical constitution of Vatican II presents a particular aspect of Francis's overall reception of the council. On the one hand, the issue of the liturgy in the Catholic Church had been one most affected by the pontificate of Francis's predecessor;[15] on the other hand, regarding the liturgy, Francis's pontificate has been marked by a reception of the teaching of Vatican II that does not reduce the council to a corpus of texts and at the same time is faithful to its trajectories—in this case, to the path toward liturgical reform introduced by Vatican II. This is one way to read the notable absence of quotations of *Sacrosanctum concilium* in *Evangelii gaudium*—a document that contains a long section on the homily.

Francis's attention to the issue of the liturgy and its connections to the ecclesiology of Vatican II is evident in *EG*. As Francis notes, liturgy is evangelizing and not part of a power struggle in the church, or a way to express an exclusive ecclesiology, or to use the gospel to ignore the deep solidarity between the church and the world:

> This insidious worldliness is evident in a number of attitudes which appear opposed, yet all have the same pretence of "taking over the space of the Church." In some people we see an ostentatious preoccupation for the liturgy, for doctrine and for the Church's prestige, but without any concern that the Gospel have a real impact on God's faithful people and the concrete needs of the present time. In this way, the life of the Church turns into a museum piece or something which is the property of a select few. (*EG* 95)

In *Laudato si'*, Francis expresses (quoting John Paul II's exhortation *Ecclesia de eucharistia*, 2003) the link between liturgy and a new church-world relationship, speaking of creation and the Eucharist "as an act of cosmic love" (*LS* 236). Also in *Amoris laetitia*, quoting again from the teaching of John Paul II, Francis emphasizes an understanding of the liturgy that connects human love and divine love, thus extending the definition of "liturgical" beyond the boundaries of the liturgical rites of the church: "The procreative meaning of sexuality, the language of the body, and the signs of love shown throughout married life, all become an 'uninterrupted continuity of liturgical language' and 'conjugal life becomes in a certain sense liturgical'" (*AL* 215).

---

15. See Faggioli, "The Liturgical Reform from 1963."

This has been a constant impulse coming from Francis: the visible statements about the liturgical reform of Vatican II—in the direction of a rejection of the plans for a "reform of the liturgical reform" of Vatican II—are substantiated by a much larger body of theology of the liturgy in his pontificate.[16]

Dei verbum: *Exegetes and Theologians*

Among all the major documents of Vatican II that need to be examined to understand Francis's reception of the council, the dogmatic constitution on revelation offers a particular point of comparison with the view of his predecessor, Benedict XVI, for whom *Dei verbum* was probably the keystone of the conciliar teaching.[17]

Francis's theological profile is not that of a biblical scholar. But certainly his preaching is in line with the conciliar recentering on the gospel of Jesus Christ as the "generative grammar" of Catholic theology and magisterium.[18] This passage from *Dei verbum*—"Through this revelation, therefore, the invisible God (see Col 1:15, 1 Tim 1:17) out of the abundance of His love speaks to men [and women] as friends" (2)—represents Francis's new incarnation of the papacy as a way to be the church not based on the gospel or about the gospel but the church *of* the gospel. In the famous passages of *EG* 222 and 231—"time is more important than space" and "reality is more important than ideas"—

---

16. Pope Francis, address to the participants of the 68th National Liturgical Week in Italy, August 24, 2017: "There is still work to be done in this direction, in particular by rediscovering the reasons for the decisions taken with regard to the liturgical reform, by overcoming unfounded and superficial readings, a partial reception, and practices that disfigure it. It is not a matter of rethinking the reform by reviewing the choices in its regard, but of knowing better the underlying reasons, through historical documentation, as well as of internalizing its inspirational principles and of observing the discipline that governs it. After this magisterium, after this long journey, we can affirm with certainty and with magisterial authority that the liturgical reform is irreversible," http://w2.vatican. va. See also the Holy See press office communiqué on July 11, 2016, which disavowed the statement by Cardinal Robert Sarah (prefect of the Congregation for the Divine Worship) and the agenda of the "reform of the liturgical reform" (an expression that the Holy See statement says "may at times give rise to error"), which the cardinal recommended to the clergy in a public lecture in London a few days before: http://press.vatican.va.

17. See the still reliable and very fascinating commentary to *Dei verbum* by Joseph Ratzinger, in *Commentary on the Documents of Vatican II*, vol. 3, trans. and ed. Herbert Vorgrimler (New York: Crossroad, 1989).

18. See Christoph Theobald, *La réception du concile Vatican II,* vol. 1. *Accéder à la source* (Paris: Cerf, 2009), 894–900.

there is an indirect but unquestionable reception of the theological insight of *DV* 8 about the relationship between human experience and God's revelation.[19]

A GENERATIVE RECEPTION OF VATICAN II

Pope Francis's reception of Vatican II is not a textual one but a "generative reception" of the council. In his pontificate, the legacy of the council lives not through quotations from the final documents but in a reception of various conciliar sources and in various ways.

The first way he demonstrates his generative reception of the council is through the use of the texts of Vatican II that do not belong to the formal corpus of the final documents of the council. The most important example of this is found in *Evangelii gaudium* 41, where he discusses the relationship between the deposit of faith and ways to express it. Here, Pope Francis quotes from John XXIII's opening speech of the council, delivered on October 11, 1962, *Gaudet mater ecclesia*—a key (and not at all obvious) source from the history of Vatican II from a hermeneutical point of view:[20]

> At the same time, today's vast and rapid cultural changes demand that we constantly seek ways of expressing unchanging truths in a language which brings out their abiding newness. "The deposit of the faith is one thing . . . the way it is expressed is another" [*Gaudet mater ecclesia*]. There are times when the faithful, in listening to completely orthodox language, take away something alien to the authentic Gospel of Jesus Christ, because that language is alien to their own way of speaking to and understanding one another. With the holy intent of communicating the truth about God and humanity, we sometimes give them a false god or a human ideal which is not really Christian. In this way, we hold fast to a formulation while failing to convey its substance. This is the greatest danger. Let us never forget that "the expression of truth can take different forms. The renewal of these forms of expression becomes necessary for the sake of transmitting to the people of today the Gospel message in its unchanging meaning" [John Paul II, *Ut unum sint* 19]. (*EG* 41)

---

19. See Severino Dianich, *Magistero in movimento: Il caso papa Francesco* (Bologna: EDB, 2016), 63–64.

20. See Giuseppe Alberigo, "Criteri ermeneutici per una storia del Vaticano II," in Giuseppe Alberigo, *Transizione epocale: Studi sul Concilio Vaticano II* (Bologna: Il Mulino, 2009), 29–45.

The other important quotation of *Gaudet mater ecclesia*, however, is in *EG* 84, about the challenges to evangelization and the lack of hope that is typical of our times:

> The joy of the Gospel is such that it cannot be taken away from us by anyone or anything (cf. *Jn* 16:22). The evils of our world—and those of the Church—must not be excuses for diminishing our commitment and our fervor. Let us look upon them as challenges which can help us to grow. With the eyes of faith, we can see the light which the Holy Spirit always radiates in the midst of darkness, never forgetting that "where sin increased, grace has abounded all the more" (*Rom* 5:20). Our faith is challenged to discern how wine can come from water and how wheat can grow in the midst of weeds. Fifty years after the Second Vatican Council, we are distressed by the troubles of our age and far from naïve optimism; yet the fact that we are more realistic must not mean that we are any less trusting in the Spirit or less generous. In this sense, we can once again listen to the words of Blessed John XXIII on the memorable day of 11 October 1962: "At times we have to listen, much to our regret, to the voices of people who, though burning with zeal, lack a sense of discretion and measure. In this modern age they can see nothing but prevarication and ruin. . . . We feel that we must disagree with those prophets of doom who are always forecasting disaster, as though the end of the world were at hand. In our times, divine Providence is leading us to a new order of human relations which, by human effort and even beyond all expectations, are directed to the fulfillment of God's superior and inscrutable designs, in which everything, even human setbacks, leads to the greater good of the Church." (*EG* 84)

In this section of *Evangelii gaudium*, with the quotations from *Gaudet mater ecclesia*, Pope Francis is reenacting Pope John XXIII's reorientation of the church's message, thus showing many parallels between the church at the end of Pius XII's pontificate and at the beginning of his own.[21] Like John XXIII, the election of Francis happened in difficult times for the church not only because of external circumstances but also because of the unstated but clear sense of exhaustion of a given

---

21. On the impact of John XXIII's *Gaudet mater ecclesia* on Vatican II, see John W. O'Malley, *What Happened at Vatican II* (Cambridge MA: Belknap Press of Harvard University Press, 2008), 93–96; Andrea Riccardi, "The Tumultuous Opening Days of the Council," in *History of Vatican II*, dir. Giuseppe Alberigo; English ed. Joseph A. Komonchak, vol. 2 (Maryknoll, NY: Orbis Books, 1997), 14–19.

theological-cultural paradigm and the need to reframe and rephrase the message of the church in a new paradigm. It is no surprise, then, that the resistance and fear of change met by John XXIII at the time of the council is similar to the reception of Pope Francis in some quarters of the Catholic Church today. Since *EG*, Francis has continued to stress the parallels between John XXIII and himself.[22] The bull of indiction of the extraordinary jubilee of mercy, *Misericordiae vultus* (April 11, 2015), quotes once again from John XXIII's opening speech of Vatican II:

> I have chosen the date of 8 December because of its rich mean-
> ing in the recent history of the Church. In fact, I will open the
> Holy Door on the fiftieth anniversary of the closing of the Sec-
> ond Vatican Ecumenical Council. The Church feels a great need
> to keep this event alive. With the Council, the Church entered
> a new phase of her history. The Council Fathers strongly per-
> ceived, as a true breath of the Holy Spirit, a need to talk about
> God to men and women of their time in a more accessible way.
> The walls which for too long had made the Church a kind of
> fortress were torn down and the time had come to proclaim the
> Gospel in a new way. It was a new phase of the same evangeliza-
> tion that had existed from the beginning. It was a fresh undertak-
> ing for all Christians to bear witness to their faith with greater
> enthusiasm and conviction. The Church sensed a responsibility
> to be a living sign of the Father's love in the world. We recall the
> poignant words of Saint John XXIII when, opening the Council,
> he indicated the path to follow: "Now the Bride of Christ wishes
> to use the medicine of mercy rather than taking up arms of sever-
> ity.…. The Catholic Church, as she holds high the torch of Catholic
> truth at this Ecumenical Council, wants to show herself a loving
> mother to all; patient, kind, moved by compassion and goodness
> toward her separated children." (*MV* 4)

The second way that Francis demonstrates his generative reception of Vatican II is his interpretation of the council *as an act* and not
simply as a corpus of final documents—as a reception in acts and

---

22. It is interesting to see that Vatican II is very present in the final document of the Aparecida conference of 2007, but in that document (largely the fruit of Bergoglio's crucial role at that conference of CELAM) John XXIII is not mentioned. Bergoglio's closeness to Roncalli seemed to have been activated, if not caused, by the conclave of 2013. Francis quotes John XXIII's theological testament and last encyclical, *Pacem in terris* (April 11, 1963), in the beginning of the encyclical "On Our Common Home," in *LS* 3.

gestures. Francis's pontificate is part of the new papacy shaped by Vatican II together with the new global media culture, the globalization of religion, and the comeback of religion in international affairs. In this sense, Francis's pontificate is not phenomenally different from the "magisterium of gestures" of his predecessors, at least since John XXIII.

But there are gestures that speak specifically to Francis's global reception of the message of Vatican II:

- His visit to the island of Lampedusa in the Mediterranean on July 8, 2013, to commemorate thousands of migrants who have died crossing the sea, as a sign of a church attentive to the signs of our times;
- The decision to open the Extraordinary Jubilee of Mercy on November 29, 2015, in Bangui, in the Central African Republic, as a sign of a church decentralizing from Rome;
- The visit to migrants and refugees detained on the Greek island of Lesbos on April 16, 2016, as a sign of the ecumenical engagement of the churches in the humanitarian crisis of our time;
- The washing of the feet of a young Muslim woman prisoner in March 2013. Francis's reception of Vatican II as an act is key to understanding his pontificate as a rejection of a neo-exclusivist Catholic ecclesiology.[23]

Gaudium et spes plays a special role in the textual as well as the nontextual, performative reception of Vatican II in Francis's pontificate beginning with his trip to the island of Lampedusa in July 2013. But the textual reception of *Gaudium et spes* constitutes an important part of his teaching for the effort of *recontextualization* of the church against the current *decontextualization* (ideologization and virtualization of the faith experience), and also in terms of recontextualization of the church's teaching in its own tradition: different moments and different voices. In this respect, the use of Vatican II documents in *Amoris laetitia* cannot be examined without a careful look at the complex relations between different sources: the systematic recourse to Jesus's preaching of the gospel; the tradition of the church, especially papal teaching of the twentieth century; and the post–Vatican II teaching of the bishops' conferences.

Francis's nontextual reception of Vatican II was found not just in personal gestures but also in institutional acts. In Francis's pontificate,

---

23. On this, see Gerard Mannion, *Ecclesiology and Postmodernity: Questions for the Church in Our Time* (Collegeville MN: Liturgical Press, 2007).

the most interesting reception of Vatican II as an act has surely been the synodal process of 2014 and 2015 leading to the exhortation *Amoris laetitia*. It is telling of Francis's reception of Vatican II that *Amoris laetitia* relies heavily and creatively on the two 2014 and 2015 synod final reports. Francis chose the texts of the final reports he wanted to quote, and he clearly takes risks vis-à-vis his opposition, making clear his mind and his ecclesiology. Francis quotes from the three paragraphs of the final 2015 report that received the highest number of negative votes.[24] They are significantly used in *Amoris laetitia*'s section on the pastoral accompaniment of difficult situations. But all this is in the context of a reception of the synodal process that follows the intention of Vatican II for the bishops' synod as a body representing effectively the church through the episcopate.

The third demonstration of Francis's generative reception of the council is his understanding of the message of Vatican II *according to the new signs of our times*. This is evident in the example of the "ecumenism of blood," which Francis has talked about since the beginning of his pontificate. There is an ecumenical landscape that has changed tragically as a consequence of the wars that target religious minorities—Christians included—in Africa, the Middle East, and Asia. What Francis called the "ecumenism of blood" is certainly part of his ecumenical outlook, as he said many times and especially in his December 2013 interview with Italian journalist Andrea Tornielli:

> For me, ecumenism is a priority. Today, there's the ecumenism of blood. In some countries they kill Christians because they wear a cross or have a Bible, and before killing them they don't ask if they're Anglicans, Lutherans, Catholic or Orthodox. The blood is mixed. For those who kill, we're Christians. . . . That's the ecumenism of blood. It exists today too, all you have to do is read the papers.[25]

The conciliar intuition of the need for a deeper look at the signs of our times is also evident in Francis's reception of the theological message of Vatican II on ecumenism and religious freedom. His ecumenism shows an intertextual reception of *Unitatis redintegratio*, *Dignitatis humanae*, and *Gaudium et spes*.

---

24. No. 84 (72 no votes); no. 85 (80 no votes); and no. 86 (64 no votes).

25. See Pope Francis's interview with Andrea Tornielli of the Italian newspaper *La Stampa*, December 14, 2013, http://www.lastampa.it/2013/12/15/esteri/vatican-insider/it/mai-avere-paura-della-tenerezza-1vmuRIcbjQlD5BzTsnVuvK/pagina.html.

This has made of Francis a global spokesperson for the defense of the religious freedom of persecuted minorities, such as the Rohingya Muslims in Myanmar,[26] and also a general spokesperson for a Catholic Church that is not concerned about its particular position in the world but about being able to advocate for causes that concern the human person today.

CONCLUSIONS

Scholars of Vatican II saw in the election of Jorge Mario Bergoglio to the papacy something that eluded those who had dismissed the council as an anomaly in the way Catholicism works. Words, symbols, and acts of the 2013 conclave and of the beginning of Francis's pontificate were clearly an echo of the 1958 conclave and of the beginning of John XXIII's pontificate.[27]

There is something especially relevant in this moment of reception of Vatican II at fifty years, that is, a fundamental shift in the status of the council as a point of reference for Catholic theologians and church leaders. There is no question that all the successors of John XXIII were "Vatican II popes" (Paul VI brought the council to a conclusion; John Paul I and John Paul II were council fathers; and Benedict XVI was one of the most important theological *periti* at the council).

But the election of Francis on March 13, 2013, has indubitably changed the landscape of the church and especially of the debate on Vatican II. The fact that Jorge Mario Bergoglio is a Vatican II Catholic—and, in a sense, the first post–Vatican II pope—has changed the nature of the debate on the council.

This meant also the liberation of the papal magisterium from the need to incorporate some of the arguments of the anticonciliar traditionalist narrative on Vatican II. One could see this from the decision announced on January 19, 2019, to abolish the pontifical commission "Ecclesia Dei" created by John Paul II in 1988, and to assign its task to a section within the Congregation for the Doctrine of the Faith.[28] This was one of the most important changes made by Francis to the structure of the Roman Curia during his pontificate, and it is particu-

---

26. See Pope Francis, "Angelus" prayer of Sunday, August 27, 2017, http://w2.vatican.va.

27. On this, see Massimo Faggioli, *A Council for the Global Church: Receiving Vatican II in History* (Minneapolis MN: Fortress Press, 2015).

28. The announcement of the Holy See of January 19, 2019, https://press.vatican.va/content/salastampa/en/bollettino/pubblico/2019/01/19/190114d.html.

larly interesting because it is a change from the decision made by John Paul II for the discussions with the Society of St. Pius X (SSPX), and from Benedict XVI, who gave "Ecclesia Dei" a role that it did not have previously under John Paul II. This decision by Francis is important because it reframed the relationship with the SSPX but also with the fragmented world of Catholic post– and anti–Vatican II traditionalism in general. The *motu proprio* constituted an interesting disclosure by Francis about how he saw the traditionalist issue in the church and how he interpreted the changes since Benedict XVI's *Summorum pontificum*, the *motu proprio* on the liturgy of July 2007. On the one hand, Francis decided that Rome had given the anti–conciliar group SSPX what could possibly be given in terms of normalization of relations; what cannot be given away is the doctrine, that is, Vatican II, which has always been rejected by the SSPX as a legitimate council of the Catholic Church. This is where Francis's decision makes an impact beyond the SSPX and on those Catholics who hoped that the commission "Ecclesia Dei" could bring a traditionalist shift to Rome. The concessions that Francis cannot make to the SSPX about reversing Vatican II are also concessions that he cannot make to traditionalists in communion with Rome. Francis's decision meant that the traditionalists could have the preconciliar liturgy but could not have the doctrine sustaining the preconciliar liturgy. This is true for both the SSPX and the traditionalists in communion with Rome.

Francis's 2019 *motu proprio* that abolished "Ecclesia Dei" is one of the clearest statements of this pontificate on the doctrinal trajectory that the pope has in mind for the Catholic Church. Francis knows that theological and liturgical traditionalism is not going away from Catholicism any time soon. But what is also typical of Francis is the idea that the interpretation of Vatican II as an exercise of textual exegesis made in a historical vacuum is not only a reduction of its meaning; it is also the subtlest form of rejection of the council. The same form of rejection can be seen in those attempts to interpret Francis's papacy outside of the history of the hermeneutics of Vatican II as an act and not just as a series of documents.

4

Catholic Social Teaching
and Forced Migration

Anna Rowlands

Before its demolition in 2016, on the outside wall of the Eritrean-led church in the "Jungle" migrant camp in Calais hung a striking picture of Christ. The large painting, created by a young refugee and former camp resident, depicted Christ knocking on the door of—what can be taken to be—the soul, the church, or the world. It is a peaceful, bucolic image framed by rolling green hills and a calm sea, and in this regard, it was in striking contrast to a second dominating image located within the grey, plastic-sheeted walls of the church's interior: an icon depicting the cosmic battle between good and evil, as recounted in Revelation 12. The war that breaks out in heaven draws the archangel into combat. The forces of evil are overcome through the power of God and the authority of his messiah, and the devil is cast down to earth. With foreboding, it is foretold that earth and sea shall be disturbed until the end of time by the one who brings conflict in his wake. There is rejoicing on earth and in heaven for the victory won for the peaceable kingdom and a prayer made through the saints for the endurance, wisdom, and faith needed to negotiate the conflicts that will blight the earth until the coming of the final judgment. This image at the heart of the makeshift Calais church depicted (as in Orthodox iconography) the archangel Michael holding a sword in his right hand and the scales of justice in his left hand.

In a tradition of CST that has been dominated for a century by christologically inflected natural law, it is notable that Pope Francis's social teaching on migration resonates with the scriptural, mystical, and narrative forms of theological reflection that mark the meaning-making evident among communities of contemporary migrants. Not only has Francis made reflection on migration a stubbornly persistent focus for his papacy, producing an almost endless stream of addresses, sermons, documents, and informal comments on all facets of human migration, but his work has been notably scriptural. Francis has made personal journeys to the sites of arrival, processing, and detention in Europe, offering a message of pastoral proximity and concrete solidarity. He has worked with civil agencies to promote the idea of humanitarian corridors, sponsoring a small number of refugees to move from Lesbos to Rome. Working through his own newly formed Migrant and Refugee Section, he has also addressed the United Nations during their recent Global Compacts migration process[1] and produced an innovative form of CST that aims to guide policy-making on migration in light of CST principles. In sum, it is difficult to see how Francis could have placed greater emphasis on the importance of migration as an epoch-defining social reality. Taken together and viewed analytically, his various initiatives constitute a turn toward the scriptural, an appeal to the duty of renewed humanitarianism at the level of the local and the formally ecclesial, and an appeal to a theological form of what could be read as rooted cosmopolitanism, imagined as a counterpoint to both liberal narratives and the rise of populism and nativism. Francis presents us with a challenge—in response to the realities of contemporary migration and the contexts into and out of which migration is happening—to reimagine the life of the common/s in terms of basic and plural human goods.

THE LONG VIEW

While we tend to date the origins of modern CST to 1891, migration has been a significant theme in the church's wider social reflection since at least the 1850s. Consequently, it is worth exploring the longer theo-historical background that forms the context of Francis's contemporary interventions.

Arguably, the initial impetus for the "modern" tradition of CST on migration emerged from the emigration of European Catholics to the so-called New World, with the migrations out of Europe to the Americas during the mid- and late-nineteenth century raising questions of provision for the religious and pastoral needs of Catholic migrants. This led to the formation of religious orders—perhaps most notably in the field of on-going migrant care were the Scalabrinians—whose

1. See https://refugeesmigrants.un.org/migration-compact.

mission was to ensure practical care and religious instruction for those on the move. The next major impetus for a development in CST on migration came with the internal and external displacement of Europeans following the Second World War. In 1952, Pius XII promulgated his apostolic constitution on forced migration, *Exsul familia*. The title comes from the reference in the first line of the document to the exilic journey of the Holy Family with the child Jesus. Acting as a text that would shape official CST on migration for half a century, *Exsul familia* complemented the pastoral and catechetical emphasis of earlier teaching, offering the beginnings of a systematic and biblical framework to guide ministry among displaced persons. Drawing on the theological trope of the Holy Family as both the model and protector for all displaced persons, Pius devotes much of the heart of the document to an outline of the practical history of Christian ministry among migrants. Emphasizing the initiatives of the institutional church that have aimed to increase the security and dignity of migrants, Pius argues for the reception and integration of migrants within stable political communities and against encampment as a solution. He argues for provision of culturally and linguistically appropriate pastoral and spiritual care and for an awareness of ways to mitigate the dreadful choices that face the destitute.

The next major migration document issued by the Vatican took another fifty-two years to arrive. Issued by Cardinal Hamao and Archbishop Marchetto, president and secretary of the Vatican's Pontifical Council for the Pastoral Care of Migrants and Itinerant Peoples, in May 2004, *Egra migrantes caritas Christi* repeats many of the earlier themes but updates the church's social teaching to reflect the changing nature of migration flows. The increasingly global and South-to-South as well as more politically (and religiously) contested South-to-North and East-to-West migration of the early twenty-first century leads the document's authors to note that any theological discussion of migration must now take account of ecumenical and interfaith responses. Addressing the question of the causes of migration in a more systematic and structural way than previous documents, *Egra migrantes caritas Christi* calls for the intensification of a search for a new economic order that better represents the universal destination of goods and, therefore, reduces the need for survival migration. The document repeats earlier teaching on the need for appropriate pastoral and missiological provision for migrants but also names internal challenges for the order of the church itself as it negotiates the relations of different Catholic cultures brought together in new forms of interaction and division in local and national church contexts.

Promising a fuller scriptural engagement with its theme, *Erga migrantes caritas Christi* delivers a much more explicitly eschatological and teleological framework for social reflection on migration. Faith is said to discover or encounter itself through its special engagement with a social "other" in migration. Faith is evident in both the prophetic act of denunciation of the forms of evil that manifest in survival and forced migratory experience: deportations, dispersals, exploitation, and criminalization; and also in the revelation of exile as our condition and salvation as our yearning. The document argues that any reflection on the meaning of migration from a Christian perspective must take as its end point (and work back from there) the ultimate purpose of human relations: the call to universal communion—what Pope Francis later rephrases in his teaching on migration as "fraternal communion."

The doctrinal focus of *Erga migrantes caritas Christi* falls initially on a hermeneutic of incarnation; meaning is drawn from the idea of the incarnation as a concrete migration of God through human history in the incarnation and the earthly ministry of Christ dominated by the exilic motif.[2] This exilic motif embraces the role of Jesus as the Incarnate Word, as itinerant preacher, and as migrant who transgresses the logic of death and thus transforms the boundaries of human suffering. There are also strong soteriological themes drawn both from the book of Revelation and a particularly strong emphasis on the Pentecost narrative. Ethical import is drawn from the Pentecostal character of the church as an ever-more-vast and varied intercultural society, held in a relationship of fraternity, communication, and difference. This Pentecostal sociality becomes, by analogy, a model for all forms of human community that are called to represent the fullness and diversity of humanity.[3] This serves as the basis for a later distinction between a church called to act without geographical borders and a political community that might make limited and provisional use of territorial borders for reasons of ensuring the universal common good.

The documents of CST on migration also offer a set of gradually developed principles of natural law aimed at orienting church engagement with concrete questions of law and politics in the context of migration. The documents propose, in the first instance, the right

---

2. See the discussion of the biblical context and figure of Christ as refugee in *Erga migrantes caritas Christi* [The Love of Christ toward Migrants] (Vatican City: Pontifical Council for Pastoral Care of Migrants and Itinerant Peoples, 2004).

3. See Catholic Bishops' Conference of England and Wales, *The Dispossessed: A Brief Guide to the Catholic Church's Teaching on Migrants* (2004).

not to be displaced or forced into emigration—a "right to remain."[4] This principle is presented less as an Enlightenment natural right and more an expression of a Thomist Catholic political anthropology. If the human person is by nature a social and political creature, oriented to negotiating one's own good as part of a common good, then achieving basic human flourishing implies the need for membership in a functioning political, economic, and ecological community. Thus both the "right to remain" and the "right to migrate" stem from the same emphasis on the social, political, economic, and cultural (including religious) protection due to the person who belongs to a covenantal political community.

Thus, the second principle of CST on migration teaches that where there is conflict, persecution, violence, hunger, or an inability to subsist, there exist natural and absolute rights of the individual to migrate and a natural right to seek sanctuary within an alternative "safe" political community.[5] This teaching is rooted in a transcendent humanism that recognizes that the well-being of the person is tied to both the good of the bounded community and a prior recognition of a meaningful global citizenship of each person through membership in the universal human family. The task of government is to form judgments about state membership—who can be admitted and recognized as a member—based on a balance of local and universal common goods, offering sanctuary in recognition of its commitment to the universal common good and the universal need for a political "home." It is the task of government to ensure maintenance of the local common good or the just life of the city, such that hospitality and reciprocal exchange between host and migrant is possible within the life of the nation. This implies a duty to think through issues of the universal distribution of goods and cultural dialogue, such that cultures are enabled to engage dialogically and labor markets act to support the basic needs of migrant and settled populations in a nonexploitative manner. The political question of borders is never wholly divorced from the questions of wider economic justice or the value of culture.

Thus a "right to migrate" implies a third principle: a moral requirement placed on existing political communities, especially the most materially privileged, to receive the migrant and hear and assess with justice their claim for admission, transit, or membership.[6] This teaching is nuanced by a fourth principle: the (imperfect) right of a sovereign political community to regulate borders and control migration.

---

4. See *Erga migrantes caritas Christi*.
5. See *GS* 65.
6. See *PT* 106.

CST has not thus far proposed a Christian cosmopolitanism based on completely open borders. Borders are recognized as legitimate only insofar as they protect the common good of the established community and are porous and humane, enabling the established community to enact its duty or obligation to offer hospitality and the right of migrants to exercise their own agency in seeking the goods of survival and life in community. Within the exercise of sovereignty, political communities are invited to include the establishment and oversight of just measures for those who arrive seeking sanctuary and for effective global governance to minimize and accommodate migration flows. Sovereignty and hospitality emerge in CST as mutually implicating; with legitimate sovereignty exercised always with reference to three prior principles: the universal destination of all goods, recognition of the prior and inalienable moral unity of humankind, and the requirement to regulate borders according to basic conditions of human dignity and social justice.[7] Spelling out this teaching in an extended reflection on refugees in *Pacem in terris*, John XXIII taught a normative and transcendent universalism in which the loss of state citizenship implies the need to restore this universal, ineradicable status in practical terms within the territory of another nation.[8]

Finally, recognition of the social and political nature of the person implies a need for multivalent forms of responsibility and judgment (migrant, civil society, and the state) to enable the meaningful social, economic, civic, and political participation of the migrant in the host community.[9] This vision suggests the need to resist capitulation to a model of integration rooted in an assimilationist model of market and state. The model for sociality is one of participation, communication, the contestation and negotiation of goods within a shared social space. The Pentecostal ecclesiology noted in *Erga migrantes caritas Christi* suggests a logic of participation and communion, seeking to foster a genuine human plurality within a harmonious whole.

There is a notable widening of social and theological analysis of migration in the encyclicals issued by John Paul II and Benedict XVI. Both refuse to treat migration as an issue separate from discussion of nuclear weapons, food security, and increases in global inequality. Consequently, they exhort the world to closer analysis of and better responses to the deep roots of displacement—including proposing

---

7. See *CV* 62.

8. See *PT* 25.

9. See John Paul II, *Message for the Day of Migrants and Refugees* (Vatican City, 2001), 3. On the question of just legislation to enable integration and participation in host communities, see also *LE* 23.

the need for new systems of international governance.[10] John Paul II judged that the impact of globalized migrations was to intensify patterns of socialization and argued for greater attention to be paid to the moral corollary of such increased socialization: practices of human solidarity. In a widely quoted passage from *Sollicitudo rei socialis*, John Paul II asserted that interdependence is a mere social fact in an increasingly globalized world, but solidarity is the moral perspective we use to interpret the meaning and possibility for virtue implicit in this fact. Solidarity is not, then, simply a duty to respect rights in the face of globalized movements of people; it calls for a deeper form of social creativity, in which our communities are refashioned as socialization gives way to concrete forms of solidarity. Benedict XVI focused particularly on the duty to create well-ordered systems to manage migration flows. Considering his reconsideration of the principle of subsidiarity, he argues that the appropriate level for moral engagement with this issue is now between states at an international level:

> We can say that we are facing a problem of epoch-making proportions that requires bold, forward-looking policies of international cooperation if it is to be handled effectively. Such policies should set out from close collaboration between migrants' countries of origin and their countries of destination; it should be accompanied by adequate international norms able to coordinate different legislative systems with a view to safeguarding the needs and rights of individual migrants and their families, and at the same time, those of the host countries.[11]

REFASHIONING THE NARRATIVE

The papacy of Pope Francis has coincided with intensification in patterns of global forced migration, the paradox of both shrinking and

---

10. In *Sollicitudo rei socialis* (On Social Concern) (1987) John Paul II reads forced migration in the context of a logic of death that refuses to engage deeper moral reflection on social changes that could lead to a "more human life" and true human development. He notes the continual failure to seek a peaceful international order and suggests that the isolationism of modern states mitigates against solutions to systemic issues that lie at the root of migration concerns. See nos. 23–25. In Benedict XVI's *Caritas in veritate* migration figures in the sociological context of all that challenges authentic human development and the opportunities for cooperation and solidarity that exist within the universal human family. See no. 62.

11. *CV* 62.

expanding forms of humanitarian response and increased public and scholarly debate about forced migration. This process is rendered most visible in the rise in the numbers of internally and externally displaced persons, a rise in long, drawn-out wars and consequent protracted refugee situations, and in increased politicization of the issue of migration. In making physical journeys to the heart of the geo-political sites that most represent our collective struggles with migration questions—to the shores where migrants arrive from sea and to in-country holding facilities—Francis is deeply aware that migrants seeking entry to northern states find that the most fundamental challenges to dignity in the migration process now often occur in the spaces between states and the internal spaces states create as structures of juridical exception. Principally, these are maritime spaces, and spaces of encampment and transit created within nation-states where law is suspended. Contemporary forced migrants negotiate the challenges of both mobility and immobility as part of their refugee journeys. The reemergence of a pastoral ministry of the borderlands has been a crucial focus for the theo-political ministry of Francis.

While this new era of migration has not yet led to the production of a further church document on migration, Francis has chosen to make migrant and refugee concerns a central focus of his papacy and has produced an unprecedented volume of teaching on the subject through homilies, addresses, and public statements. He has established a new body to oversee the Vatican's migration and refugee work and through this new body has issued a brief, interesting document to coincide with the United Nations' Global Compacts on Migration. On the one hand, Francis has adopted a theological approach that owes less to natural law and public reason traditions (while nonetheless repudiating neither) and more to a liberationist and Ignatian engagement, and public conjuring, with Scripture. This teaching should be read in the context of Francis's wider teaching that the church must become a church of the poor. He has used preaching and a homiletic style to great—sometimes ecclesially and politically contentious—effect as a form of public apologetics. On the other hand, the brief text prepared for the UN process arguably reinvigorates and extends the Catholic natural law tradition of public reasoning on migration. Francis's papacy marks both a point of deep continuity with the natural law teaching outlined above, which he does nothing to repudiate, and significant novelty when viewed through the lens of his homiletic, informal, and directed policy interventions on migration.

Francis's best-known address on migration was made during a 2013 homily on the island of Lampedusa. The homily places the wider political dynamics that shape the migration experience in the context of Christian narratives of creation, fall, and redemption.[12] Francis begins with a reflection on the first two questions that God asks humanity in Scripture: Adam, where are you? Cain, where is your brother?[13] Francis interprets these passages as stories of human disorientation, of the first signs of a tendency in humankind to lose our place within creation, to lose our orientation as creatures toward a creator. Thus, to Fall is to be disoriented and to lose our bearings. It is striking that Francis juxtaposes an account of the disorientation of the "settled" in relation to the orientation of the displaced. This appears as a narrative and doctrinal reframing of a debate the church has couched in more rationalist language concerning the human search to secure particular individual, public, and common goods. Francis offers a profoundly theological perspective to a debate that tends to be framed as an external legitimation about sovereign borders: in order to identify what might be going wrong politically in our failure to respond adequately to the challenge of the displaced, we must first come to recognize our own disorientation.

Francis explains this disorientation not only in terms of a classic account of the Fall but also in terms of the particular conditions of late modernity that seem to mitigate against our ability to perceive and know our disorientation. In various addresses and homilies, Francis grounds indifference to migrants in a culture of individualism that he thinks breeds anxiety and cynicism and in a capitalist market culture that reduces people to narrow economic value yet simultaneously fails to deliver real economic value. He also criticizes a therapeutic narcissism that he calls a culture of "well-being." Our own transient cultural ways breed indifference toward truly transient people. That we—the disorientated "settled"—have forgotten how to inhabit space, place, and time well seems to be the conclusion he wishes us to draw. While many contemporary secular studies of migration point to the way that state border policies disorder time for migrants—protracted journeys, lengthy waits, and traumatic experiences that seem to foreclose future promise—Francis's theological contribution to this debate is to both echo these insights and to throw the mirror back on the disordered relationship to temporality of the "settled." Thus, globalization, which creates ironically the transience of the settled, produces as its

---

12. Text of Pope Francis's homily on Lampedusa (July 8, 2013) is available at http://w2.vatican.va.

13. The narrative of Cain and Abel is a trope to which Francis has returned on numerous occasions, most recently in his treatment of integral ecology in *Laudato si'*.

by-product the globalization of indifference. In turn, the equally anti-theological by-product of the culture of indifference is that we ourselves become anonymous: we seem unable to understand ourselves as named, particular, and responsible persons in relation to named, particular, and responsible others. "The globalization of indifference makes us all 'unnamed' . . . without names and without faces."[14] And thus we all cry out but often with the wrong object as the focus of our cries and our perceived "settled" woundedness. Francis emphasizes that this dynamic of anonymity is the opposite of the creator–creature relationship, through which we are named, and as named beings called to account for other named beings.

This approach to the ethics of migration deals less with the external borders of the nation-state and more with the prior internalized borders of the human will as the "matter" at the heart of a properly theological ethics. These two sets of borders—one geopolitical and one interior to the human self—are not opposed to each other as matters to be treated by two different kinds of "specialists" but rather are read dialectically against each other. There is no repudiation of a theological critique of the moral function of borders, no spiritualization of forced migration. Francis's constructive theological response to this situation is rooted in an appeal, via scriptural narrative, to a renewed natural-law personalism mixed with a strong communitarian dimension. He emphasizes both universal kinship and familial relations (literal and figurative) alongside a person-centered culture of political decision-making and a necessary respect for the basic dignity and rights of the person that go way beyond the narrow offerings of current legislative regimes. Read one way, Francis can be interpreted as renewing a Maritain-like personalist appeal to the rights inherent in the person as such, much in line with—but updating—the tone of teaching on forced migration in *Pacem in terris*.

However, more unusually in the canon of modern CST, there is also a more mystical-political turn discernible in Francis's recent addresses. Francis argues that the capacity to break through cultural indifference comes not only through an in-principle affirming of the rights due to the person as such but that such a recognition becomes possible when one adopts a contemplative gaze. He suggests that a contemplative gaze is necessary to reorient perception toward the universal dimensions of kinship. He tackles this in two ways: through the theme of "suffering with" as an antidote to indifference (the theme of his Lampedusa sermon) and through a more constructive vision of the relationship

---

14. See text of Pope Francis's Lampedusa homily at http://w2.vatican.va.

between the heavenly and earthly cities. He notes that contemplating the life of the New Jerusalem allows us to see differently the life of the earthly city. With strong echoes of St. Augustine's "two cities," he hints that those who are able to see the connections between the heavenly city (manifest in the communion of saints) and the cities we live in now will be able to break through the pervasive culture of indifference. The "fruits" of this contemplation—which implies, although does not make explicit, a Pauline logic of gift—are a spirit of dialogue and encounter. This dialogue and encounter do not exist only as interesting ends in themselves but as the basis for a new creativity: new forms of service, justice, and love that the Spirit can inspire through such contemplative-led engagement. The first form of social action in relation to migration is thus conceived as a receptive one, for both "host" and migrant alike. Through openness to this receptive and creative movement, including when such Christian engagement is interfaith, the Christian encounters Jesus Christ. This is the flesh on the bones of Francis's call that we see "fraternal communion" as the necessary context of the upholding of rights and as the end goal of a Catholic ethics of migration. The process of moving beyond ourselves through contemplation to receive the gift that enables us to perceive our social reality in its fragmented forms returns us, via the other, in reciprocal gift exchange and dialogue, to (and beyond) ourselves. Contemplation becomes the way to see what concretely *is* in all its stark difficulty and possibility, and to be moved by it. The process of attending to issues of migration is thus thoroughly theological for Francis; a transcendent account is the necessary ground for an ethics of seeing and being with others in a context of structural and social sin; and the social dimension of reality is the necessary, unavoidable grounds of our ongoing Christian conversion toward a life of communion.

The addresses, documents, and homilies delivered by Francis have also utilized and developed the basic categories and principles of the social encyclicals. Francis develops the fundamental theological vision we noted above into a corresponding analysis of institutional and social processes. In *Laudato si'*, Francis connects the failure of law to respond to the pressing challenges brought by increased forced migration to a deep failure in civil society. Indifference to migrant suffering in Europe suggests not just the failure of government or the individual but—of central concern to CST—"the loss of that sense of responsibility for our fellow men and women upon which all civil society is founded."[15] This hints at both a modern liberal conception

---

15. *LS* 25.

of the basis of good law—*nomos* emerging from the social body acting both as legislator and the entity shaped by law—and also a continued complex Catholic philosophical view of social life rooted in plural forms of associational life, thus extending the insight beyond a social contractarian view of the constitution of good law.[16]

In later addresses, Francis argues that solutions to the current suffering of migrants lie at the level of nation-states, within regions, as well as at the level of local civil (including ecclesial) society. He suggests that "solutions" lie within a newly generated, mutually constituted political space in which all levels of social organization play their part. He calls for an expansion of humanitarian corridors organized by networks of civil actors and of local Catholic parishes and organizations acting as refugee hosts. Francis's teaching offers a more place-based and communitarian vision of migrant response than his two predecessors, emphasizing the constantly interconnected relationship of the local and global and states that the global is encountered in concrete terms through the particular. His proposals are focused not only on law and rights but also on a commitment to a reconstituted political order.

While the theological themes of Francis's teaching are striking, it is worth noting that his interventions on forced migration have also been novel in more political and ecclesiological terms. While Francis acts and speaks as a resolutely global figure utilizing global platforms and networks, his focus has taken the form of calls for a renewal of local faith-based action. While the teaching of his immediate predecessors focused much more heavily on calls for global governance structures and greater cooperation between states, Francis has refocused Catholic migration teaching on the potential for avowedly local, place-based humanitarianism and civil action. While Francis's calls have been made in both overtly scriptural language as well as a universal language of justice and solidarity, his calls can be read as parallel to movements within humanitarian policy toward localized responses to reception, protection, and integration of forced migrants. Such an emphasis is strongly theologically informed and also mirrors wider trends in refugee response.

The stories told by contemporary South-to-North migrants indi-

---

16. While clearly not a source of influence, it is worth noting the parallels between what Francis hints at in his comments on the failure of civil society vis-à-vis the failure of law and Seyla Benhabib's concept of jurisgenerativity as a crucial part of renewing law in relation to the claims of migrants. See Seyla Benhabib, *Exile, Statelessness and Migration: Playing Chess with History from Hannah Arendt to Isaiah Berlin* (Princeton, NJ: Princeton University Press, 2018).

cate that the failures of nation-states to provide well-ordered and just processes for reception, handling, and later integration of migrants impact not simply the dignity of the migrant but also the overall possibility of a just outcome. Their stories also indicate that local humanitarianism—both from local citizen hosts and between refugee hosts and other refugees—remains a major source of assistance for those on the move or those migrants trapped in forms of increasing immobility or stuckness during transit. This is especially clear in South-to-South migration contexts but also applies to South-to-North migration. While CST as a formal, disciplined body of thought has yet to fully address such insights drawn from shifting migrant experience and remains a largely top–down body of work, Francis's teaching clearly nudges church social teaching in the direction of a more dialogical engagement with migrant experience and with a more localized and reciprocal ethics of response. Francis has chosen to highlight significant barriers to integration at the local level as well as the necessary responsibility local hosts take and must take for engaging with displaced people. He has not repudiated the call for greater international cooperation through global management bodies made by his two predecessors and has engaged in direct ways with the UN Global Compacts processes, but his emphasis has fallen more heavily than his predecessors on local and more informal faith-inspired humanitarianisms. This shift should be read in theological, political, and pastoral terms.

Francis updates and expands the natural-law principles outlined by his predecessors in two ways. Following the motif of his pontificate, he presents the principles more accessibly and concretely. Engaging in an act of translation, he simplifies previous natural-law-based migration teaching into the simplified form of four verbs: to welcome, to protect, to promote, and to integrate. "Conjugating these four verbs is a duty," says Francis, "a duty of justice, civility and solidarity." He defines welcome as provision of safe and legal programs of reception, providing personal safety for arriving migrants, and access to services. "Protecting" implies availability of relevant and accurate information, defending basic rights independent of legal status and a duty to provide special care for child migrants. "Promoting" is defined as ensuring the conditions for the development of migrants according to their own needs and capacities and those of native citizens. Francis places greater emphasis than his predecessors on the duty of state and civil society to promote mutual integral development of migrants and citizens and to facilitate state and local actors in developing new forms of sustainable hospitality. Supporting integration implies providing opportunities for intercultural encounter and active citizenship. Francis addresses the question of culture by reminding Europeans that this is not simply a question of reflecting on the impact of the arrival of perceived cultural "others" but also a matter of the internal erosion of a vision of "integral humanism" core to European ideals. Francis calls this vision "the finest fruits of European civilization." The vacuum left by liberal individualism and the commodification of reason causes fear and cynicism to take root. Francis is clear that migration does raise cultural and theological questions, but those questions are as much about the atrophied moral performance of Western and European projects and its attendant politics of identity as they are about the presence of cultural "others" and demographic change.

Francis also updates the church's social analysis of contemporary migration trends and integrates the principles of CST into this picture. He proposes that the key causes of contemporary displacement are armed conflict and social violence, poverty, economic crisis and exploitation, ecological change and climate vulnerability, political instability, and corruption. He proposes that the current practice of border closing can itself constitute a form of cooperation with moral evil when shown that it leads to intensification of vulnerability and the criminal exploitation of forced migrants. Borders do not serve the good when they intensify rather than mitigate vulnerability, even for nonmembers. Such a claim is rooted in his wider account of a priori universal human kinship as well as a thoroughly historical appeal to moral action and its effects in a globalized, interconnected world. For both reasons, he repeats that the only possible ethical response to forced migration flows—whether economic or political—is solidarity.

To understand what Francis means when he refers to solidarity requires us to remind ourselves of its earlier definition in the social teaching of John Paul II. Solidarity as a principle does not aim to invoke a weak universal benevolence but rather a structural orientation toward ensuring the dignity and development of the human person. He connects this ethic of solidarity to a critique of reductionist views of the human person that dominate debates about migration, in which the person is reduced to economic, legal, or political concerns. Francis notes that such reductionism offends against the principle of human dignity and is most visible in debates about legal and illegal migrants and when deciding national priorities for legal pathways. The use of humanitarian reason as part of a system of categorization is not exempt from this critique.

Francis repeats both the paternal and fraternal corporate themes of earlier CST, emphasizing the particular threat to the family posed by current migration patterns shaped through inadequate or hostile policies.[17] The separation of families, the increased risk of exploitation arising from the closure of borders, and the failure of dignified reception processes and the inherent trauma of forced migration are all noted as threats to the dignity of the family. The moral framework through which Francis views migration continues to be that of the natural mobility of humankind and (without fundamental contradiction) a natural search for roots and a common life through which the human person comes to self-knowledge and fulfillment and is enabled to transcend the narrow borders of the self through acts of love and service. Francis continues to teach that, even when migrant journeys are brought about by loss, disaster, and evil, God finds ways to wrest blessing; and God's command to love of neighbor requires an openness to cooperate with that process of wresting blessing in the context of loss.

TWO CONCLUDING
POLITICAL-THEOLOGICAL CONSIDERATIONS

To place Francis's work on migration within the long view might also lead us to read his contribution alongside the wider streams of (often overlooked) *informal* Catholic social and political thought.[18] Over the last two years, I have been particularly struck by the surprising parallels between Francis's rendering of both the reality of forced migration and debates about migration (it is politically necessary to make some distinction between the two) and the mystical, political writings of the mid-twentieth-century French philosopher Simone Weil. A French-Jewish refugee who wrote from within the Christian philosophical tradition and who died in exile in her thirties in mid-war England, Weil wrote powerfully of migration in the context of what she cast as the "uprootedness" of modern societies. She considered that visibly uprooted peoples (the displaced) were the tangible signs of a deeper, less immediately visible all-pervasive, cultural-economic system that

---

17. Here I am using the distinction James Chappel draws between paternal and fraternal traditions in *Catholic Modern: The Challenge of Totalitarianism and the Remaking of the Church* (Cambridge, MA: Harvard University Press, 2018).

18. It is interesting to note, as an aside, that many of the plural and highly diverse new lay movements that are taking root across the global context are drawing on the informal and unofficial tradition of Catholic social intellectual and activist thought and less than one might expect on formal CST. This is, I think, a notable current trend. One example can be found in the sources noted on the website of the French movement *Limite*, www.revuelimite.fr.

created a culture of uprootedness as a common, shared condition. Her intention was not to extend the idea of displacement gratuitously to whole populations and thus rob the term of any meaning but to name the processes of (post)industrial capitalism that, she understood, disoriented persons from rightly oriented relations to place, time, nature, production, and the other. She considered that the structures of capitalist markets and the workplace, the operation of private property, class systems, and liberal systems of political representation to each and in combination manifest and reproduce such uprootedness.[19]

Interestingly, akin to Francis's emphasis on the disorientation of the settled, Weil suggested that this uprootedness produced blindness to the conditions and deep causes of displacement. Her remedy takes the form of training in a process of individual and communal attention to the other and to the conditions of affliction. I doubt very much that Weil has been a direct influence on Francis, and there are certainly tensions between Weil's mystical, political theology and a doctrinal Catholicism (her unorthodox Christology and theodicy as starting points), but nonetheless, the parallels in thinking are striking and interesting to a contemporary reader. Both Francis and Weil view an ethics of migration as necessitating a broader account of the disorientation of cultures; both insist on the need for a contemplative-political response to displacement; and both view a willingness to enter into contexts of suffering as a necessary part of an ethical path. Yet neither wishes to make suffering in itself useful or justifiable. Neither valorizes the refugee as such but focuses on the moral obligations that stem from the mere fact of displacement and its complex material causes. Both refuse to view questions of refugee rights separately from forms of social, legal, political, and economic (dis)order.

By attending to the parallels between Weil's and Francis's renderings of the mystical politics of migration, we can begin to place Francis's social teachings not only within the line of official CST but also within the tradition of twentieth-century political theology, more specifically a mid-century tradition of thought that did not win out at the end of the war and consequently, until recently, was largely forgotten. Weil, prefiguring Francis's insights on disorientation, suffering, and attention, was nonetheless a strong critic of Maritain's personalism and

---

19. See Simone Weil, *The Need for Roots* (New York: Routledge, 2011). For Weil's work on refugee writing and reflection on the conditions of love and force as it pertains to uprootedness, see "The Iliad, or the Poem of Force," in George Panichas, *The Simone Weil Reader* (New York: Moyer Bell, 1977). See also Simone Weil, "Fragments, London 1943," in *Oppression and Liberty* (London: Routledge, 1965).

the early stages of its embrace by the church. She issued a critique of the turn toward human rights language and the uses of theology to ground these claims and preferred a philosophy of mutual obligation and what she called the *impersonalism* of duty for the other.[20] Francis is perhaps not only resurrecting and developing aspects of the church's social teaching in his remarks on migration but also returning us in rather interesting (if incomplete and almost certainly accidental) ways to resources from a lay Christian philosophical path not taken in the immediate aftermath of the Second World War—a path that might be fruitful for the church to revisit and one in which refugee political theologians were prominent thinkers. Given Francis's teaching in *Laudato si'* and the turn toward a more comprehensive social ecological account of our times—toward an account of the systematic denaturing of our ways of living and dying—it is worth noting that there is a wider tradition that Francis might continue to weave together and develop as the intellectual theological hinterland that might challenge our current denatured political gaze. This is a collaborative task that might be shared among lay political theologians, migrant communities who are again reflecting theologically and politically, and the papacy of Francis.

A second theo-political challenge relates to oft-repeated journalistic and theological mischaracterizations of Francis's teaching on migration as a form of liberal cosmopolitanism. This is an unhelpful and inaccurate categorization for two reasons. As we have explored above, Francis's teaching on migration is strongly theologically rooted and sits in some evident tension with the neoliberal philosophies such analyses assume cosmopolitan thought to rest upon. Yet, such a categorization tends to be as poor a reading of the varied and pluriform cosmopolitan tradition as it is of Francis's own contribution. Seyla Benhabib argues that in its classical eighteenth- and nineteenth-century and contemporary forms cosmopolitanism tends toward two different traditions: "positive" and "negative."[21] Negative traditions of cosmopolitanism drawn from a Cynic heritage tend to rest on sentiments of necessary nomadism and universalism emanating from either a desired detachment from the particularities of place or from recognition of the inevitable, sometimes catastrophic failures associated with the life of the city. We despair of the fragility of the particular and invest in the universal. By contrast, "positive" cosmopolitan

---

20. See Weil, *The Need for Roots.*

21. See Benhabib, *Exile, Statelessness and Migration,* and (for her discussion of different lineages of cosmopolitanism) see *Dignity in Adversity: Human Rights in Turbulent Times* (Cambridge: Polity Press, 2011), 1–20.

accounts, drawing from a Stoic genealogy, do not suggest such an inherently agonistic or broken relation of the universal and particular, and instead ground the ethical life of the particular person and place in what is already and transferably universal. The sharing of reason makes possible the sharing of law, belonging, and cohabitation. We begin from what is universal and work toward the particular.

It is this second strand of cosmopolitanism—seen by postliberals as both anthropologically flawed and easily co-opted by late capitalism—that is the assumed point of universal reference for cosmopolitanism among many current commentators. It is such contemporary cosmopolitans that David Goodhart seeks to immortalize in his recent work on the rise of populism, *The Road to Somewhere*, cast in his terms as the "citizens of anywhere."[22] To characterize Francis as a liberal cosmopolitan in these prelapsarian political terms makes little sense. Nonetheless, Benhabib's "negative" tradition of cosmopolitanism does have an important and almost entirely overlooked theological lineage in eighteenth- and nineteenth-century Christian and Jewish thought that is worth noting. Jewish traditions of cosmopolitan thought drew from the dark experience of exclusion, forced nomadism, and expulsion of the Jews and insisted on the need for a political-theological cosmopolitanism that was capable of addressing the persistent failures of political communities to provide membership for all human persons. This tradition held onto both the abiding importance of place and rootedness, even the sacredness of this, but recognized the persistent uprooting of people from place, the continuous history of the generation of placeless persons, that impelled a necessary cosmopolitanism. The tradition of CST, including Francis's contribution to reflection on migration, does not fit neatly into either Cynic or Stoic, "positive" or "negative" genealogies of cosmopolitanism; they cut across both and speak in a different voice. We are living through a time when the public contestation of ideas that draw from both kinds of cosmopolitan traditions and from long traditions of nativist populism has become brittle and deadly; and with it the life of the commons (beyond mere citizenship) is also brittle and threatened. With both this debate in mind and with the reality of increasingly large numbers of displaced and displaced-immobile people globally, a willingness to engage with the terms of this debate and to retrieve and rethink its theological forms seems important intellectual-apologetic and pastoral-prophetic ground for the church. There is, arguably, a form of theological cosmopolitanism in Francis's thought, but it is neither that of the crude com-

---

22. David Goodhart, *The Road to Somewhere: The Populist Revolt and the Future of Politics* (London: C. Hurst, 2017).

mentators nor easily situated in the landscape of crumbling secular cosmopolitan options. Nonetheless, if it can continue to stretch and open itself to responding to the fundamental challenges unfolding around us, it has something compelling to say to a necessary but ever more fragile life of a truly common good.

5

A Latin American Pope

Óscar Andrés Cardinal Rodríguez Maradiaga, SDB

Pope Francis was born on December 17, 1936, in Buenos Aires, into a family of Italian immigrants. He went to public school. He studied to be a chemical technician and, at twenty-one, decided to enter the Jesuit novitiate. He graduated in philosophy and was ordained to the priesthood at thirty-three years of age. Soon after began a rapid career in the Society of Jesus.

At the age of thirty-seven, he became the superior (provincial) of the Jesuits in his country. In 1992, he was appointed auxiliary bishop of Buenos Aires, one of the most populated cities of the continent, and in 1998, he became the archbishop of the church there. Created a cardinal in 2001 by John Paul II (at the same time as myself, so we can call ourselves to be "of the same graduating class"), he then became the president of the Episcopal Conference of Argentina, a position he held until 2011.

He has been recognized by all for renewing the church of Argentina and is an austere person, of deep spirituality, and devoted to the secular traditions of Catholicism. He never lived in an elegant mansion and always traveled by public transportation. His trips to Rome were in economy class. Bergoglio has distinguished himself by his speeches denouncing poverty, corruption, and what he calls political "tension."

ELECTION

The Argentinian cardinal, Jorge Mario Bergoglio, was elected supreme pontiff at seventy-six years of age and chose to be called Francis in honor of St. Francis of Assisi. He succeeded Pope Benedict XVI and is the 265th successor of Saint Peter. He is the first pontiff to be called Francis, the first Latin-American, and the first Jesuit to hold the seat of Saint Peter. He was elected on Wednesday, March 13, 2013, in the fifth round of voting during the conclave, which began the day before, in the Vatican's Sistine Chapel, at which were present 115 cardinals from fifty nations. After the white smoke appeared around 7 p.m., everyone was eager to meet the new pope.

Following the white smoke announcing that a new pope was chosen, the bells of St. Peter's Basilica pealed, confirming the decision. An hour later, the windows of the central balcony (loggia) of St. Peter's Basilica in the Vatican, overlooking St. Peter's Square, were thrown open, and the famous *Habemus papam* ("we have a pope") proclaimed the name of Bergoglio. Bergoglio wasn't on anyone's short list—only the Holy Spirit knew. He took office six days after his election on the feast of St. Joseph, March 19, 2013.

Francis wore a white robe and a stole, but not the typical red cape. This was the sign that he wanted to be a pope of simplicity. He looked out on the plaza with deep emotion and offered a simple *Buonasera*, Italian for "Good evening." "Before all else, I want to ask you a favor: I want to pray for our Emeritus Pope Benedict XVI. Let us all pray together for him that the Lord bless him and Our Lady protect him"; this was followed by a greeting and message to the world in Italian and an Our Father, a Hail Mary, and a Glory Be. It was a simple start for a simple man.

A NEW "JOURNEY"

The day of his election, in a brief introduction to the whole world, the new pope announced that he was now starting "a journey" for which he asked us to pray for one another so that there might be a great sense of community: "I hope that this journey of the church which we begin today might be for evangelization." In addition, he asked all to pray in silence, that God might assist him in his work.

Today, we know that the journey that the pope has undertaken is that of the poor, of synodality and collegiality, and of the spiritual renewal of the church. All those roads lead to Christ. They are not three personal choices but three vital impulses that the church needs, according to the deliberations of the cardinals during the preconclave meetings and that any elected pope would have to assume as an imperative, taking into account the global reality of the church and the deep transformations of society.

To follow this journey is to follow the inspiration of the Holy Spirit, who led Jesus into the desert (see Mark 1:12). All of us at some point in our lives, after having sought in vain the meaning of our existence, have set our sights toward the river of history. We have left aside the task of finding our own way in order to let the One who is the Way seek us out. We have stopped probing our own concerns in order to let he who is Truth share his concerns with us. We no longer live for ourselves for he who is Life offers us an abundant life that we might share it with others.

This is precisely what Jesus experienced when he went into the wilderness: he stopped for a moment on his journey and was touched by the questions that God addressed to him through the lives of his people. It was in this context of silence and solitude that he went about discovering what his Father was asking of him. It was there that he felt the trials and temptations. Pope Francis came to Rome where he has encountered not a few difficulties that he needed to face from the moment he assumed the path of the poor, the journey of synodality, and the spiritual renewal of the church. Difficulties and hostilities have tried to overshadow his prophetic mission, seeking to confuse, worry, and scare him, just like Christ when he was tempted in the wilderness, but we know that the Holy Spirit chose Francis, taking him to a remote place, to the existential desert of Rome, and the Spirit who began his good work in Francis has the power to bring it to a blessed completion.

ETHNICITY

The faithful, amazed and proud, call Francis the "first Latino pope," Spanish-speaking, Argentinian-born; but for some American-born Latinos, there is a problem. Pope Francis's parents were Italian. In Argentina, there are many grandchildren and even sons and daughters of Italians. Most of the surnames are Italian, to the point that, in some schools in Buenos Aires, Córdoba, and San Miguel, you would find the same names as in a school in Rome, Turin, or Treviglio. They share the same cultural roots, the same ancestral patterns, and a wide variety of items that speak of a multicultural, multiracial, and multinational Argentina.

The fact has revived debate in the United States about what it means to be Latino. Those who question the pontiff's Latino identity recognize that he is Latin American and is a great source of pride for Spanish-speaking Catholics around the world. But for some that doesn't mean that he is "Latino." These seem to be a minority, but they have taken a toll on the debate in the United States around this man and this moment, which are so unique. Are the Italians Latinos? Some say no, others say yes, that the quintessential Latinos are from the Lazio region, which is the cradle of the Italian language; and insofar as Italian is a romance language, so are Spanish, French, and Portuguese.

The day of Francis's election, a newspaper asked, "Should a Latino have native blood?"[1] Regardless of his ethnicity, the controversy reveals the importance of the man known to Latino Catholics around the world until recently as Jorge Mario Bergoglio. His two given names are completely Castilian, although his two surnames (Bergoglio and Sivori) are Italian. There we see the result of an authentic inculturation and a genuine assumption of the Hispanic cultural condition of the predominantly Castilian environment that Jorge Mario Bergoglio would grow up in, without renouncing his authentically Italian origins.

The roots of the debate are anchored in history and geography. Latin America is a complex region of deep racial expressions and class. Elites tend to be of white European origin. The poor tend to be the dark-skinned descendants of indigenous or African peoples. Latinos can be of any race; many identify themselves as Latino and white, or black and Latino. And so the inevitable debate after the elevation of this son of Italians, of white complexion, born in the most European city in South America that has always been identified with Rome, Madrid, and London. Of course, if one is born in Latin America, speaks Spanish, knows their history and their culture, has a passport from a Latin American nation, and has the cultural sensitivity of a Latino, then he is Latino. Pope Francis, I can assure you, loves the tango, drinks the traditional infusion "mate," and is a big fan of the soccer club San Lorenzo de Almagro. In other words, he is an Argentinian.

A MARIAN POPE

After extending his first blessing and indulgence *Urbi et Orbi*, to the city of Rome and to the whole world, he then, before departing, announced that on the following day, Thursday, he was going to pray to Our Lady for the protection of the church.

Although perhaps it goes unnoticed in his preaching, the presence of the Virgin Mary in his homilies and catechesis is constant. Some time ago, he declared that his devotion to the Virgin was to be attrib-

---

1. Dennis Romero, "Jorge Mario Bergoglio: Is the New Pope Latino?," *LA Times*, March 13, 2013.

uted to the Salesians of Don Bosco from his student days in the College Wilfrid Baron of the Holy Angels, in Ramos Mejía, Argentina.

Francis's unwavering spirit of renewal combines with a strong and tender devotion to the mother of God. Francis is a person of strong faith and simple piety. In front of any image of the Virgin, he always devotes loving looks and glances; and among all the Marian devotions there is one to which he feels particularly drawn: La Desatanudos, the "Untier of Knots." The devotion originated in Germany and is widespread in Argentina.

Commenting on the need for vigilance in times of personal confusion, Francis evokes the guidance of the Russian fathers to "seek refuge under the mantle of the holy Mother of God." This Marian shelter, the pope reminds us, "forms part of the liturgy as well, by which the believer declares to find safety under the *presidium* ("refuge") of Mary: *sub tuum presidium confugimus, Sancta Dei genitrix* ("under your protection we take refuge, holy Mother of God"). In this way, not praying to Mary in times of need is like being an orphan.

Those who follow Francis are familiar with his visit before and after every trip to the precious Byzantine icon of the *Salus Populi Romani*, the patron saint of the city of Rome, of which he is bishop.

It is also not uncommon to see Francis praying the Hail Mary with the pilgrims who arrive in St. Peter's Square, and among the objects he carries in his pocket can be found the rosary. Yes. It is a rosary that already has a guardian—quite young, by the way, but appointed by the pope in person. It was February 15, 2016, during his visit to Mexico. He said to this boy, "I'm going to bless you and name you custodian of my rosary. And you will always look after it, is that right? And occasionally, pray for me?"

In Mexico, before the Virgin of Guadalupe, he prayed in silence for about twenty-five minutes while a crowd was waiting for him outside.

At the beginning of his pontificate, standing in front of the image of Our Lady of Fatima, he asked her to take care of the poor and those who are excluded.

These are constant gestures that express a form of simple but not childish faith. This is true because, for the pope, the Virgin is so fundamental to the church, just as a mother is to a family.

We noted earlier that Pope Francis loves soccer. Well, his devotion to the Virgin led to soccer, as I will explain: the Salesian priest Enrique Pozzoli, who baptized Jorge Mario on December 25, 1936, was also a fan of San Lorenzo, and he believed that the blue and red colors of the team were provided by the Virgin Mary Help of Christians for this traditional soccer team, of which the pope is an intense admirer.

ST. JOSEPH

Devotion to St. Joseph is one of the most popular devotions through-out Latin America and Italy, and Pope Francis is clearly devoted to him. When Pope Francis speaks to us of St. Joseph, he always calls him a custodian, which is his job, to take care of and be in charge of what came unexpectedly to him, a son, whom he had not fathered, and to take care of the woman he loved.

In St. Peter's Square, while celebrating the Solemnity of St. Joseph on March 19, 2013, which officially began his pontificate, Pope Francis said that the mission God entrusted to St. Joseph was to be *custos*, "the protector," of Mary, Jesus, and the church. He exercised that role, Francis said, "discreetly, humbly, and silently" and always "with lov-ing care." And he did so, he added, "by being constantly attentive to God, open to the signs of God's presence and receptive to God's plans, and not simply to his own." St. Joseph, he noted, is a "strong and courageous man, a working man; yet, in his heart, we see great tenderness"—a sign of strength of spirit and "a capacity for concern, for compassion, for genuine openness to others, for love."[2] In fact, his strong devotion to this saint explains why we find the "flower of St. Joseph" in his papal coat of arms.

After all, it was at St. Joseph's Basilica in Flores where Jorge Ber-goglio had a spiritual awakening that led him to the priesthood as a child. On September 21, 1954, Jorge Bergoglio, aged seventeen, was going to meet his friends to celebrate Spring Day, and, while passing the church, he felt a strong urge to enter. It was there that he received the vocational call of which St. Joseph was the mediator.

On January 16, 2015, while celebrating Mass in the Mall of Asia in Manila, he shared with the crowd the following revelation: "I also want to tell you something very personal. I really like St. Joseph, because he is a strong and silent man. On my desk I have an image of St. Joseph sleeping. And while he's sleeping, he takes care of the church! Yup! He can do it; we know that. And when I have a problem, a difficulty, I write a piece of paper and put it under St. Joseph, because he dreams about it! This gesture means, Pray for this problem!"

Like Pope Francis, I, too, am surprised by the silence, humility, and all that St. Joseph teaches us. Would that all spouses and fathers were devotees of this great saint and that we imitated his great vir-tues. Without a doubt, this would change society in which every day,

---

2. Edward Pentin, "The Inauguration of Pope Francis Focuses on St. Joseph and Protecting Others in Love," *National Catholic Register*, March 19, 2019, http://www.ncregister.com.

the percentage of fathers and husbands away from home seems to increase.

LIFESTYLE

Francis's personal habits, although very admirable, are not those of a great patriarch but rather those of a "dad" or, if you prefer, a loving and kind grandfather. I know him very well and can attest that he evokes all the simplicity, naturalness, and poverty of which the gospel speaks:

- As archbishop and cardinal of Buenos Aires, he preferred discretion and was no friend of widely advertised media conferences.
- Being the archbishop and cardinal of Buenos Aires, he refused to live in the Archbishop's Palace and preferred to stay in a small apartment before he was named pope in 2013.
- In Buenos Aires, he used to get around by foot, subway, and bus.
- As archbishop and cardinal of Buenos Aires, he never accepted an invitation to go to a restaurant. He used to cook his own food.
- He didn't like to travel to Rome, and when he did, it was always in economy class.
- He never liked to demonstrate the attributes of a cardinal. That is why, on his trips to Rome, it was common to see him with a simple black coat, to avoid the ostentation of the vivid red outfit of the cardinals.

His humility has made him immensely popular, a smiling figure walking among the crowds in St. Peter's Square. He speaks in very personal terms about those forgotten by the global economy, whether they be migrants drowned in the sea or the women with no choice but to engage in prostitution. His deep criticism of environmental destruction has captured the world's attention because of the emphasis he puts on the theme that the hardest hit by wild greed are always those who are poorest.

HEARTH, HOME, AND FAMILY

The experience of his Italian-Argentinian family lifestyle and the influence of the family environment during his childhood and youth have deeply set the tone for Pope Francis. His style is cordial, affectionate, and friendly; he calls things by their name, with tenderness, but also with clarity. His was a family where everything was communicated openly, where all was shared and life was made bearable because there was no selfishness—a life without masks and with a family atmosphere of intimate confidence and expressed affection, always enthusiastic. That is why Francis learned to form an intimate circle of indispensable friends, and why he chose, on arriving at the Vatican, to live in the residence of Santa Marta and not be isolated and inaccessible. The warmth of the people (the smell of sheep) is something particular to his sensitivity and his family and parental style. In that, certainly, the pope is Latin American.

DEEDS MORE THAN WORDS

We could write a book of anecdotes, a kind of new "Little Flowers of Francis"—similar to the book that bears that name but refers to St. Francis of Assisi—about the many symbolic actions, prophetic and pedagogical, that the pope has displayed in many different scenarios. Pope Francis or simply Francisco, with his eloquent and spontaneous deeds, gives enough material to write of the teachings and testimonies that his actions, so striking and relevant, provide as a clear translation of his doctrine, of his overall thinking, of the new paradigm of bishop of which he is the designer and promoter in the church.

Francis's gestures coincide fully with his written doctrine and sometimes not only are its authentic interpretation but also its genuine translation, insofar as they bring his words to life, into concrete action. Pope Francis will be remembered as the person who, as the Acts of the Apostles says of Jesus, taught by doing (see Acts 10:38). There was no split between what Jesus said and what he did, because he taught as he did things; he taught by doing. His gestures, his miracles, were very clear signals that the kingdom of God was already among us.

They say that St. Francis of Assisi asked a disciple to accompany him to a town to preach. The disciple accepted, enthusiastic about the possibility of learning to preach. He knew that he had to learn how to reach people with the word of God. So they went out to preach, but on their long journey through the town they never pronounced a single word. Once back at the convent, the young friar asked Francis of Assisi why he had not preached. St. Francis's response was that they had done so, by their example. Pope Francis speaks to the world more with gestures, words, language, and his life than with his encyclicals.

6

The Ignatian Roots

Antonio Spadaro, SJ

We just celebrated the fifth anniversary of the election of Pope Francis. "How has the church changed in these five years?" This has been the question that many have frequently sought to answer by bringing together analyses and opinions. Nevertheless, it risks being a question that overlooks an important fact: the church lives in continuous change, because it is on a journey with the history of men and women. And every pontificate has had an influence on its times and has contributed, in one way or another, to the journey of the church in the world. Like every pontiff, Francis is called to express his own view on the world and the church.

In particular, Pope Francis's proposal is "prophetic," that is, realized by those who know how to bestow its true relationship with God's plan through the passage of time.

Some commentators have wanted to read the changes in the course of Francis's pontificate with an exclusively sociological perspective and have condensed the theme of "reform" to the reform of the Roman Curia. It's a short-sighted prospective.

Already at the beginning of his pontificate, Francis affirmed that the reform of the Curia could only be the expression of a profound, interior reform of the church.[1] When I asked the pope if he wanted to reform the church, he responded that he simply wants to put Christ ever more at the center of the church; then Christ would be the one to do the necessary reforms.

It's not a coincidence that, when he became the pope, Cardinal Bergoglio chose the name "Francis." He did not do it only to highlight

---

1. Antonio Spadaro, "Interview with Pope Francis," in *La Civiltà Cattolica* 3 (2013): 449–77.

the gospel ties with the poor and the least, but he did it because he feels the mission of Francis of Assisi is his: "rebuilding" the church, beginning, like the saint of Assisi, as the mason who rebuilds a chapel. His is, and it needs to be, essentially a spiritual reform.

In this sense, Francis's objective was that of launching internal reforms of the Curia, but not that of bringing them all and right away to completion. Humility prevents him from imagining himself as the Don Quixote of reform. Rather, "it is like cleaning the Egyptian Sphinx with a toothbrush," to use one of his eloquent images.[2] This is the ironic and shrewd observation that has guided him since the beginning of his pontificate.

The narrative that nothing has left port is patently false. Francis "puts his hand" to things and unties the knots one by one, within the limits of the possible. Those instead who would imagine a Don Quixote like *deus ex machina* may be disappointed. The pope knows that mistakes can be made, and he has the humility to recognize them and to try other roads. Then he "tests" the quality of the processes and he consults. This is why the group of cardinals, the so-called C9, exists. But Francis doesn't believe in *prêt-a-porter* (ready-to-wear) solutions. He has never believed in them. Reform is a step-by-step process. In other words, this is a pontificate of seeds. The quantity of seeds it is spreading is broad and greater with respect to that of the first harvest.

Central to Francis's pontificate is discernment, and, for Bergoglio, discernment is Ignatian: although it is carried out in the environment of the heart, of interiority, its raw material is always the daily reality that echoes and reverberates in that intimate space. It is an interior attitude that pushes him to be open and to find God everywhere he wants to be found, and not only in already well-known and well-defined places. Above all, he is not afraid of the ambiguity of life, and he faces it with courage.

The energy fields of attraction and repulsion—positive and negative—created around the pope, of which he is the catalyst of the positive, both inside and outside of the church, demonstrate that this discernment is happening, whether it be the mobilization for peace in Syria or of the effect of the encyclical *Laudato si'*. He aggregates the good and forces evil to reveal itself.

The pontificate of Francis is a pontificate of spiritual discernment. He is guiding the church through the *Spiritual Exercises*. And it is by no means an accident that the pope decided to celebrate the Feast of the Chair of St. Peter on February 22, 2018, not in a solemn celebra-

2. See Pope Francis, "Christmas Discourse to the Roman Curia" (December 21, 2017).

tion at St. Peter's accompanied by choruses of *Tu es Petrus* but closed in silence, in the *Spiritual Exercises*, with the Curia, at Ariccia (Rome). Pope Francis is a Jesuit, and the experience of the *Spiritual Exercises* has shaped his life.

Let us recall and consider the figure of another pope who will help us to understand Francis better.

POPE MARCELLUS II

After the death of Julius III on April 9, 1555, Marcello Cervini, cardinal of the Basilica di Santa Croce, was elected pope. He had been one of the papal legates at the Council of Trent, where he was able to get to know the Jesuit theologians.

From the beginning of the council, some Jesuits were present as theology experts. We have a letter in which Ignatius gives instructions to his confreres about how to behave at the council.[3] The interesting thing is that he does not enter at all into doctrinal and theological issues but is concerned about the living testimony offered by the Jesuits while there. This already gives us an idea of how Ignatius intended the reform of the church. For him, it was not so much a matter of reforming the structure as reforming the people from within. For example, he recommends that, following in his own path, they go visit the sick in hospitals, "confessing and consoling the poor, bringing some material help if possible, and having them pray [for the council]."[4]

Marcello Cervini argued that the reform of the church could not only be founded on the removal of some abuses but had to be radical, that is, it had to start from the "self-renewal of the pope and the Curia." But he also saw clearly that this self-renewal had to go hand in hand with an incisive conciliar reform. "The world cannot be disappointed by the reform that was expected by the council," he wrote to his trustee Maffei, "or the last error will be worse than the first." On his election, Ignatius, in letters addressed to the whole Society of Jesus, revealed his intentions regarding the reform of the church.[5]

From these letters, we can infer that Ignatius's desire was to have a pope who had done the entire *Spiritual Exercises*. It may well be that,

---

3. See *Monumenta Ignatiana, Epp.* 1.386–89. Quotations are from the Italian edition: Ignazio di Loyola, *Gli scritti,* a cura dei Gesuiti della Provincia Italiana (Rome: Adp, 2007), 1017–1019. The numbering of the letters follows this edition.

4. See *Monumenta Ignatiana, Epp.* 1.387.

5. They are quoted and commented on extensively in E. Cattaneo, "La riforma della Chiesa secondo sant'Ignazio di Loyola," in *La Civiltà Cattolica* 4 (2013): 341–451.

at the Council of Trent, the then-Cardinal Marcello Cervini, being in contact with the Jesuits Laínez and Salmerón, had come to know, and maybe even done, at least in part, the *Exercises*. Regardless, his disposition was perfectly in accordance with them.

Ignatius was convinced that, starting from the "reform of one's own life" and keeping one's eyes fixed on the poor and humiliated Christ, one could not but necessarily achieve a structural reform of the church.

And this is what Francis really wants: he simply wants to put Christ ever more at the center of the church; then Christ would be the one to do the necessary reforms.

Pope Francis is a Jesuit pope, and his idea of the reform of the church corresponds to that of Ignatius. The reform is indeed a spiritual process that also affects, by connaturality, the ecclesial structure. Ignatian spirituality is the "dark chamber" of deep or, we could say, "chemical" elaboration of Bergoglio's experiences as bishop first and then as pope. Francis is a "product" of the *Spiritual Exercises*, and his vision of church reform is rooted in the "reform of life," which is the outcome of the *Exercises*.

A REFORMER IS ONE WHO "EMPTIES HIMSELF"

If we read what Francis has said of the Jesuits, we understand why he feels that he ought to "empty himself." In his homily at the Church of the Gesù, Rome, on January 3, 2014, he said:

> The heart of Christ is the heart of a God who, out of love, "emptied" himself. Each one of us, as Jesuits, who follow Jesus should be ready to empty himself. We are called to this humility: to be "emptied" beings. To be men who are not centered on themselves because the center of the Society is Christ and his Church. And God is the *Deus semper maior*, the God who always surprises us. And if the God of surprises is not at the center, the Society becomes disoriented.

Reform, for Francis, is rooted in this emptying of self. If it were not so, if it were only an idea, an aspirational project, the fruit of one's own desires, even if good, it would become yet another ideology of change.

During my interview with him in 2013, Francis gave a key definition of the Jesuit (and hence of himself): "A person whose thought is incomplete, whose thought is open." And again: "The Jesuit always thinks again and again, looking to the horizon, toward which he must advance, with Christ at the center."

In this sense, Pope Francis is a man whose thoughts are "incomplete, open." And this requires, as he himself affirmed in the course of the interview, on the one hand "research, creativity, generosity," and, on the other, "humility, sacrifice, courage." This attitude is especially called upon in difficult times.

For Francis, being men and women of discernment means being men and women of "incomplete thought," of "open thought." The road that Francis intends to follow is truly open for him, and he refuses easy conclusions: the journey reveals itself by walking. Thus, at times he opens discourses without closing them right away or drawing from them hurried implications, leaving space for dialogue and debate, even among those who have high ecclesial responsibilities.[6]

On this journey, the pope does not believe that "a definitive or complete word on every question which affects the Church" (*EG* 16) should be expected from his magisterium. In fact, "neither the Pope nor the Church has a monopoly on the interpretation of social realities or the proposal of solutions to contemporary problems" (*EG* 184). Then, "in her dialogue with the State and with society, the Church does not have solutions for every particular issue" (*EG* 241).

There is a deep sense of "incompleteness" in Francis's vision. He said in a audience he gave to the Jesuit writers of my review, *La Civiltà Cattolica*:

> The crisis is global, so then it is necessary to address our gaze to the dominant cultural convictions and the criteria by which people believe that something is good or bad, desirable or not. Only a truly open thought can confront the crisis and the understanding of where the world is going, of how the more complex and urgent crises, geopolitics, the challenges of the economy and the grave humanitarian crisis tied to the drama of migrations that is the true knot of global politics of our days, are confronted.

NONIDEOLOGICAL DISCERNMENT

The spirituality of Ignatius of Loyola is a historical spirituality, connected to the dynamics of history. Better yet, it is what drives history and organizes and gives shape to an institution. The spiritual ministry of Ignatius is institutionalized in service to the church, giving shape to the Society of Jesus and its ability to dialogue with culture and history.

---

6. *EG* 32, on the conversion of the papacy; *EG* 51, on the discipline of the sacraments; and *EG* 104, on the role of women.

This is, in fact, the background against which a more complex picture emerges, which is of paramount importance to understand Bergoglio's way of proceeding during his pontificate. He observes that in Ignatius's life is found the internal coherence of his project. But what is exactly Ignatius's "project"? Is it a theoretical vision ready to be applied to reality, to force it within its parameters? An abstraction to be applied to reality?

Nothing of the kind. "His project is not a planning of functions, nor an assortment of possibilities. His project consists in making explicit and concrete what he had experienced in his inner world," as Bergoglio has expressed it.[7] Considering this, the question about what Pope Francis's "program" is does not make sense. The pope has no clear and distinct ideas to apply to reality, but he proceeds based on his spiritual experience and prayer that he shares in dialogue and in consultation with others.

This procedure is called "discernment": it is the discernment of God's will in our daily lives. As noted earlier, although it is fulfilled within the heart, the inner self, its raw material is always that daily reality that reverberates in that intimacy. It is an inner attitude that drives us to be open to dialogue, to the encounter with others, to finding God wherever he wants to be found, not only in narrow or well-delimited and restricted confines. Our actions and decisions, therefore, must be accompanied by a careful, thoughtful, and prayerful reading of the signs of the times. For Bergoglio, the world is always on the move; the ordinary perspective, with its measures for classifying what is important and what is not, does not work. The life of the spirit is guided by other principles.

And we cannot practice discernment on ideas, even ideas of reform, but on what is real, on histories, on the concrete history of the church. For Francis, realities are always more important than ideas (see *EG* 231–33). Therefore, the starting point is always historical, and we must first recognize that *Dios trabaja y labora por mí en todas cosas criadas sobre la haz de la tierra* (God works and labors for me in all things created on the face of the earth, *Sp. Ex.* 236) and that the world is God's "construction site."

In the last five years, Pope Francis hasn't followed a defined strategy that has been dreamed up in a bureaucratic ivory tower; he hasn't applied an abstract or theoretical five-year plan. He proceeds through discernment, opens eyes, touches wounds, listens . . . and makes his decisions in the chapel, not in the "office." He makes some choices,

---

7. J. M. Bergoglio, *Chi sono i gesuiti* (Bologna: EMI, 2014), 20.

even important ones, not because they were "planned" but because he perceived in his prayer they were necessary. His ability to surprise comes from here, but also his ability to throw straight, feeling neither the strength of the wind inside nor the media pressure outside. He feels them, but he is not susceptible to them.

AN OPEN AND HISTORICAL PROCESS

The task of the reformer is to initiate or accompany historical processes. This is one of the fundamental principles of Bergoglio's vision: time is greater than space (*EG* 222–25). To reform means to start open processes and not to "cut heads" or conquer spaces of power. It is with this same spirit of discernment that Ignatius and his first companions faced the challenge of the Reformation.

Francis is the pope of processes, of "exercises"—a superior who, in his own words, should be "a leader of processes and not a mere administrator."[8] This is, from his viewpoint, the form of true "spiritual government."[9] Bergoglio's pontificate and his willingness to reform are not and will not be only "administrative," but they are processes intended to inspire and accompany. Some may be fast and dazzling, others extremely slow.

The process is therefore truly open; only God knows when it will end and its outcome. It is other and far more than a human project, and is "more than our expectations"[10]—even if they are the pope's. In *Meditaciones para religiosos*—a series of reflections written when Bergoglio was provincial of the Argentine Jesuits—he explains the spiritual and practical dynamics of the process. He uses a very effective image from the gospel: "We are encouraged to build the city, but perhaps we need to tear down the model we were drawing in our head. We must take courage and let God chisel our face, even if this means smoothing out some of our tics that we thought were gestures."[11] The *pars destruens*, which consists in doing away with the "model," is functional for leaving the chisel in the hands of God. Here is another interesting example for understanding Francis's vision.

---

8. J. M. Bergoglio, *Nel cuore di ogni padre: Alle radici della mia spiritualità* (Milan: Rizzoli, 2014), 88.

9. Ibid., 90.

10. Ibid., 81.

11. Ibid., 274.

Another remarkable example is the movement given to the entire church with the Third Extraordinary General Assembly of the Synod of Bishops. The event was conceived as a process set in motion by an extensive questionnaire addressed to all the People of God; it then converged into the extraordinary synod and opened a year of reflection before it reconverged in an ordinary assembly of the same synod. But the dynamics of *parresia* (candid openness), clarity, and freedom of expression and listening in which the process was experienced initiated in the entire church a dynamic that has also frightened many. Yet, it is precisely in the distant 1980s that Bergoglio established his confidence in processes, thus expressing a radical trust in the Holy Spirit. The wisdom of discernment "implies surrendering to God's will, and this, in turn, means to stop controlling processes with purely human criteria."[12] And again, "In the course of processes, to wait means to believe that God is greater than ourselves, that God is the same Spirit who governs us" (*Sp. Ex.* 365), and the "'Master' who allows the seed to grow."[13]

The pope lives a constant dynamic of discernment, which opens him to the future. It opens him also to the future of the reform of the church, which is not a project but an exercise of the spirit that does not see only in black and white, as those who always want to fight "battles." Bergoglio sees shades and stages; he seeks to recognize the presence of the Spirit in our human and cultural reality, the seed already planted through its presence in the events, feelings, desires, and the deep tensions in our hearts and in social, cultural, and spiritual contexts. And the seed is not the tree; it is often buried and thus invisible to the eye. This is what was expressed by the 34th General Congregation of the Society of Jesus, which took place in 1995: "In exercising their priestly ministry, the Jesuits try to see what God has already done in the lives of individuals, societies and cultures, and to discern how God will continue that work" (no. 177).

It is an interior attitude that drives us to be open inwardly to dialogue, encounter, finding God wherever he wants to be found and not only in narrow or well-defined and restricted confines. It does not fear the contradictions in our lives but faces them with courage. It is not an intellectual knowledge but one that integrates the values of the heart and mind.[14] The actions and decisions, therefore, should be rooted deeply inside and must be accompanied by a careful, medi-

---

12. Ibid., 94.
13. Ibid., 96.
14. Ibid., 130.

tative, and prayerful, reading of the signs of the times, which are everywhere.[15]

A PROCESS TO FIND THE GREATEST IN THE SMALLEST

The principle that sums up this evolutionary view is the motto *Non coerceri a maximo, contineri tamen a minimo, divinum est,* which can be translated as, "not to be limited by the greatest and yet to be contained in the smallest—this is the divine." The motto is part of a long literary epitaph composed by an anonymous Jesuit in honor of Ignatius of Loyola. Friedrich Hölderlin liked it so much that he affixed it as a motto to his *Hyperion.* And we know how much Bergoglio loves Hölderlin's work, so much so that he cited the German poet in the two days after his election as he greeted the cardinals in the Clementine Hall.

For Pope Francis, this epitaph means that, within the horizon of the kingdom of God, the infinitesimal can be infinitely large, while infinity instead can be a cage. It seems a paradox, but not for God who became man. The great reform project is realized in the slightest gesture, the little step. God is hidden in what is small and what is growing, even if we are incapable of seeing it. It's a thought that has accompanied Bergoglio at least since the years in which he was provincial superior, as documented in an essay entitled *Conducir en lo grande y en lo pequeño,* perhaps one of his most significant, given that the pope cited it several times during the interview with me.[16]

The perception of the divine enclosed in the smallest space and not restricted in the larger one is therefore a fundamental criterion. Without it, you will have "the charlatan priest, who in his comings and goings shows the inability to get established in God and in the concrete history with which he is bound"; or we will have "the elaboration of grand plans without any attention to the concrete mediations that will make them possible."[17] That paradoxical epitaph becomes the principle of the pope's pastoral action, and also of his leadership and assessment of reality.

A PROCESS THAT NEEDS IMAGINATION

In the talk that Francis gave to the Jesuit writers of *La Civiltà Cattolica* last year, he said: "We need to penetrate ambiguity, we need to enter

---

15. Ibid., 229.
16. Ibid., 91–102.
17. Ibid., 156.

in there, as the Lord Jesus did assuming our flesh. Rigid thought is not divine because Jesus has assumed our flesh, which is not rigid except after death." The direct consequence of this need to penetrate ambiguity is expressed in the pope's following sentences: "This is why I like poetry so much and, when it is possible for me, I continue to read it. Poetry is full of metaphors. Understanding metaphors helps to make thought agile, intuitive, flexible, acute. Whoever has imagination does not become rigid, has a sense of humor, always enjoys the sweetness of mercy and inner freedom."

He even quoted some verses of Baudelaire on Rubens where he writes:

> *la vie afflue et s'agite sans cesse,* / *Comme l'air dans le ciel et la mer dans la mer* (life moves and whirls incessantly, / Like the air in the sky and the tide in the sea). Yes, life is fluid and is agitated relentlessly like the air in the sky and the tide in the sea. The thought of the church must recover genius and understand ever better how man and woman are understood today to develop and deepen right teaching. And this genius helps us to understand that life is not a painting in black and white. It is a painting in colors: some clear and others dark; some soft and others vivid. But in any case, nuances prevail. And this is the space for discernment, the space in which the Spirit agitates the sky like the air and the sea like the water.

In Fyodor Dostoyevsky's *Notes from the Underground* (published in 1864), the protagonist supports the idea of "two times two making five," spending several paragraphs considering the implications of rejecting the statement "two times two makes four." Pope Francis likes Dostoyevsky and, in particular *Notes from the Underground*.

What does it mean? Why the refusal of reason and logic? This is hilarious. Dostoyevsky's purpose is not ideological. His poetic image means that dealing with free will—and dealing with God and human beings means to deal with free will, sin, and grace—is not dealing with machines, nor is it dealing with mathematics. In 2006, Pope Benedict XVI, talking with young people, said: "God is not just mathematical reason but . . . this original Reason is also Love"; and Pope Francis, in a homily at Casa Santa Marta on December 14, 2015, said: "Human calculations close the heart, they block freedom." Discernment doesn't match with any kind of rigidity and needs an open way of thinking.

A PROCESS THAT FACES LIMITATIONS, CONFLICTS, AND PROBLEMS

Bergoglio is not a "maximalist." He does not believe in a rigid idealism, nor in "ethicism" or spiritual "abstractionism."[18] Limits, conflicts, and problems are integral to our spiritual journey.

The relationship between desire and limit is advantageous, realistic, humanizing: it highlights our smallness, and opens us to the greatness "ever greater" of God.

Indeed, God helps us to accept our limits, because he "communicates in a *limited* way"; thus, we must "accept the limits of our pastoral expression (so distant from the notion of the one who has the solution to all the world's problems, who knows neither waiting nor hardship, and who lives driven by frenzy and delusions)."[19]

We do not even need to be afraid of conflicts, which sometimes disturb and frighten us. Talking to superiors of the male religious orders in November 2013, Pope Francis used a beautiful image: "We need to caress conflicts." But for Bergoglio, the distinctive trait of the Society of Jesus is to "make possible the harmonization of contradictions."[20] He then makes a quick list of contradictions: We Jesuits have been contemplatives and men of action; of discernment and obedience; men of "consolidated" works as well as of missions that seemed almost incursions; men who devote themselves to what they do with total commitment and, conversely, with great generosity (men equally Jesuits when shaping peoples and when all they had to call home was a simple cart: so were our missionaries).[21]

Contradictions are part of a fruitful history. And indeed, so are problems. So much so that it is not always appropriate to resolve them, writes Bergoglio. A problem may not always need to be solved immediately, on the spot. There is a discernment that involves history and verifies times and moments.[22] Sometimes, a problem can be solved without wanting to face it immediately. It is therefore necessary to understand the processes taking place, even giving up the things of the moment. A real temptation is to "want to separate the wheat and the weeds prematurely."[23] These are important words in order to understand the timing of Francis's vision of the reforming process.

18. Ibid., 37.
19. Ibid., 132.
20. Ibid., 83.
21. Ibid., 84.
22. Ibid., 84.
23. Ibid., 129.

A PROCESS THAT DEALS WITH
TEMPTATIONS AND RESISTANCES

Temptations and the struggle against them are also part of this process. The reform process for Bergoglio is a competitive process. The pope has a "militant" vision of reality. This dramatic quality comes from St. Ignatius of Loyola and his *Spiritual Exercises*, especially from his meditation "on the two standards" (*Sp. Ex.* 136–48), which should be read carefully.[24] Ignatius depicts a battlefield in which are contrasted "Christ, our supreme master and lord," and "Lucifer, the mortal enemy of our human nature." For Bergoglio, there is an inevitable dimension of belligerency in the Christian *modus vivendi*. "The Christian life is a battlefield,"[25] and "our faith is revolutionary, and foundational in itself. It is a *fighting faith*."[26] "Discernment is an instrument of struggle."[27]

A remarkable temptation is the one that presents itself under the appearance of good and has the most disastrous and pervasive effect of pulling the church away from reality, from history. We experience it when figures seek to replace the pope to defend the doctrine, or when they sow uncertainty and confusion, even letting us believe that orthodoxy is in danger. These temptations generate distortion "because the *opium of nostalgia*, so characteristic of the traditionalists, which distracts us from the creativity of a faithful memory, is blinded."[28]

Francis, like all the popes, has generated opposition outside and inside the church. Why? The deep root of this pontificate is faith that God is active and at work in the world. Some believe that God has retreated, that by now the world is lost to evil and that the church herself must retreat from the world and its dust, to keep herself pure and beautiful.

For some, Catholicism must be conserved for a minority of the pure who preserve doctrine in a jewel box and who are not contaminated in the world, in history, in reality. Francis sees fluidity between the public square and the church, between *ecclesia e agora*, not hostility. For him, the church must always be open to the "public square," to let the people enter, yes, but above all, to let Christ go out without locking him in. The vision of Christ who wants to go out of the temple for his

---

24. Ibid., 162–69.
25. Ibid., 194.
26. Ibid., 128.
27. Ibid., 165.
28. Ibid., 107 (emphasis added).

mission is opposed to the idea of a Christianity made up of a small group of the pure.

For Francis, the gospel is the talent to spend and to bear fruit. The church must go out to the street, get dirty, and perhaps hurt. The opposition attacks and contrasts this vision of the church as a "torch" that walks and goes everywhere. The opposition would prefer the image of a "lighthouse" that stays put where it is, in its static condition: it attracts and comforts, but it does not accompany. The opposition to Francis is opposition to the council.

Strikingly, while so far the opposition has essentially been "grammatically" correct, that is, criticizing the actions of the pontiff in office while safeguarding his figure and ministry, it now often appears completely "ungrammatical," that is, not able to speak ecclesial language and even divisive on the decisive questions such as ecclesiastical authority or the liturgy. That has even involved other prelates and has required the intervention of the Press Office of the Holy See to correct mistaken interpretations. In a serious case, the pontiff himself had to intervene.[29] To that is added also the use of *fake news* spread by a dense network of blogs and social media that declare themselves as "Catholic."

The fact remains, however, that the pontificate of Francis is intimately and profoundly dramatic. As noted above, Ignatius depicts a battlefield on which our friend "Christ, our chief captain and lord," and "Lucifer, mortal enemy of human nature," confront each other. For Bergoglio there is an inevitable warlike dimension in the Christian *modus vivendi* (way of life). In short, Christian life is a struggle. And at times the "enemy" proclaims himself dressing in the habit of the good guys. And at times the "friend," to express himself, chooses the word from a "distance." The Spirit blows where and as it wants.

Sometimes in his discourses, both as cardinal and as pope, the word "struggle" appears. And his struggle is always consoled by the certainty that the Lord has the last word on the life of the world: He is always present in history, that it is not abandoned to itself.

TENSION BETWEEN SPIRIT AND INSTITUTION

In conclusion, it must be said that, for Pope Francis, the reform of the church is experiencing a strong and fruitful dialectic tension between

---

29. Cf. C. Giraudo, "'*Magnum principium*' and Liturgical Inculturation in the Wake of the Council," in *La Civiltà Cattolica* 4 (2017): 311–24.

Spirit and institution. In his apostolic exhortation *Evangelii gaudium*, he wrote: "The Church has to accept this unruly freedom of the word, which accomplishes what it wills in ways that surpass our calculations and ways of thinking" (*EG* 22). There is a dialectical and intraecclesial tension in Francis's remark regarding Spirit and institution. One never denies the other, but the former must animate the latter in an effective, incisive way to counter the "ecclesial introversion" (*EG* 27)—as St. John Paul II called it—which is always a great temptation.

The pope also wrote: "I do not want a Church concerned with being at the center and which then ends by being caught up in a web of obsessions and procedures" (*EG* 49). He then says that the church is a "people of pilgrims and evangelizers, transcending any institutional expression, however necessary" (*EG* 111).

Finally, note this fruitful tension between the church as a "pilgrim people" and as "institution," which reflects two of Pope Francis's favorite definitions of the church, as it is also evident in the interview he gave to *La Civiltà Cattolica*, the "pilgrim people of God" (*Lumen gentium*) and "holy Mother the hierarchical church" (St. Ignatius of Loyola).[30] The reform of the church, for Francis, is essentially to ensure that the holy Mother the hierarchical church is always the pilgrim People of God.

The truly great question that pulses in the heart of Francis's pontificate is this: How do you proclaim the gospel to anyone, regardless of his or her existential condition? His model is the encounter of Jesus with the disciples of Emmaus, and he asks pastors to accompany people by staying alongside them even when men and women enter into the night, wandering alone without a goal, as he said to the Brazilian bishops just four months after his election.

What should we expect in the future from this pontificate? We will come to understand this in time, because as the poet Antonio Machado said, *Se hace camino al andar* (The path opens up along the way).

---

30. Ignatius of Loyola, *The Spiritual Exercises of St. Ignatius* (New York: Vintage Spiritual Classics/Random House, 2000), rules 352–62, 365.

7

"He Drinks from His Own Wells"

Thomas J. Massaro, SJ

In considering the papacy of Francis, it is natural to look for unifying threads within the many initiatives and accomplishments of the Argentinian pope's time in office. Ethicists and moral theologians (to limit the scope of this potentially unwieldy inquiry at the outset) will hasten to enumerate a long list of highly significant teachings and preferred themes of Francis, on the levels of both personal and social ethics. These include teachings stemming from economic inequality and injustice, contributing to healthy family life, promoting environmental sustainability, supporting migrants and refugees, and building a more peaceful world. Francis has advanced these social and ethical concerns through eloquent written and spoken words—from formal documents to off-the-cuff comments in impromptu press conferences and wide-ranging interviews in formats unprecedented in papal history. No less important are the many symbolic actions that enact the pope's commitment to social justice and his deep concern for the excluded and marginalized person. With a genius for rich gestures of empathy for the suffering and solidarity with the poor, Francis proposes a renewal of church mission and corporate discipleship that has touched millions throughout the world. In so many venues available to him—from encyclical letters to Twitter messages to heartrending visits to refugee camps—Francis invokes signature themes of mercy, dialogue, discernment, and a culture of encounter and accompaniment that feature profound ethical import.

Rather than dwelling on the task of describing the pope's ethical teachings (through word and example), we will probe beyond what is observable to identify unifying elements in the moral teachings of Pope Francis and what really makes Francis tick in this area of ethical teachings. What are the formative influences that most account for his concerns and shape his words and actions? Of course, any leader will be influenced by a variety of factors in his or her personal and intellectual background, and a prominent place must be reserved in our analysis of Francis for such items as his family origin, his Argentinian citizenship, and a variety of other experiences and marks of identity in his long and eventful life. But my thesis is that no factor comes close to rivaling the pope's "Jesuit DNA" in accounting for his ethical teachings and moral leadership as universal pastor. The Society of Jesus not only formed Francis in a literal sense (Bergoglio spent approximately fifteen years in the Jesuit program of priestly formation), but in innumerable ways, his religious order shaped every aspect of his thought and ethical commitments. Even beyond the conclusions he reaches, the style and method with which he approaches matters of ethical import display the distinctive fingerprints of his Jesuit origins.

IGNATIAN SOURCES

The title of this chapter deliberately employs a metaphor involving the everyday human act of drinking water. Spiritualities are often likened to a source or font from which flow nourishing (indeed, life-giving) riches. The Ignatian spirituality imbibed throughout the process of formation by Jesuits (and likewise by so many members of the wider Ignatian family through retreats, spiritual direction, and various other means) seems to have a remarkable ability to infuse all that one does. Once we discover a particularly nourishing source of water, we tend to drink deeply indeed! In the ethical arena, adopting the distinctive Ignatian approach to the spiritual life sets a particularly strong agenda of commitments and moral obligations—identifying priorities and core values on both personal and social levels. Throughout its history, the Society of Jesus has been associated with a certain brand of "Christian humanism" that has inspired many elements of its pastoral and educational work—including such familiar motifs as the holistic notion of *cura personalis*, the flexible open-endedness of "finding God in all things," and fervent dedication to the "service of faith and the promotion of justice."[1]

---

1. This phrase constitutes the subtitle of Decree 4 ("Our Mission Today: The Service of Faith and the Promotion of Justice") of General Congregation 32, promulgated May 8, 1975, and appearing in English translation in *Documents of the 31st and 32nd General Congregations of the Society of Jesus* (St. Louis: Institute of Jesuit Sources, 1977), 411–38.

Of course, none of the analysis developed below denies the existence of other metaphorical wells from which Pope Francis certainly and evidently drinks. There remains ample room to recognize further sources that have influenced him. Without a doubt, one of these is Franciscan spirituality, replete with its own distinctive style and sets of concerns, which the pope clearly holds in high regard. In response to an interviewer's question about his choice of a papal name, Francis lifts up this influence, explaining his eagerness to honor St. Francis of Assisi, but quickly elevates the Ignatian influence on his thought and spirituality to a considerably higher place.[2] Another obvious influence is the distinctively Latin American cultural context that so clearly shapes the perspective of the first pope from the Southern or Western Hemispheres. Indeed, for contemporary audiences, invoking the metaphor of "drinking from our own wells" immediately calls to mind the work of Gustavo Gutiérrez, the Peruvian priest and founder of liberation theology, whose magisterial volume on the distinctive history and spirituality of the Latin American church is called *We Drink from Our Own Wells: The Spiritual Journey of a People*.[3] There is surely no need to offer further disclaimers or disavowals of reductionism in the analysis that follows. The claim here is not that being formed as a Jesuit has determined all of Pope Francis's moral commitments and priorities but simply that the pope's Jesuit "layer" or Ignatian inheritance provides the strongest guidance to his ethical agenda, as the single most influential factor in the chosen style, method, and content of his moral teachings.

We will explore this theme in five sections, each representing a major feature of the Jesuit inheritance that is reflected in the ethical teachings and moral commitments of Pope Francis. These five items may appear at first glance to be rather disparate—representing as they do a mix of ethical priorities, commitments, procedures, methods, and value orientations—but each captures a distinctive facet of the over-

---

2. The pope replied as follows to a question in July 2013 about the strength of Jesuit influence on him despite a long absence (since he became a bishop in 1992) from actually living in a Jesuit community or participating in a Jesuit apostolate: "I feel I am a Jesuit in my spirituality, in the spirituality of the Exercises, the spirituality that I have in my heart. I have not changed my spirituality, no. Francis, Franciscan, no. I feel Jesuit and I still think like a Jesuit." Cited in Philip Endean, ed., "Writings on Jesuit Spirituality by Jorge Mario Bergoglio, S.J.," *Studies in the Spirituality of Jesuits* 45, no. 3 (Autumn 2013): 2.

3. Gustavo Gutiérrez, *We Drink from Our Own Wells: The Spiritual Journey of a People* (Maryknoll, NY: Orbis Books, 1984). The epitaph of this volume, which includes the book's title phrase taken from Saint Bernard of Clairvaux, appears on p. vii. The original Latin runs, "*Bibet de fonte putei sui primus ipse.*"

all Jesuit charism that informs Francis as he shapes his own ethical agenda. The five are: (1) an Ignatian orientation that emphasizes both spiritual freedom and practical material assistance in service to the neediest; (2) an emphasis on social transformation and activism; (3) an appreciation for the value of viewing ethical issues through a structural lens; (4) the practice of careful moral discernment; and (5) a commitment to reconciliation and peacemaking. To associate these with both Pope Francis and the Jesuit charism in no way implies that these five are somehow absent elsewhere; indeed, many moral teachers of various backgrounds, including recent popes, display these qualities and priorities in abundance. As we shall see, Francis—like Jesuits in general—enacts each of these general features of a socially responsible approach to ethical issues in ways that yield highly practical guidance to pressing social problems of our age.

SPIRITUAL FREEDOM AND MATERIAL CONCERNS

Nearly a half-millennium of Jesuit spiritual practice has bequeathed to Francis, as to all who honor Ignatian spirituality, particular moral priorities. The phrase "our way of proceeding" that Ignatius used often in the *Constitutions of the Society of Jesus*, of course, means many things, but primary among them is the cultivation of a spiritual freedom that allows the practitioner to grow beyond inordinate worldly attachments. To opt to forgo all ostentation and self-aggrandizement (well captured in Ignatius's triad of spiritual dangers: riches, honor, and pride) is central to this approach. It is important to add at the outset that practicing the virtue of asceticism by no means implies a denigration of the material world or indifference to the physical needs of others. That is why the admiration by so many for the personal comportment of Francis (especially his deliberate rejection of many of the trappings and privileges of church office before and after his election to the papacy) is paired with appreciation for his simultaneous commitment to lifting up the poor and those who are marginalized. Preferring a cramped ride on a bus to a chauffeured limousine goes hand-in-hand with advocacy for and direct assistance to low-income neighbors. An Ignatian perspective on the relation between the material and the spiritual allows one to embrace simplicity of lifestyle and voluntary poverty for oneself while simultaneously taking with utmost seriousness the struggle of the majority poor of the world for a decent livelihood. The "Principle and Foundation" that Ignatius places at the start of the *Spiritual Exercises* provides the orientation to develop and enact the proper disposition of material things; the CST principle of "the universal purpose of created things"[4] (that is, to serve the life of all rather than the arbitrary desires of some for luxury or superfluity) suggests how this spiritual insight possesses normative ethical force for the church and its mission.

Not only does Pope Francis display an appreciation for this Ignatian approach to material goods, but he communicates an ardent passion to accompany the materially poor—often including in his travel itineraries visits to hard-pressed neighborhoods and struggling communities despite the inevitable constraints of papal office (regarding time, security, and protocols for papal travels). Francis never appears as fully alive as when he is meeting with common people in humble circumstances, whether in hospitals for the indigent, prisons, refugee camps, or migrant detention centers. If circumstances allowed, he would no doubt prefer to express his close identification with the poor in even more frequent encounters, as he did even as archbishop in Buenos Aires (where he earned the moniker *un obispo callero*, or "a bishop of the streets"). To invite others into this set of concerns, Francis marked November 19, 2017, as the first World Day of the Poor observed by the Catholic Church, establishing the penultimate Sunday of the liturgical year henceforth as an annual occasion for the worldwide community of the faithful to lament the persistence of poverty. Indeed, Francis frequently displays his rootedness in Jesuit spirituality in calling attention to both the spiritual and the material needs of the outcasts of society. Notwithstanding the carping of detractors who accuse Francis of staging contrived photo opportunities while mingling with the poor, the pope's personal practice of the culture of accompaniment and the culture of encounter represents an utterly genuine effort to enact principles at the core of his ethical teachings. That he presents this proclivity as more than a matter of personal taste only adds to the ethical import. While he displays an almost instinctive personal desire to mix with the less fortunate and a unique "popular touch," his efforts in this regard are also part of a deliberate effort to communicate core elements of the Christian faith to a worldwide audience, whom he ardently hopes will share his ministry to and with the poor.

Where do these practices and priorities originate? Surely, to some extent, in the background of the Bergoglio family, who never rose very high into the ranks of the middle class and never lived far from the *villas miserias* (the infamous "neighborhoods of great suffering") of Buenos Aires. An even more direct connection runs to the many years when Jorge Mario Bergoglio served as novice director and rector of

---

4. This phrase appears in *PP* 22. *GS* 68 substitutes the word "common" for "universal."

formation communities, when he was particularly firm in requiring his young Jesuit charges to engage in especially frequent experiences of humble service and direct accompaniment with the poor of Argentina (not to mention the onerous requirement that they tend the livestock on Jesuit seminary properties). Bergoglio greatly admired Pedro Arrupe, the Spanish Jesuit who as superior general inspired the founding in 1980 of the Jesuit Refugee Service (J.R.S.), whose constant mission triad is direct service, accompaniment, and advocacy for the refugees of the world. There is no room for a standoffish *noblesse oblige* approach in this paradigmatic work of the international Society of Jesus in the past four decades; direct contact and accompaniment of the poor are indispensable dimensions of the Jesuit commitment to social justice today that are abundantly reflected in the ethical priorities of Pope Francis.

It is especially instructive to note precisely how the pope speaks about the Christian vocation to reach out to the poor and outcast of society. Francis invokes the themes of culture of accompaniment, culture of encounter, and culture of solidarity so often that papal observers may think of these phrases as a verbal tick of sorts. For every desirable attitude, there is a culture of that quality (matched, of course, by the inverse: by way of symmetry, he has often referred to the regrettable culture of indifference and the culture of exclusion). But beyond the occasions when he relies on these rhetorical flourishes, Francis has advanced church teachings and practices that address the plight of the needy and marginalized of our world in a number of spectacular ways. His apostolic exhortation *Evangelii gaudium* (his first major writing, "The Joy of the Gospel," released on November 24, 2013) contains several sections highlighting themes regarding poverty and its remedy. Paragraphs 52 to 75 denounce a number of causes of human suffering, including a financial system that dominates the poor, an idolatry of money that warps human relations, and an economy of inequality and exclusion that, he is not afraid to claim, kills. Paragraphs 186 to 237 of that programmatic document again turn to social and economic issues, lamenting unjust practices and calling for a greater inclusion of the poor in society as part of the church's evangelizing mission. As if to put flesh on this particular skeleton of key social concerns, Francis launched a startling papal initiative the next year. He convened and personally addressed large gatherings of representatives of grassroots organizations of communities struggling for worker rights, land, employment, and social justice. The three World Meetings of Popular Movements (which met in Rome in 2014, in Bolivia in 2015, and again in Rome in 2016, and which have spawned a further series of regional meetings) provided favorable settings for Francis to leverage his influence in calling the world's attention to dire needs and desperate struggles for the basics of life (the alliterative triad of land, labor, and lodging, or, in Spanish, *tierra, trabajo, techo*). No pope had ever done anything quite like this before Francis sponsored this initiative.

A final face of the culture of encounter worth mentioning here involves dialogue across religious boundaries, which especially in recent decades has emerged as an important complement to any church effort to reach across socioeconomic boundaries. Interreligious dialogue has long been a priority of the Society of Jesus, eager as it has been to engage in ambitious programs of inculturation even centuries before that term was ever used (witness the efforts of Matteo Ricci in China as early as the sixteenth century, and Robert de Nobili and John de Brito in India in the seventeenth century). In *Laudato si'*, his 2015 encyclical letter addressing the environmental crisis, Francis displays his particularly ardent desire to engage resources, leaders, and adherents of all the world's religious traditions in common efforts to care for our common home. In this document, Francis reiterates his deep concern for the poor by highlighting the insight that it is the poor who are the first victims of pollution, climate change, and environmental degradation. In citing the phrase "cry of the earth, cry of the poor," associated with his fellow South American Leonardo Boff, Francis signals his desire to put the poor at the center of all efforts for the renewal of the church's ecological concern, just as the truly marginalized people have garnered special attention throughout the history of Jesuit ministries.[5] It is more than mere coincidence that the Society of Jesus had convened an impressive international task force and published an ambitious special report on ecology with similar expressions of concern for the suffering of the poor shortly before his election as pope.[6] The orientation of Ignatian spirituality toward right use of the common gift of the creator inspired both sets of efforts at ecological justice.

SOCIAL TRANSFORMATION AND ACTIVISM

In mentioning the urgency of ameliorating poverty, the above paragraphs already anticipate the second of the five themes: an emphasis on activism and social transformation that are evident both in Francis and the broader Jesuit tradition. If the Ignatian perspective fosters a

---

5. See Leonardo Boff, *Cry of the Earth, Cry of the Poor*, trans. Phillip Berryman (Maryknoll, NY: Orbis Books, 1997).

6. Task Force on Ecology of the Social Justice and Ecology Secretariat of the Society of Jesus, "Special Report on Ecology: Healing a Broken World," *Promotio Justitiae* 106 (2011): 1–67.

particular vision of spiritual and material reality, as well as the ends to which they are directed, then the style with which it proceeds is rightly characterized as activist and socially engaged. Starting with the dictum (found in the "Contemplation to Attain Divine Love" in the *Spiritual Exercises*) that "love ought to show itself in deeds more than in words," the Jesuit tradition displays an unmistakable impulse toward both personal and social transformation. The Ignatian motto *simul in actione, contemplativus* (a contemplative in action) further encourages the practitioner to avoid any manner of self-absorption that might prevent genuine other-directed service. Not satisfied merely to observe or even diagnose social problems and injustices, the Ignatian-inspired person or group eagerly engages social reality in order to contribute to solutions. The responsible practitioner of this activist spirituality seeks to forge a better world, making prudential interventions large and small to improve whatever lies within one's control. While external effectiveness never replaces fidelity to one's vocation as the hallmark of a life well lived, being a catalyst for social change emerges as an outgrowth of genuine Ignatian spirituality.

The call of Ignatius to "the *magis*"—to render ever greater service to church and world—is answered by every generation of new initiatives undertaken by Jesuits and other members of the Ignatian family. The Society of Jesus may be accused of many things, but stasis and apathy should not be among them, at least not in recent decades, which have witnessed the renewal sparked by Vatican II. The motif of the *magis* has inspired initiatives of great creativity and ambition in pastoral, spiritual, and educational work. Jesuits and their colleagues continually experiment with new methods of adapting the *Spiritual Exercises* to new social contexts, sharing these riches through innovative spiritual direction, group reflection, and retreat modalities. Along with pastoral and social ministries, the apostolate of Jesuit education has similarly undergone renewal, experimenting with nontraditional ways of providing educational services tailored to the specific contexts of local communities—often in ways geared to the particular needs of those of modest means. If not always "setting the world on fire" in a dramatic way, Ignatian-inspired social engagement has at least issued significant challenges to the status quo, laying the foundation for imagining alternative practices to advance social justice. If the Holy Spirit is indeed trying to enter the world to subvert the inherited order, then the agents of the gospel working at Cristo Rey schools, the Jesuit Volunteer Corps, the Center of Concern, Nativity schools, and the Ignatian Solidarity Network (among many other organizations founded by Jesuits) would be highly promising allies.

The papal ministry of Francis clearly reflects these energies directed toward world transformation. Like his Jesuit confreres on all continents, he too assumes an activist stance, frequently calling his listeners beyond apathy, complacency, and indifference to deeper social engagement and outreach to marginalized groups. The central motifs of his preferred ecclesiology—which include "pastors with the smell of the sheep," "the church as a field hospital after battle," and "a church that goes out into the streets"—all evoke action, energy, and even experimentation. Even before his election as pope, Francis had earned a reputation as an agent of change in the sharply divided political arena of Argentina, organizing Catholics on numerous occasions to advocate for more socially responsible public policies.[7] A provocative homily he delivered on September 16, 2013, six months into his papacy, which included the phrase "a good Catholic meddles in politics,"[8] raised some eyebrows at the Vatican and elsewhere, but probably none in Argentina. If this constituted a "church-state boundary violation" involving advocacy for the unwarranted intrusion of religion into politics, it was nothing new for the Jesuit pope. The homily borrowed phrases and thoughts from many previous public statements during his time as bishop in Buenos Aires—words that express his consistent support over the decades for an activist stance in which religious convictions motivate actions for social change. To reduce religion to "a private affair of the heart" with no public implications is to truncate the faith. While such direct encouragement of political engagement (though prescinding from rank partisanship) alarmed some observers, members of the Ignatian family have come to appreciate how such calls to represent religiously inspired ethical values in the political order express the faith without distorting the Christian gospel.

ADOPTING A STRUCTURAL LENS

A third item that Pope Francis draws from his "Jesuit DNA" is an appreciation for the value of viewing issues of social ethics through a

---

7. See the account of the political activism of Bergoglio in Argentina in the early years of the twenty-first century in chap. 7 ("Gaucho Cardinal") of Austen Ivereigh, *The Great Reformer: Francis and the Making of a Radical Pope* (New York: Henry Holt, 2014), 253–301. As auxiliary bishop and then as archbishop of Buenos Aires, he tussled with successive Argentine governments over social priorities, public policies, and even the austerity budgets that harmed poor citizens in innumerable ways.

8. See "Vatican Insider" coverage of this homily at "Francis: A Good Catholic Meddles in Politics," http://www.lastampa.it.

structural lens. The success of any effort to transform the world and to encourage social change will rely on knowledge of the social, political, and economic structures that shape social relations and either foster or hinder the attainment of right order. While good intentions and a yearning for justice are commendable, effective transformation and the lasting attainment of proper social order depend on concrete adjustments in such social structures as cultural and economic institutions that too often restrict opportunities for social advancement of the poor. The tools of what has come to be known as *social analysis* have gained wide currency within Catholic circles in recent decades, often presented as a specification of the see-judge-act methodology of the pastoral circle that is a staple of CST.[9] The opening pages of *Gaudium et spes*, the primary social teaching document of Vatican II, had encouraged the faithful to "read the signs of the times." In the United States, a ground-breaking book by Jesuit Peter Henriot and Joe Holland (both at the time researchers at the Jesuit-sponsored Center of Concern, a think tank located in Washington, DC) introduced social analysis to a broad audience.[10] Many Jesuit-led pastoral planning projects around the world also pioneered the practice of social analysis informed by structural perspectives, including the Society of Jesus's own most recent statement on justice in the global economy, published in 2016 by an international task force of Jesuits and lay colleagues convened by the Social Justice and Ecology Secretariat in Rome.[11]

The leadership of Francis on moral issues clearly benefits from his having inherited the "structural eye" that has become part of the Jesuit charism today. On every topic across the range of his ethical teachings, Francis displays an appreciation for the role of large institutions in human social life. This insightful affirmation of the importance of structures enriches not only his *diagnosis* of social problems but also his *prescriptions* for changes that will benefit the social order if we can successfully leverage our systemic thinking. His approach to the following five topics, in particular, reflects this pattern of approach.

First, his treatment of economic justice in *Evangelii gaudium*, mentioned above, makes frequent reference to structures of sin as the

---

9. See *MM* 236, which cites this methodology.

10. Joe Holland and Peter Henriot, SJ, *Social Analysis: Linking Faith and Justice*, rev. and enl. ed. (Maryknoll, NY: Orbis Books, 1983). The Center of Concern itself had previously published shorter booklet versions of the text, starting in 1980.

11. Task Force on the Economy, "Special Report on Justice in the Global Economy: Building Sustainable and Inclusive Communities," *Promotio Justitiae* 121 (2016): 1–35.

deep and sometimes hidden causes of exclusion and so much human suffering.[12] Alleviating the wounds of poverty will require concerted effort to overturn evil structures and to reverse the effects of unjustly applied power. Providing an adequate remedy will entail deep social reforms that will benefit the poor by preventing egregious situations of inequality that currently frustrate their legitimate aspirations for human dignity.

Second, in *Laudato si'*, Francis treats environmental degradation in general, and climate change in particular, with a similar structural perspective. He repeats about a dozen times in the course of the encyclical the insight that "everything is connected"—a structuralist mantra of sorts. In a chapter titled "The Human Roots of the Ecological Crisis," he identifies several root causes of the horrendous situation whereby "the earth, our home, is beginning to look more and more like an immense pile of filth," as he laments in paragraph 21. The extended foray of Francis into social analysis in this encyclical reveals a range of destructive human activities (such as unrestrained profit seeking and irresponsible reliance on fossil fuels) and cultural attitudes (such as "tyrannical anthropocentrism" and "the technocratic paradigm") that have contributed to the dire crisis we face.

Third, in his exhortation *Amoris laetitia*, Francis offers an analysis of the crisis of family life in our day in similarly structural terms. Not satisfied to attribute accelerating family breakdown merely to personal weakness or sin in isolation, the pope probes a number of sometimes overlooked systemic causes that contribute to the growing crisis, including such cultural and economic factors as chronic unemployment, rampant consumerism, underresourced educational systems, and the coarsening of popular culture that frustrates even the most sincere efforts to sustain marriages and to raise children in the ways of tenderness and other virtues. While the Catholic approach to family life is generally framed through a pastoral and theological lens, Francis dares to apply a structural lens that identifies deep social imbalances as the cause of so much human hardship and disappointment.

Fourth, on a topic that is quite evidently close to his heart, Francis proposes an analysis of the refugee crisis that does not shy away from identifying the disturbing root causes behind the displacement of at least sixty-five million persons from their homelands. Speaking in a variety of venues, including in the course of tearful visits to refugee

---

12. For example, *EG* 59 refers to "evil crystalized in unjust social structures," and *EG* 188 affirms the importance of "working to eliminate the structural causes of poverty." *EG* 189 explicitly calls for "structural transformations."

camps and detention centers in various lands, Francis consistently calls attention to several factors that contribute to the unprecedented number of people on the move in the world today: the effects of climate change, endemic violence perpetuated by street gangs and drug cartels, diminishing economic opportunities, and ethnic discrimination, among many other root causes.[13] Anyone willing to challenge the global anti-immigrant backlash and probe the true root causes of today's migration crisis will heed the repeated calls of Francis to welcome our neighbors in distress as victims of circumstances beyond their control rather than to portray them as threats to national security and proper social order.

Fifth, Francis consistently views the escalation of violent conflict in so many parts of the world through a structural lens. On many occasions, including his historic addresses to the United Nations General Assembly and the United States Congress in September 2015, Francis highlights a key causal factor contributing to violence: the global arms trade, in which powerful manufacturers and suppliers, driven by the greed for profit, conspire to create the conditions that allow for continued carnage. While violence takes many forms, from armed conflict between states to organized terrorism to the coercive activities of drug cartels and human traffickers in many lands, applying the tools of social analysis reveals many disturbing patterns behind global conflicts. Asking penetrating questions regarding incentive structures, covert supply lines, and illicit funding sources reveals many unsettling truths about the global arms bazaar. Without doubt, a primary cause of the rampant bloodshed is a lucrative and unregulated arms trade that enables the death-dealing proliferation of weapons, both small arms and major weapons systems, at levels unprecedented in human history. As with each of the previous topics illuminated by a structural perspective, good intentions alone are not adequate to address the problem; we must expose, challenge, and correct corrupt patterns of human behavior. Francis not only preaches a message of peace, but has insistently voiced his whole-hearted support for concrete measures, such as universal ratification and implementation of the 2013 United Nations Arms Trade Treaty, which will address the structures that sustain arms proliferation. The section below on the related topic of peacemaking will connect these efforts of Francis to

---

13. Francis describes many of these causes in his 2015 World Day of Peace message, even though his main focus in this document is on the specific plight of those migrants who are victims of human trafficking. See the text of this January 1, 2015, document subtitled "No Longer Slaves, but Brothers and Sisters" at http:// w2.vatican.va.

support these global structural changes to the Jesuit tradition of concern for peacemaking and reconciliation.

CAREFUL DISCERNMENT

From its founding, the Society of Jesus has been associated with the practice of careful discernment. In the *Spiritual Exercises*, Ignatius highlighted the importance of "testing the spirits" and making deliberate and well-informed "elections" or decisions regarding one's vocation. For our present purposes, it is especially valuable to note that careful decision making proceeds on both the individual and collective level, and the process of "communal discernment" has received much attention in recent literature in spirituality and church governance. Discernment is both a spiritual practice with rich connection to prayer and a practical exercise in which following sound procedures for weighing the merits of various courses of action pays rich dividends.

The papal ministry of Francis displays nearly daily evidence of careful attention to the process of discernment, and it is often evidently Ignatian in its cast. While most items that cross the desk of a pope require decisions that are primarily administrative in nature (charting courses of action that involve finances, personnel, and scheduling), it is in matters of especially momentous ethical import that the Ignatian cast of this pope's discernment is most evident. Perhaps the best example of a sustained effort to hear the authentic voice of God for the church today is how Francis has handled deliberations on the family. Even before he ascended to the papacy, the topic of challenges to family life had been identified as the focus of the worldwide synod of bishops meeting to be held in October 2015. Francis recognized immediately that such an important topic (and one fraught with potential controversy) deserved more prolonged deliberation than the rather cramped traditional three-week synod format would allow. He called an additional (and quite rare) extraordinary synod to be held in October 2014, and encouraged dioceses around the world to gather information from the faithful by means of a thirty-nine-item survey. He encouraged unusually broad participation in the multiyear synod process through several other means, including delivering unusually rousing opening addresses that challenged the hundreds of delegates gathered in Rome to speak candidly, even with boldness—something that typical synod proceedings rarely display. Six months after the second synod on the family, Francis published the exhortation *Amoris laetitia* (April 2016), which draws richly upon the proceedings of the two synods and contained additional fruits of his own discernment on how the church can extend proper pastoral care to struggling families today.

Rather than focus on the controversies that swirled around every step of this process, we serve present purposes best by noting just a few qualities of the common discernment conducted by Francis. Both the process and its results (that is, the teachings contained in *Amoris laetitia*) are redolent of core Ignatian themes and Jesuit practice over the centuries. Above all, Ignatian discernment is characterized by a commitment to careful listening and a deep respect for the opinions of the people most affected by a given decision. In spiritual terms, this is described in terms of the imperative of listening to the Holy Spirit. Ignatius himself displays great confidence that the authentic voice of God can be discovered in many ways and places (an aspiration captured by the phrase "finding God in all things"), not only in traditions, established rules, and the will of authorities. This attention to local voices is related to the CST notion of subsidiarity, a principle that prioritizes the local level in decision making whenever possible. Francis frequently affirms the wisdom of bottom-up rather than top-down discernment, upholding the local level in ways that allow for pastoral flexibility and special accommodations rather than uniformity and rigid adherence to standardized norms. For example, in 2017, he authorized local bishops' conferences to play a greater role in the determinations of liturgical texts in vernacular languages, and in *Amoris laetitia* he signaled (primarily through footnotes such as number 351 dealing with sacramental help for Catholics in irregular marital situations) a new openness to local pastoral solutions to departures from inherited church disciplines.[14]

On both these occasions, decisions enacted by Francis have been met by sharp criticism from voices favoring a stricter approach to the exercise of church authority. Francis shows no signs of backing down—not because he favors utter laxity or a disregard for church rules but because of his appreciation for the Ignatian practice of discernment. To read the *Constitutions* that Ignatius wrote for the new order he founded or to observe the style of Jesuit governance as practiced over the centuries is to see evidence of a great confidence that the voice of the Holy Spirit indeed speaks in multiple ways. For example, Jesuit superiors conduct with each Jesuit under their care an annual "account of conscience," which is a formal opportunity to share one's experience of God and the promptings of the Spirit, and it provides the

---

14. Pope Francis, apostolic letter, *Magnum principium* (September 3, 2017), http://w2.vatican.va.

raw material for the Society's decision making at all levels. At its best, discernment is primarily inductive rather than deductive in emphasis, fostering processes of planning that are revisable rather than rigid. The resulting flexibility with and openness to many sources of wisdom reflect not a disregard for authority but a respect for the many ways that God speaks and that sometimes challenge and transcend humanly constructed rules and procedures, however useful they are as guideposts along the way to the future. As a long-time Jesuit superior and instructor in the ways of Ignatian spirituality, Francis has gained a deep appreciation for these values and principles, so it is no surprise that his way of proceeding as pope reflects these approaches, especially in shaping and promulgating moral teachings regarding healthy family life.

Another way of speaking about these same features of Jesuit spirituality and governance that have clearly influenced the moral teachings of the current papacy is to invoke the theme of conscience. Roman Catholic moral theology has consistently held a singularly high regard for the operations of the individual conscience, delineating over the centuries its premier role in guiding the individual to sound moral decisions. The documents of Vatican II upheld and extended this tradition and *AL* 37 reaffirms the inviolability of the voice of conscience on the part of all members of families, adding the wise final sentence: "We have been called to form consciences, not to replace them."[15] While there will always exist some tension between the role of humanly fashioned rules and the open-endedness of respecting a free conscience, through this document, Francis proposes a synthesis that reflects the Jesuit inheritance. While established church regulations governing marriages play an important role, ultimately supporting the gospel-based principle of the indissolubility of sacramental marriage, there remains no substitute for listening closely to the people most affected by the pain of marital breakdown and demonstrating respect for their free consciences while applying pastoral care. Francis affirms the legitimate role of local pastors to guide affected parties to an appropriate resolution, deliberately declining to lay down a new set of hard-and-fast general guidelines for the management of specific cases.[16] Proposing this teaching and applying it with pastoral

---

15. See *GS* 16 and the entirety of *Dignitatis humanae*, which constructs a new teaching on religious liberty on the foundation of respecting the free consciences of all people.

16. *AL* 300 states that "neither the Synod nor this exhortation could be expected to provide a new set of general rules, canonical in nature and applicable to all cases." Further clues to the role of discernment in these sensitive matters are easily found

sensitivity are works of careful discernment. What motivates the labor of Francis and pastors around the world who apply his teachings is, above all, love. Those familiar with Jesuit spirituality recognize the influence of the Ignatian notion *caritas discreta*—a discerning love that seeks to help souls by applying both prudence and care to their spiritual journeys. Honoring their sincere search for a way forward in the concrete circumstances of often messy lives requires wisdom, reverence, and a love that challenges, but ironclad rules are seldom among the helpful tools of such a pastor.

Ignatian discernment is often described as the Jesuits' gift to the church, but not all members of the church have received it so warmly. Those who resist or reject it outright often display a commonplace human defensiveness in the face of novelty and uncertainty. Anyone gripped by inordinate fear of the unknown, such as the perceived threat of compromising doctrinal clarity, will likely cast a suspicious eye on the open-endedness proposed by an Ignatius or a Francis. Culture warriors who prefer a defensive crouch over the prospect of revised practices in church and society are unlikely to muster the flexibility and spontaneity necessary to support free Ignatian discernment. Another factor creating resistance to the Ignatian vision involves one's view of what constitutes spiritual authority. A cramped view of divine revelation may prevent one from imagining God speaking freely through the experience and voice of common people, so revisions of long-standing customs and loci of authority are unwelcome. These are the most common rationales for resisting innovations in church governance (such as those proposed by Francis) and in apostolic priorities (such as those repeatedly pioneered by the Society of Jesus in its nearly five centuries of living out Ignatian spirituality).

What makes those influenced by Ignatian spirituality, including Francis himself, so eager to press the case for careful listening to the faithful in all their diversity? What explains the commitment to continually "testing the spirits" to discern new places where God may be leading? One adjective that has often been employed to describe a characteristic Jesuit stance is humanistic. Whatever else this intriguing word might mean in various contexts, it captures an attitude of commitment to the broadest possible construal of what allows people to thrive. The humanistic impulse affirms what is valuable in all disci-

---

in the outline of *Amoris laetitia*. Chapter 8 is called "Accompanying, Discerning, and Integrating Weakness" and includes the section titles "Gradualness in Pastoral Care," "The Discernment of 'Irregular' Situations," and "Rules and Discernment." It is important to note that none of these sections contain wholesale changes in church doctrine, as Francis has maintained on many occasions.

plines and endeavors, not rejecting anything that is potentially helpful simply because its source or expression might appear at first alien or potentially threatening. This openness to a variety of sources, even to unsettling surprises, reflects a certain magnanimity of character that a person of faith can display only when he or she possesses confidence that the contents of faith and reason will ultimately cohere. The support of Ignatius and Francis for the engagement of the faith with many disciplines of secular learning and with all human cultures, and their enthusiastic pursuit for dialogue with other religions, mark them as notable humanistic seekers of truth. The constant call of Francis to participate in the culture of encounter is just the latest expression of the centuries-long Jesuit project of building bridges wherever newly constructed walls threaten to divide people further. This goal of advancing the unity of humankind is given to all of us by the gospel, and the means are matters for our ongoing discernment.

COMMITMENT TO RECONCILIATION
AND PEACEMAKING

Although it may not appear as foundational within Jesuit spirituality as items such as discernment, the call to the *magis*, and the aspiration for spiritual freedom to transform the world to benefit those who are marginalized, the theme of reconciliation helps fill the Ignatian well from which Francis drinks. Francis rarely misses an opportunity to advocate for disarmament and to publicize the urgent need to reach peaceful resolutions of conflicts. The papacy provides numerous occasions to exercise this ministry of reconciliation—from the tradition of papal messages for World Day of Peace[17] to papal visits to nations suffering from violence[18] to the capacity to leverage its diplomatic standing to foster back-channel negotiations between rivals (a service Francis provided as the United States and Cuba moved to normalize relations in 2014).

---

17. These annual World Day of Peace messages, released each December in anticipation of the January 1 celebration, may be accessed at http://w2.vatican.va.

18. Francis embarked on twenty international trips in his first four and a half years as pope. Many featured themes involved the need for peace and reconciliation. In November 2015, Francis visited the Central African Republic, against the admonitions of security advisors, while even the capital of Bangui was very much a conflict zone. His visit to Colombia in September 2017 was timed to support recently signed peace accords aimed at ending decades of civil strife. His April 2017 visit to Egypt came just weeks after a tragic series of fatal terrorist attacks.

To appreciate how central the theme of peacebuilding is within the Jesuit charism, it is helpful to recall that Ignatius was himself a soldier, a knight struck by a cannonball at the battle of Pamplona in 1521. His subsequent conversion (while convalescing for months in the castle of his Basque family) to a new way of life included a renunciation of violence (symbolized by the act of laying down his soldier's sword before the Virgin of Montserrat at a Benedictine abbey along his pilgrim way to Jerusalem). Upon his ordination as a priest, he took up (with exemplary seriousness) the priestly mandate to serve as an agent of reconciliation for all. He understood this solemn mission not only in terms of individual spiritual or sacramental reconciliation (dealing with spiritual directees or penitents in the confessional), but inter-party reconciliation on larger societal stages as well. Part Seven of the Jesuit *Constitutions* (which deals with the mission and ministries of the Society) explicitly mentions "the reconciliation of quarreling parties" as a key activity by which the newly founded order would produce apostolic fruit and contribute to the progress of souls.[19] Not only does peacemaking recommend itself as a helpful component of any pastoral activity, but fostering social peace and resolving large-scale discord is a promising way to advance the common good and assist the poor, who invariably suffer most from internecine conflict and war.

It is little wonder that the early generations of Jesuits took up with such assiduous dedication the specialized ministry of serving as mediators and arbitrators in the local clan feuds that convulsed many villages in the Italian peninsula, among other parts of Europe where the first Jesuits found themselves. The early Jesuits frequently worked with civic leaders to defuse the grudges and animosities that fueled often bloody simmering civil strife—a situation captured vividly by William Shakespeare in his fictional portrayal of the feud between the Capulet and Montague families of Verona, the backdrop for the tragedy *Romeo and Juliet*. The Protestant Reformation and the subsequent wars of religion produced additional Jesuit heroes—some of them missionaries and martyrs targeted for their efforts to promote dialogue among separated brethren and to reconcile estranged members of the Christian family. Not only did the hard work of peacemaking engage the energies of Jesuits of the sixteenth century, but the legacy of these efforts has lived on in the imaginations of Jesuits through the centuries. Jesuits intent on brokering peace have positioned themselves in royal courts, in international agencies, and on the front lines of nego-

---

19. These words are contained in number 650, which appear on page 298 of *The Constitutions of the Society of Jesus and Their Complementary Norms* (St. Louis: Institute of Jesuit Sources, 1996).

tiations to resolve conflicts in South Africa, Northern Ireland, and the Near East, to name just a few settings in dire need of reconciliation in recent decades. Though today we would employ more sophisticated labels for these efforts, including the terms peacebuilding and conflict transformation, one need not search very long before locating Jesuits continuing these ambitious efforts to advance the peace that God promises in Scripture.

Pope Francis is, without doubt, the most prominent of the present-day Jesuit peacemakers. Having led the Jesuit province of Argentina through that nation's horrific "Dirty War" of the 1970s and 1980s, he came to Rome already thoroughly familiar with the horrors of war and with a determination never to take for granted the benefits of peace. Whether it is through hosting an elaborate solemn prayer vigil to prevent escalation of aerial bombings in war-torn Syria (as he did on September 7, 2013), launching the record-setting Twitter hashtag #prayforpeace, or hosting the leaders of Israel and Palestine in the Vatican gardens for a shared day of prayer (as he did on June 8, 2014), Francis finds many creative and effective ways to advance the peace process.

Many additional peacebuilding initiatives of Francis could be cited. Just as remarkable as the sheer volume of his activity for peace is the style with which he undertakes his campaigns for reconciliation between parties in conflict. We have already had occasion above to note how Francis has employed his characteristic structural lens to expose the ghastly global arms trade that fuels the preventable violence of terrorist gangs and proxy wars around the world. Part of the solution to violence, Francis instructs us through symbolic actions as well as explicit teachings, is supporting institutions that bolster the conditions that foster peace, including international covenants, coalitions, and organizations working to prevent conflict. Another emblematic strategy of Francis is the slow and sometimes hidden effort to build partnerships and relationships of trust among key players on the global scene. His customary rounds of ceremonial meetings with heads of state and NGO officials are, for Francis at least, not merely perfunctory photo opportunities but rather precious opportunities to build up a network of trust, good will, and useful contacts. If the diplomatic motto "peace is a by-product of relationships" still holds some truth, then the deliberately cultivated style of Pope Francis—one that emphasizes personal diplomacy as well as skillful engagement of key institutions—is a promising approach indeed. This pope named for a beloved saint, Francis of Assisi, whose most ardent desire was to be "an instrument of God's peace," displays a remarkably deep spiritual commitment to be a peacemaker in this new millennium, as Jesuits have aspired to be since the middle of the last millennium.

CONCLUSION

The sections above treat five points of intersection between the ethical teachings and moral leadership of Francis, on the one hand, and the tradition of Jesuit spirituality and apostolic practice, on the other. By considering three potential objections, we shed some further light on this project.

First, it might well be argued that weightier themes than those appearing on this list of five deserve top billing. No short list would be complete, of course, and there is ample room for amiable disagreement about which qualifying items (that is, where the requisite overlap occurs) are most central. It could well be that Pope Francis himself, if presented with this analysis, would suggest further elements of the Jesuit inheritance that have inspired his leadership as universal pastor. Surveying the activities and writings of this papacy, perhaps the most likely of these alternative items would be the themes of mercy and dialogue—two signature themes of Francis since he assumed office and two features frequently associated with the Society of Jesus. In each case, at least two of the five sections above offer some coverage, which may merit expansion or at least more explicit labeling.[20]

Second, a skeptical reader might well harbor lingering doubts about the claims offered here regarding lines of causality and influence. As with any project seeking to establish intellectual influences on a public figure with a profile as complex as Francis's, it is simply unrealistic to expect to draw airtight explanations. Correlation is not identical to causality. Providing evidence that a theme or characteristic exists in the Jesuit tradition and in the moral leadership of Francis does not, admittedly, prove the origin of what we find in Francis's ethical teaching. Nevertheless, the general influence of the Jesuit DNA of Francis is undeniable. After all, he lived the common Jesuit life for thirty-four years (from the start of his novitiate in 1958 until his ordination as a bishop in 1992), contributed richly to several corporate Jesuit apostolic works, and has for decades participated in regular retreats and daily prayer according to the Ignatian style of spirituality. Even if not for

---

20. Much more extensive treatment of themes such as dialogue and mercy appear in Thomas Massaro, SJ, *Mercy in Action: The Social Teachings of Pope Francis* (Lanham, MD: Rowman & Littlefield, 2018).

his explicit disavowal of any other dominant spiritual influences,[21] it would be hard to imagine that he had not imbibed deeply from this well during the most formative years of his young adult life. We need not look far at all to identify "what makes Francis tick," for it is most likely hidden in plain sight.

A third possible objection is that the analysis above is overly focused on the practical and external, and does violence to a purer, more genuine construal of spirituality, which is a term that should be reserved to those things that are eminently internal to each person. As this argument runs, for all the specific things Francis says and does externally, we deceive ourselves if we imagine that we enjoy much access to his internal spirituality, inspired as it may (or may not) be by Ignatian elements. While reminders of the possibilities of reductionism, hubris, and self-deception are valuable, in the case of this particular academic project, the voice of caution that might undercut our endeavor turns out to be overscrupulous in nature. We are, after all, examining the public words and actions of a global religious figure who deliberately shapes his moral teachings to serve public purposes. This essay has not pretended to peer very far into the inner life of Francis or to pierce his very soul; rather it has attempted to read the readily evident signs of his ethical priorities. His chosen spiritual values and characteristics quite obviously exert great influence on his formal ethical teachings, which themselves address practical matters such as economic justice, the environment, family life, the treatment of refugees, and peacemaking. Admittedly, spirituality can never be reduced to any set of worldly concerns, but neither does it serve any purpose to posit an artificial separation between spirituality and what is observable. In the case of Francis, as with Ignatius and all those he has inspired, reliable indeed is the commonsense observation that a healthy person's inner life and outward actions will closely cohere. Upon the solid foundation of Ignatian spirituality and the Jesuit tradition he has lived, Francis has constructed exemplary and challenging moral teachings on many topics, and his activist agenda of promoting love, social justice, and practical reform will remain with us for a long time.

---

21. As noted above (see n. 2), regarding the strength of Jesuit influence on him despite a long absence (since he became a bishop in 1992) from actually living in a Jesuit community or participating in a Jesuit apostolate, the pope stated: "I feel I am a Jesuit in my spirituality, in the spirituality of the *Exercises*, the spirituality that I have in my heart. I have not changed my spirituality, no. Francis, Franciscan, no. I feel Jesuit and I still think like a Jesuit." Cited in Endean, ed., "Writings on Jesuit Spirituality," 2.

8

Mercy

Marcus Mescher

Mercy is the defining characteristic of Pope Francis's leadership. His words and actions have made visible a discipline of mercy, which does more than illuminate God's character and purpose; it offers an expansive imaginative framework to spark new possibilities for moral agency and growth. Before Francis, mercy received limited attention in the canon of CST. Francis's signature message of mercy retrieves a central moral duty in Scripture, provides a focal lens for CST, and prompts a "revolution of tenderness" capable of inspiring personal conversion and social change. This chapter examines this message in three stages: we first unpack the rich and diverse meaning of the word mercy and explore its undervalued role in CST; we then analyze how mercy functions as the crux of Francis's moral imagination; and finally, we explore how mercy expands possibilities for living the principles of CST.

INTRODUCTION

Mercy has characterized Pope Francis's pontificate from its beginning. His chosen name indicates his commitment to humility, simplicity, as well as his special concern for the poor and the planet. Jorge Mario Bergoglio decided to take the name "Francis" after his election, following an embrace with his friend, Brazilian Cardinal Hummes, who insisted, "Don't forget the poor." During his introduction at St. Peter's Square, Francis broke with tradition by asking the 150,000 people gathered to pray for him before offering his first blessing as pope. When he was introduced to his brother cardinals, Francis refused to use a platform to elevate himself over them. Francis chooses to live in a small suite in the Vatican guesthouse rather than the Apostolic Palace. Religious and secular news outlets report his regular efforts to help the needy, including a construction project to make the Vatican more hospitable to those experiencing homelessness in Rome. The most iconic images of his time as pope include his warm embrace of a man covered with tumors, tender gestures of welcome to young children, washing the feet of prisoners, and celebrating Mass around the globe with refugees and migrants. Francis's pedagogy of mercy combines these richly symbolic actions with public statements and official documents that emphasize the need for mercy to infuse and inspire the lives of each Christian and the church's social mission. Francis reinforces the biblical witness of mercy as "God's identity card" and the heart of the Christian moral life. In response to the alienating effects of sin, Francis embraces mercy as essential for healing wounds and building communion with all creation. He also augments the meaning of mercy beyond loving-kindness, generosity, and forgiveness by highlighting its connection to humility, fidelity, tenderness, fortitude, and solidarity. Through his signature message of the primacy of mercy, Francis expands our theological and moral imagination and provides ready access to the principles and practices that constitute CST. This represents an important development for the church's tradition, since the documentary heritage of CST does not consistently connect mercy to work for social justice.

WHO GOD IS AND WHAT GOD WANTS

As the newly elected pope, Francis was asked, "Who is Jorge Mario Bergoglio?" He replied: "I am a sinner. This is the most accurate definition. It is not a figure of speech, a literary genre. I am a sinner."[1] Francis reveals a person in touch with the experience of God-who-is-mercy. In *The Name of God Is Mercy*, Francis writes:

---

1. Antonio Spadaro, "A Big Heart Open to God: An Interview with Pope Francis," *America*, September 30, 2013, http://www.americamagazine.org. Note also that this reflects Francis's Jesuit background, both in terms of the first week of the *Spiritual Exercises* as well as the opening lines of the 32nd General Congregation, Decree 2: "What is it to be a Jesuit? It is to know that one is a sinner, yet called to be a companion of Jesus as Ignatius was: Ignatius, who begged the Blessed Virgin to 'place him with her Son' and who then saw the Father himself ask Jesus, carrying his Cross, to take this pilgrim into his company" (no. 1).

The centrality of mercy, which for me is Jesus' most important message, has slowly evolved over the years in my work as a priest, as a consequence of my experience as a confessor, and thanks to the many positive and beautiful stories that I have known . . . [mercy] means opening one's heart to wretchedness. And immediately we go to the Lord: mercy is the divine attitude which embraces, it is God's giving himself to us, accepting us, and bowing to forgive . . . we can say that mercy is God's identity card.[2]

Francis understands God's character and purpose through the lens of the gerund "mercifying," *doing* mercy.[3] His emphasis on mercy communicates that God is known through the experience of receiving mercy, and, moreover, God expects mercy from and for God's people. The Incarnation, according to Francis, represents an invitation for humanity to join God in a "revolution of tenderness."[4] Tenderness is often shorthand for Francis's theological and moral understanding of mercy.[5] He describes the mission of the church as mediating mercy freely offered and received, being people who practice forgiveness more than judgment and who work ardently for reconciliation.[6] Mercy is the criterion for being a credible Christian, the inspiration for the church to be, as Francis exhorts, a "field hospital" and a place without frontiers, a "mother to all."[7]

To help the church become more attentive and responsive to the experience of God's mercy and more intentional about incarnating God's mercy in the world, Francis proclaimed the Extraordinary Jubilee of Mercy in 2015 by proposing:

---

2. Pope Francis, *The Name of God Is Mercy*, trans. Oonagh Stransky (New York: Random House, 2016), 8–9.

3. Ibid., 12.

4. *EG* 88.

5. Francis explains his understanding of tenderness as using "our hands and our heart to comfort the other, to take care of those in need. Tenderness is the language of the young children, of those who need the other." He explains that tenderness is like parents who respond to a baby in his or her own incomprehensible babbling — not to condescend, but to connect — "adapting to the little child, sharing the same level of communication. This is tenderness: being on the same level as the other." See Pope Francis, "Why the Only Future Worth Building Includes Everyone," *TED*, April 2017, https://www.ted.com.

6. Pope Francis, *The Church of Mercy: A Vision for the Church* (Chicago: Loyola University Press, 2014), 28. Francis highlights four characteristics — humility, meekness, magnanimity, and love — as instrumental in building a church that is a "house of communion" and a "house that welcomes all" (26–32).

7. *MV* 9; Spadaro, "A Big Heart Open to God"; see also *EG* 210.

We need constantly to contemplate the mystery of mercy. It is a wellspring of joy, serenity, and peace. Our salvation depends on it. Mercy: the word reveals the very mystery of the Most Holy Trinity. Mercy: the ultimate and supreme act by which God comes to meet us. Mercy: the fundamental law that dwells in the heart of every person who looks sincerely into the eyes of his brothers and sisters on the path of life. Mercy: the bridge that connects God and man, opening our hearts to the hope of being loved forever despite our sinfulness.[8]

Some might wonder whether such an emphasis on mercy might mute the prophetic call to denounce the causes of sin and suffering and announce the changes required by justice. After all, if one pushes the idea of "being loved forever despite our sinfulness," then it might be tempting to adopt a less ascetic discipleship or a more permissive morality. On the contrary, Francis appeals to mercy as the motivation for condemning corruption and seeking to heal social disorders.[9] Mercy does not convey a therapeutic image of God who is distant or disinterested, or a God who withholds judgment on human sinfulness; it does not endorse moral laxity. Rather, mercy prompts the acknowledgment of one's sinfulness, dependence on God's forgiveness, and continuous desire for conversion. Cognizant of the alienation produced by sin—resulting in separation from God and neighbor—Francis exhorts the church to heal these wounds by receiving and extending mercy.

Surrounded by temptations to despair in a world marked by doubt and divisions, mercy galvanizes trust in God and hope that change is possible. Mercy softens stubbornness in judgment about oneself and others, energizing into motion the sluggish inertia of indifference or apathy. Mercy is less a cognitive presumption that God will forgive than a visceral encounter with God-who-is-love.[10] Some critics fear that such a focus on mercy will eclipse the pursuit of truth, but Francis asserts that "mercy is doctrine . . . mercy is true" and any opposition between mercy and truth distorts the logic of God.[11] Mercy is not

---

8. *MV* 2.

9. See Jorge Bergoglio, "Sin and Corruption," in *The Way of Humility* (San Francisco: Ignatius Press, 2014). Thanks to David Cloutier for this insight.

10. Pope Francis, "Message for World Mission Day" (May 15, 2016), https://w2.vatican.va.

11. Pope Francis, *The Name of God Is Mercy*, 62, 66. Francis adds that mercy generates freedom from a legalistic mentality (which he calls the "logic of the scholars of the law") that, through prejudice and rigidity, confines ourselves and

acquiescing to lower standards, or a laissez-faire credo such as "live
and let live." Mercy does not replace judgment; mercy informs judgment. It requires great resolve to be merciful rather than condemn,
surrender, or abandon. For these reasons, Francis is quick to assert
that mercy is a sign of strength, not weakness.[12] Mercy—as humble
and steadfast, gracious and unconditional, faithful and tender—communicates who God is and what God wants.

Many Christians, however, reduce mercy to kindness, an openness
to forgive, or acts of generosity. In the Catholic moral tradition, mercy
may be known as the preeminent virtue, according to Thomas Aquinas.[13] Mercy is practiced by seven spiritual and seven corporal works,
ranging from comforting the sorrowful and patiently bearing wrongs
to feeding the hungry and welcoming the stranger. James Keenan
characterizes these as the very "heart of Catholicism," adding his own
definition of mercy as the "willingness to enter into the chaos of others
to answer them in their need."[14] Yet the biblical witness of mercy—
communicating God's character and purpose—reaches beyond these
spiritual and corporal works, encompassing a rich and diverse significance for Christian faith and discipleship. As Scripture demonstrates,
mercy is circumscribed when it fails to signify humility, fidelity, tenderness, fortitude, and solidarity.

The biblical words for mercy (*hesed* and *eleos*) appear nearly three
hundred times and convey far more than loving-kindness, forgiveness, or generosity. For example, *hesed* is the first word used to describe
God, who is merciful and gracious, slow to anger, abounding in steadfast love and faithfulness (Exod 34:6–7). *Hesed* refers to God's unconditional and unlimited love that is always faithful, never fails, a love
marked by tenderness and overabundance (Josh 2:12; 1 Sam 20:14–17;

---

others from experiencing the welcome embrace, transformation and redemption
through which God is "transmuting condemnation into salvation" (66).

12. Francis asserts, "Tenderness is the path of choice for the strongest, most
courageous men and women. Tenderness is not weakness; it is fortitude. It is the
path of solidarity, the path of humility. Please, allow me to say it loud and clear:
the more powerful you are, the more your actions will have an impact on people,
the more responsible you are to act humbly." See Pope Francis, "Why the Only
Future Worth Building Includes Everyone."

13. *Summa Theologica* II-II.q30, a4. Thomas writes, "In itself mercy is the greatest
of the virtues, since all the others revolve around it and, more than this, it makes
up for their deficiencies. This is particular to the superior virtue, and as such it is
proper to God to have mercy, through which his omnipotence is manifested to the
greatest degree."

14. James Keenan, *The Works of Mercy: The Heart of Catholicism* (Lanham, MD:
Rowman & Littlefield, 2008), xv.

Isa 54:8–10). *Hesed* reflects God's goodness that endures for a "thousand generations" (Exod 20:6) as well as God's unlimited forgiveness of sin (Num 14:18–19; Mic 7:19). Mercy grounds the interdependent web of relationships as part of God's covenant with God's people (Lev 19:2, 18; Deut 15:4, 7; Ps 13:6). As the basis for the covenant with Yahweh (Deut 5:2, 10; Hos 2:16–21; Isa 55:3), *hesed* signifies solidarity among God's people, illustrated by fidelity and obligation (2 Sam 7:11–16). *Hesed* highlights the gratuitous love of God that embraces all creation, including nonhuman creatures (Deut 7:7–9; Ps 33:5; 111:4; 136:1; 145:9; Dan 7:9–14). It communicates God's will to save humanity and restore the human family to the Promised Land (Ps 25:6; Jer 42:12). *Hesed* defines faithfulness (Hos 6:6; Mic 6:8) and characterizes those who love God (Ruth 1:8; 2:20; 3:10). The Hebrew Scriptures make clear that *hesed* is inseparable from justice, judgment, piety, compassion, and salvation (Ps 72:1–4; 82:3; 140:13), serving as the essential norm for relationships with God and one another.

Eleos appears in the Christian Scriptures dozens of times and fortifies the witness of the Hebrew Scriptures that mercy describes God's own being (Luke 6:36; 2 Cor 1:3; Eph 2:4) and how God treats God's people (Luke 1:58; 1 Pet 2:10). As the incarnation of God-who-is-mercy, Jesus's teachings and practices orbit around mercy (Matt 5:7; Mark 5:19). Mercy is the way to love one's neighbor and inherit eternal life (Luke 10:25–42); it is the standard for unlimited forgiveness (Matt 18:21–35). Paul adds that mercy makes faithfulness possible (Rom 12:1–2; 2 Cor 4:1). *Eleos* is the core of God's desire for God's people (Matt 9:13; 12:7; 23:23). Even when the word doesn't appear in the passage, mercy is the fulcrum of several key Gospel stories, whether the father's forgiveness of his prodigal son (Luke 15:11–32), Jesus's forgiveness of the woman caught in adultery (John 8:1–11), or what separates the sheep from the goats in the Last Judgment (Matt 25:31–46). Mercy is an expression of wisdom (Jas 3:17) and the reason for hope (1 Pet 1:3). In the end, mercy triumphs over judgment (Jas 2:13); it is the expression of God's justice (Ps 51:11–16; Matt 9:13). Borrowing a phrase from St. John of the Cross, mercy is "the measure by which we shall be judged," the ultimate criterion of the Christian moral life.

For these reasons, it is both curious and lamentable that mercy does not play a more prominent role in the canon of CST. In the hundreds of pages of documents that constitute CST, mercy is rarely invoked as a theological warrant or moral resource for social justice. In *Rerum novarum*, Leo XIII quotes Gregory the Great to insist that one should be a steward of God's providence in serving others: "He that hath abundance, let him quicken himself to mercy and generosity; he that hath art and skill, let him do his best to share the use and the utility hereof with his neighbor" (*RN* 22). Aside from this appeal to mercy as motivation for serving a needy neighbor, mercy is not explicitly linked to social responsibility or structural change in many of the lengthy treatises that comprise CST. Mercy goes unmentioned in *Quadragesimo anno, Pacem in terris, Dignitatis humanae, Laborem exercens, Centesimus annus,* and the 1971 World Synod of Catholic Bishops' document "Justice in the World." Mercy is mentioned just once or twice in many documents such as *Mater et magistra* (including the same quote by Gregory the Great), *Gaudium et spes, Populorum progressio, Octogesima adveniens, Familiaris consortio,* and *Laudato si'*.[15] In these and other cases (including *Sollicitudo rei socialis* and *Caritas in veritate*), mercy is referenced less as a resource for serving the needy (which is still more in the spirit of charity than justice) than as a divine attribute.[16] It is not until *Amoris laetitia* that mercy is reclaimed as central for right-relationship with God and neighbor on the personal, social, and institutional levels; Francis's emphasis on mercy translates to almost forty references in this document.[17] In light of the fact that *Amoris laetitia* largely focuses on the intimate bonds shared between spouses or parents and children, it remains the case that the canon of CST has not yet robustly marshaled the theological and moral significance of mercy for affirming the dignity and rights of all persons in society, dismantling racism and sexism, combating xenophobia, advancing restorative justice,

---

15. See, for example, *MM* 119 (the other reference is from Ps 84:9: "mercy and truth have met each other," *MM* 262); *GS* 42 (briefly mentioning the "works of mercy"); *Populorum progressio* makes no appeal to mercy but does call Christians to "be moved by this sad state of affairs" in the world and to "echo the words of Christ: 'I have compassion on the crowd'" (*PP* 74; cf. Mark 8:2); *Octogesima adveniens* states that disciples should be like Jonah, who proclaimed "the good news of God's mercy" (*OA* 12); *Familiaris consortio* alludes to God's mercy in the paragraphs on the Sacrament of Reconciliation (*FC* 58); the lone reference to mercy in *Laudato si'* quotes a line from Pope Benedict XVI in 2005 on ascending from created things "to the greatness of God and to his loving mercy" (*LS* 77).

16. See, for example, *SRS* 36. Pope John Paul II also asks Christians to place the world's needs before Mary's "eyes of mercy" in the final paragraph (*SRS* 49); and Benedict XVI, *CV* 79. This is also true in the U.S. Catholic bishops' 1986 pastoral letter "Economic Justice for All," which mentions mercy six times (nos. 36, 37, 42, 44, 50, and 364), almost always in terms of God's gift to humanity, not the basis for cultivating communion or working for economic justice.

17. In addition, Francis mentions compassion six times in *Amoris laetitia*: as a core trait for God and Jesus (*AL* 28 and 38), constitutive of love shared within the family (*AL* 92 and 175); and as the necessary posture of the church toward families (*AL* 200 and 308). Compare this to John Paul II's single reference—to Jesus's compassion—in *FC* 41.

building inclusive and equitable communities, and participating in civic life for the common good.

In a related observation, some biblical scholars suggest that the Greek word *charis* (grace) in the Christian Scriptures is a closer equivalent to *hesed* than *eleos*. Identifying mercy with grace reinforces the idea that, insofar as grace is God's self-gift, God makes Godself known through mercy. Moreover, *charis* serves as another theological resource for moral responsibilities viewed through the lens of cooperation with God in fostering right-relationships and building a just social order. Like mercy, grace is also underdeveloped in many documents that comprise CST. In the same papal documents listed above, grace is most often mentioned between one and three times and almost always depicted in a highly individualistic paradigm. Grace is typically presented as a gift for personal sanctification at work in the hearts of individuals[18] and as special assistance from God.[19] Several documents restrict the function of grace to the sacramental life, in particular, Baptism and Eucharist.[20] This oversimplification of grace ignores the significance of God's triune nature, which implies that grace, as an experience of God's self-gift, is more accurately described as an experience of loving communion.[21] Like mercy, experiencing grace is a direct sharing in the divine life, a catalyst for personal moral growth as well as social transformation.[22] Yet CST almost exclusively presents grace as a gift operating on human life instead of a relationship empowering human and divine cooperation, as Aquinas describes.[23] Like grace, mercy is not only a matter of personal salvation or sanctification; it is also the means by which humans live as a "new creation" (2 Cor 5:17) or as "risen beings" who cooperate with God's self-gift to build the "not yet" fully realized reign of God in the

---

18. Cf. *GS* 22 and *LS* 205 and 233.

19. Cf. *RN* 21 and *SRS* 25, 28, 48.

20. Cf. *GS* 89, *LS* 236, and *AL* 38.

21. Donald L. Gelpi, *Grace as Transmuted Experience and Social Process, and Other Essays in North American Theology* (Lanham, MD: University Press of America, 1988). Gelpi writes, "The fact that the divine experience subsists as an eternal social process provides the pattern, the norm for the historical gracing of human experience. We become graced by being drawn socially into the experience of interpersonal communion shared by the divine persons" (54).

22. Gelpi claims the "eruption" of grace in history "transmutes natural and sinful feelings into an experience of social communion in hope, faith, and love" (ibid., 54).

23. See Thomas Aquinas, *Summa Theologica* I-II q.111, art. 2, "Of the Division of Grace," in *St. Thomas Aquinas Summa Theologica*, trans. Fathers of the English Dominican Province, vol. 2 (Notre Dame, IN: Ave Maria Press, 1981), 1136–37.

world of the "already."[24] Highlighting the interpersonal qualities of mercy and grace helps prevent them from being confined to matters of personal piety or holiness. Portraying mercy and grace as resources provided by God for magnifying moral agency expands the Christian moral imagination of what God is helping to make possible for the church and world.

For too long, mercy has been viewed largely as a gift received from God and inspiration for individual service to others in need. In contrast to this impoverished understanding of mercy and its limited treatment in CST, Francis's words and actions deepen and broaden the meaning and significance of mercy. Francis's emphasis on mercy inspires a renewal of the biblical witness that includes adopting a posture of humility, practicing fidelity to God and neighbor, displaying fortitude through tenderness, and fostering the mutual concern and responsibility that generates solidarity. Through this example, Francis reveals new possibilities for the church's commitment to justice and reconciliation on the personal, social, and structural levels. This means calling the church to be more inclusive and welcoming, to engage culture and society for the common good, and to accompany those pushed to the peripheries. By consistently emphasizing mercy as the defining characteristic of who God is and what God wants for and from God's people, Francis highlights how God's unlimited self-gift makes it possible to imagine—and build—a more faithful church and a more just social order.

MERCY EXPANDS THE MORAL IMAGINATION

Mercy is the crux of Francis's theological vision, the true north of his moral compass, the spark that inflames his imagination of what is possible for Christian faith and discipleship. Francis stresses the centrality of mercy not just to rehearse biblical themes but as an invitation to stand afresh in wonder and awe at the unconditional and unending tenderness of God, to receive and be received by a God who never tires of forgiving us "in ways that are continually new and surprising."[25] Francis envisions a church renewed by the inexhaustible spring of

---

24. Jon Sobrino makes this claim, in drawing from Karl Rahner's description of Jesus's resurrection as more than a historical event, a "permanent prevailing" that allows Christians "to experience the repercussions of Jesus' resurrection as such in our own lives here and now." See *Christ the Liberator: A View from the Victims*, trans. Paul Burns (Maryknoll, NY: Orbis Books, 2001), 13, 31.

25. *MV* 22.

God-who-is-mercifying so that, in all times and places, its members can be tributaries of this superabundant source of humility, fidelity, tenderness, fortitude, and solidarity.

Francis's attention to mercy—both as God's gift and as what God expects from God's people—inspired his call to build a "culture of encounter" that bursts the "soap bubbles" of vain self-concern. It confronts the "globalization of indifference" that abdicates responsibility for the suffering of our neighbor.[26] It involves a recognition of the presence, power, and love of God in the sacrament of our neighbor as well as prompting an "ecological conversion" to a "sacrament of communion" with every member of creation and with the earth, our common home.[27] Mercy is the crux of Pope Francis's moral imagination, which is why he shows special concern for those who are vulnerable, marginalized, and living in "irregular situations."[28] He insists that mercy is the test of the church's welcome, especially to those pushed to the edges of society. It is not enough for the church to extend welcome to all; the church must "go forth" into the world to "reach all the 'peripheries.'"[29] Francis asserts that "the way of the Church is not to condemn anyone for eternity; it is to pour out the balm of God's mercy on all those who ask for it."[30] Mercy is the path to holiness, the defining trait for the followers of Christ.[31] For this reason, mercy cannot be confined to personal piety or sanctification; it inspires social and ecological responsibilities in the pursuit of justice. This emphasis on mercy adopts a different approach from the top-down, principles-to-practice dominant paradigm in CST; instead, Francis aims for a moral conversion in the church from the ground up through personal attitudes and habits that extend beyond kindness, forgiveness, and generosity by also including humility, fidelity, tenderness, fortitude, and solidarity. Without these virtues, there can be no trust or mutuality, no way to overcome the divisions fomented by rigidity, fear, or judgment, and no hope for reforming unjust systems and structures.

Francis's repeated references to God-who-is-mercifying unmask the image of a god who condemns people of a certain belief or lifestyle,

26. Pope Francis, "Homily," Mass at Lampedusa (July 8, 2013), https://w2.vatican.va.

27. *LS* 5, 9.

28. *AL* 78, 296–305.

29. *EG* 20.

30. *AL* 296.

31. Pope Francis states that mercy is the work of God in the world and the "criterion for knowing who his true children are" (*AL* 310). Francis defines holiness as "seeing and acting with mercy" (*GE* 82), following the example of Jesus Christ, who demonstrates that mercy is "the beating heart of the Gospel" (*GE* 97).

who expects more than finitude allows, or who is uninterested and uninvolved in human affairs. Recasting theological imagination away from a fault-finding god yields important implications for the Christian moral life. It makes room for moral failure without assuming condemnation; it adopts a more gentle and flexible posture in place of a rigid fixation on following rules. It replaces anxious concerns about purity or perfection with humility to seek conversion and redemption. Attunement to mercy is emancipatory. Mercy is a grace of liberation from doubt and despair, from dwelling on sin and feeling trapped by it. Mercy does not ignore sin or its harm to relationships with God, self, and neighbor. Instead, mercy seeks to heal shame, stigma, suspicion, and division. It aims to warm, soften, illuminate, and forge union between God and all creation. It is not pixie dust or a panacea but an experience of the tender caress of God that inspires astonishment at what more is possible as mercy is shared in and through each person:

> Only one who has been caressed by the tenderness of mercy truly knows the Lord. The privileged place of encounter is the caress of Jesus' mercy regarding my sin. This is why you may have heard me say, several times, that the place for this, the privileged place of the encounter with Jesus Christ is my sin. The will to respond and to change, which can give rise to a different life, comes thanks to this merciful embrace. Christian morality is not a titanic, voluntary effort, of one who decides to be coherent and who manages to do so, a sort of isolated challenge before the world. No. This is not Christian morality, it is something else. Christian morality is a response, it is the heartfelt response before the surprising, unforeseeable—even "unfair" according to human criteria—mercy of One who knows me, knows my betrayals and loves me just the same, appreciates me, embraces me, calls me anew, hopes in me, has expectations of me. Christian morality is not a never falling down, but an always getting up, thanks to his hand which catches us. This too is the way of the Church: to let the great mercy of God become manifest.[32]

Mercy inspires a Christian morality that replaces "never falling down" with "always getting up." Trusting in the vast tenderness of God grows the capacity for compassion and courage. Compassion and courage are crucial for cultivating a moral imagination that looks to the future with hope inspired by humility, fidelity, tenderness, for-

---

32. Pope Francis, "Address to the Communion and Liberation Movement" (March 7, 2015), https://w2.vatican.va.

titude, and solidarity. Instead of viewing imagination as fantasy or illusion, it is better understood as a "vehicle for liberation."[33] Imagination is the fruit of one's deepest desires, illuminating what one hopes for oneself and the world.[34] It does not disdain or reject the world, but embraces the world in its complex, fallen state.[35] In the face of sin, suffering, and injustice, the imagination is an exercise of resistance to evil as well as resilience in promoting the good. It is an invitation "into a different wavelength," an energizing "transformed consciousness" in alert wonder at what is, and awe at what more is possible.[36] The moral imagination is "the capacity to imagine something rooted in the challenges of the real world yet capable of giving birth to that which does not yet exist."[37] Imagination is a practice of hope and love, affirming the goodness in every member of creation, and inspiring collaboration. Imagination is at its fullest and freest when it is a shared exercise, marked by mutuality and equality among persons.[38]

The Christian moral imagination frames a vision of what is good, right, true, and just. And yet, because of finitude and sin, this vision is always susceptible to blind spots. Mercy makes it possible to seek out blind spots without fearing the vulnerability of being wrong. As Francis asserts, to embrace mercy is to dedicate oneself to an examination

---

33. So argues Johann Baptist Metz, who envisions the restoration of memory — especially the "dangerous memory" of the Paschal Mystery — as precipitating the restoration of imagination that resists the acceptance of suffering as complacent with the status quo. See Metz, *Faith in History and Society: Toward a Practical Fundamental Theology*, trans. J. Matthew Ashley (New York: Herder & Herder, 2007), 177–78.

34. William Lynch insists that hope is impossible without imagination. He posits, "Hope is, in its most general terms, a sense of *the possible*, that what we really need is possible, though difficult, while hopelessness means to be ruled by the sense of the impossible. Hope therefore involves three basic ideas that could not be simpler: what I hope for I do not yet have or see; it may be difficult; but I *can* have it — it is possible." See William F. Lynch, *Images of Hope: Imagination as Healer of the Hopeless* (Notre Dame, IN: University of Notre Dame Press, 1974), 32.

35. Lynch explains, "We must *go through* the finite, the limited, the definite, omitting none of it lest we omit some of the potencies of being-in-the-flesh. . . . We waste our time if we try to go around or above or under the definite; we must literally go through it." See William F. Lynch, *Christ and Apollo: The Dimension of the Literary Imagination* (New York: Sheed & Ward, 1960), 7.

36. Michael Paul Gallagher, "Theology and Imagination: From Theory to Practice," *Christian Higher Education* 5 (2006): 83–96, at 87.

37. John Paul Lederach, *The Moral Imagination: The Art and Soul of Building Peace* (Oxford: Oxford University Press, 2005), 29.

38. Lynch states, "In mutuality, each of the parties helps the other to become himself . . . such a unity is creative. . . . Real mutuality also communicates freedom . . . [and] includes a profound wishing together" (*Images of Hope*, 171).

of conscience, healing, and transformation.[39] William Spohn explains the connection between moral perception, imagination, and conversion:

> The main components of moral perception are habits of considerateness and attentiveness to the data, virtues of respect and empathy, imagination capable of understanding the other's hopes and fears, experience that has taught us how to place this situation in a larger perspective, honest self-knowledge about our preferences and prejudices, and humility to seek the advice of others to expand our own vision. The story of Jesus calls his disciples to develop the capacity to see justly and lovingly. Conversion requires confronting our blindness and reluctance to be engaged with people who are threatening or repulsive. The transformation of moral perception begins with admitting that we are blind, or at least quite selective in our compassion.[40]

Mercy is a key resource for expanding the moral imagination because it is allergic to partiality and acquiescing to a sinful status quo. Mercy helps to sustain the waiting that comes with the hopeful expectation of the imagination. Mercy is useful for resisting panic or passivity. It works with the imagination to avoid condemnation, "foreclosing judgment on ourselves," a kind of "internalized form of brainwashing," an inclination toward becoming "our own executioners."[41] Mercy sharpens moral perception while multiplying the scope, like a set of lenses that enhance vision both near and far, increasing sensitivity to recognize human dignity and the pursuit of solidarity. Mercy implies proximity with God and others. By drawing near another, it seeks to build bridges across division and distrust through empathy, the artful work of imagining what it is like to be someone else. Mercy aids discernment in order to better grasp what God is calling and empowering each person to be and to do so that the church and world more richly reflect God's character and purpose.

Pope Francis has suggested that this is a time of particular need for imagination. Along with restlessness—the refusal to accept mediocrity and the commitment to be audacious in seeking to change the

---

39. *MV* 19, 21.

40. William Spohn, *Go and Do Likewise: Jesus and Ethics* (New York: Continuum, 2006), 98–99.

41. Lynch explains, "If the last word were ours, we would indeed be badly off. It is imagination and hope, even when they look at our worst, that leave room for another and a better world" (*Images of Hope*, 256).

world—as well as incompleteness—always being open to the God of surprises—Francis envisions imagination as crucial for being available to the new work of the Spirit in the world today. He explains:

> This is the time of discernment in the Church and in the world. Discernment is always realized in the presence of the Lord, looking at the signs, listening to things that happen, the feelings of people who know the humble way of the daily stubbornness, and especially of the poor. But we need to penetrate ambiguity, we need to enter in there, as the Lord Jesus did assuming our flesh. Rigid thought is not divine because Jesus has assumed our flesh, which is not rigid except after death. This is why I like poetry so much and, when it is possible for me, I continue to read it. Poetry is full of metaphors. Understanding metaphors helps to make thought agile, intuitive, flexible, acute. Whoever has imagination does not become rigid, has a sense of humor, always enjoys the sweetness of mercy and inner freedom.[42]

Imagination makes it possible to translate theology from prose to poetry and moral theology from obligation to passion. It speaks to and from one's deepest desires, surmounting the banality that strips the potency of the gospel. Imagination functions on a cognitive level just as much as it does a spiritual and religious level: it dismantles the limitations placed on God, one another, and oneself. Imagination is prophetic, finding a healthy balance between an overaffirmation and overrejection of the world. Imagination is creative, opening access to the spiritual and moral resources necessary for building the reign of God and resisting the antireign of God (that is, forces that dehumanize, deprive, and divide). This raises the moral question of how imagination is exercised: Which values are embraced, which are rejected, and who benefits or suffers from these choices? As a "key battleground for meaning, values, and in particular for religious faith," the imagination is "where the quality of our lives is shaped and where we shape our vision of everything. Imagination is the location both of our crisis and of our potential healing. It is vital for the quality of our seeing, because it can save us from superficiality and torpor and awaken us to larger hopes and possibilities."[43] What problems are solved because of

---

42. Pope Francis, "Discourse to the Community of *La Civiltà Cattolica*," *La Civiltà Cattolica*, February 9, 2017, https://www.laciviltacattolica.it.

43. Michael Paul Gallagher, "Culture and Imagination as Battlegrounds," Shaping the Future: Networking Jesuit Higher Education for a Globalizing World Conference in Mexico City (April 21–25, 2010), 3, 7.

the solutions we imagine, what problems remain unresolved because they do not capture our imagination, and what does that say about how we exercise—or fail to exercise—our moral agency? Moral growth develops in direct proportion to one's capacity to stretch one's moral imagination.

Mercy keeps the moral imagination trained on justice, since, as Francis attests, "mercy is the fullness of justice and the most radiant manifestation of God's truth."[44] Explicitly joining mercy to justice— a rare occurrence in the canon of CST[45]—points to the need to connect the moral imagination with social analysis. In the United States, Christians are twice as likely as non-Christians to blame the poor for their state in life.[46] Not only does this judgment reflect a lack of mercy, but it points to a failure to understand the complex circumstances and structural inequalities that often contribute to poverty. A moral imagination inspired by mercy can cultivate the curiosity that seeks to understand these root causes. Opposed to abstraction or hypothetical daydreaming, this is a curiosity that activates a social analysis of how power is exercised in systems and structures. Curiosity mobilizes the moral imagination through an approach to "social realities with an abiding respect for complexity, a refusal to fall prey to the pressures of forced dualistic categories of truth, and an inquisitiveness about what may hold together seemingly contradictory social energies in a greater whole."[47] In this way, the imagination functions with clear-eyed realism, or even what might be described as a "pessimism" that "is a terrain-based understanding of the social setting. What it seeks to engage is a deep understanding of human affairs, the true nature of how change happens, and the necessity of integrity as a condition for surviving manipulation and mendacity."[48] Combining social analysis with the moral imagination makes it easier to grasp the root causes of

---

44. *AL* 311. This line represents the most explicit link between mercy, justice, and truth in the canon of CST.

45. Even with the limited number of documents that mention the relationship between God's mercy and justice (see, for example, *SRS* 36; *CV* 6 and 79), in most cases, the canon of CST restricts mercy to a gift from God or act of kindness to others in need, rather than the humility, tenderness, forgiveness, fortitude, and solidarity that can generate the relationships and structures necessary for creating a more just social order.

46. Julie Zauzmer, "Christians are more than twice as likely to blame a person's poverty on lack of effort," *Washington Post*, August 3, 2017, https://www.washingtonpost.com.

47. Lederach, *The Moral Imagination*, 36. Lederach observes that the root of curiosity has to do with both "cure" and "care." It would seem that mercy also attends to both.

48. Ibid., 55.

social and ecological problems before applying moral wisdom from CST to strategize the kinds of habits, relationships, and policies that will better promote human dignity and rights, economic and ecological justice, the common good and solidarity.

Francis's embrace of mercy and his appeal to the imagination represent important areas of growth in the canon of CST, especially when the moral imagination is marshaled for complex social analysis. Most documents in CST draw from Scripture and Tradition to present moral principles intended to persuade Christians and people of good will to modify their beliefs and practices. However, not enough documents incorporate social analysis in order to interrupt—and even better, prevent—the systems and structures that dehumanize, deprive, and divide. For example, although *Laudato si'* explicitly condemns the corruption, inefficiency, and waste in local government (no. 44) and denounces the global debt crisis as "structurally perverse" (no. 52), it does not discuss the harmful effects of free market capitalism; and, moreover, it fails to reference racist and sexist beliefs and policies that result in indigenous communities, women, and people of color enduring the worst effects of climate change and ecological degradation. A moral imagination inspired by mercy can expose these harmful systems and structures while also envisioning economic practice based on mutual respect, responsibility, and cooperation instead of exploitation of labor, resources, and the natural environment, often justified by the top priority to maximize profit.[49]

By linking mercy to humility, fidelity, tenderness, fortitude, and solidarity, Francis provides an expansive imaginative framework to spark new possibilities for moral agency and growth that is both personal and social. As the church responds to Francis's call to be merciful and exercise the imagination, more individuals and communities can join the work to heal alienation and separation. This can take shape through identifying social problems, accessing theological and moral resources, and collaborating for social change. This collective, ground-up approach can fill in holes left by the traditional top-down approach of CST, including blind spots in perception, incomplete teachings, or

---

49. One example is Mondragón, a Spanish co-op founded in 1956 by Fr. José María Arizmendiarrieta. Inspired by the principles of CST, Mondragón now boasts over seventy thousand employees in a variety of fields and is lauded for the way it involves its employees in decision making, its treatment of female workers, and respectable wages. For a more detailed account, see William Foote Whyte and Kathleen King Whyte, *Making Mondragón: The Growth and Dynamics of the Worker Cooperative Complex* (Ithaca, NY: Cornell University Press, 1991); Fernando Molina and Antonio Miguez, "The Origins of Mondragón: Catholic Co-Operativism and Social Movement in a Basque Valley," *Social History* 33, no. 3 (2008): 284–98.

inadequate attention to personal and shared dispositions and habits. It can empower the church to move from witnessing the "Francis moment" to building the "Francis movement."

FROM THE "FRANCIS MOMENT" TO THE "FRANCIS MOVEMENT"

Division and polarization wound the church and world today. These wounds are caused by misunderstanding and assumptions, disrespect and dismissal of others, and "culture wars" that widen separations and exacerbate hostility. In response to these crises, Francis presents mercy as the "moral center" of the Christian life, that which is capable of bringing people together across differences. By reiterating that mercy begins with recognizing one's sinfulness, he makes clear that no one can be considered superior to another. In this way, mercy is what connects each human to every other human, as all stand in need of healing. Francis explains:

> If you don't recognize yourself as a sinner, it means you don't want to receive [mercy], it means that you don't feel the need for it. Sometimes it is hard to know exactly what happened. Sometimes you might feel skeptical and think it is impossible to get back on your feet again. Or maybe you prefer your wounds, the wounds of sin, and you behave like a dog, licking your wounds with your tongue. . . . If we do not begin by examining our wretchedness, if we stay lost and despair that we will never be forgiven, we end up licking our wounds, and they stay open and never heal. Instead, there is medicine, there is healing, we only need to take a small step toward God, or at least express the desire to take it. A tiny opening is enough.[50]

Francis's focus on sin is not to encourage anyone to wallow in guilt or feel overcome with unworthiness. Instead, he reinforces the message that God extends Godself to each and all to ease the universal struggle with sinfulness. He insists, "God forgives everyone, he offers new possibilities to everyone, he showers his mercy on everyone who asks for it. We are the ones who do not know how to forgive."[51] Human failure to receive and extend forgiveness warps Christian identity and relationships. It leads to a "diseased" social imaginary and an inability

50. Pope Francis, *The Name of God Is Mercy*, 57–58.
51. Ibid., 80.

to cultivate the vulnerability and trust necessary for robust, inclusive, and equitable communities.[52] Francis often describes the Christian vocation as a bridge builder (as opposed to a wall builder), as "artisans of peace" who advance the "culture of encounter."[53] This requires humility and fidelity as well as courage, especially given the risks involved in trying to mediate conflict.[54] It also requires levity and a curiosity that seeks to discover common ground. Given the acrimonious debates that fill cable news and the echo chambers that reinforce biases on social media, such work is decidedly countercultural. To embrace mercy in the face of such division and polarization is to resist actively

> a public and increasingly private atmosphere of imagery and language so rancorously divisive and often violent with respect to difference that it threatens to bury our most basic capacities for empathy, intimacy, and love beneath an avalanche of narcissism, political self-interest, and distraction. All of which add up to a very different kind of presence and power at work in our relational lives and shaping our conception of the real at every level.[55]

It is precisely in the midst of this ecclesial and social context that Francis's boundary-breaking imagination envisions a church and world transformed by experiencing God-who-is-mercifying. For this

---

52. Willie Jennings contends that Christianity has "yielded a form of religious life that thwarts its deepest instincts of intimacy. That intimacy should by now have given Christians a faith that understands its own deep wisdom and power of joining, mixing, merging, and being changed by multiple ways of life to witness a God who surprises us by love of differences and draws us to new capacities to imagine their reconciliation. Instead, the intimacy that marks Christian history is a painful one, one in which the joining often meant oppression, violence, and death, if not of bodies then most certainly of ways of life, forms of language, and visions of the world." See Willie James Jennings, *The Christian Imagination: Theology and the Origins of Race* (New Haven, CT: Yale University Press, 2010), 9.

53. Cf. Pope Francis, "Thirst for Peace: Faiths and Cultures in Dialogue" (September 20, 2016), http://w2.vatican.va.

54. Christine Hinze observes, "Undertaking bridge discourse is risky: one takes the chance of offending, or being written off, by everyone. No matter how sincerely attempted, building bridges or hybrid publics across ideological differences is arduous and uncertain work. But amid our fractious cultures, we are deeply interconnected, and grave issues urgently require our collaborative attention." See Christine Firer Hinze, *Glass Ceilings and Dirt Floors: Women, Work, and the Global Economy* (New York: Paulist Press, 2015), 24.

55. Christopher Pramuk, *Hope Sings, So Beautiful: Graced Encounters across the Color Line* (Collegeville, MN: Liturgical Press, 2013), 132.

"Francis moment" to become a "Francis movement," the church—as individuals, as local communities, and as a global institution—needs to adopt habits that reach beyond voluntary acts of kindness, forgiveness, and generosity. Instead, for personal and communal transformation to take root, people, relationships, and institutions need to be marked by greater humility, fidelity, tenderness, fortitude, and solidarity. Consistently receiving and extending mercy is the path to peace and justice.[56]

To share in Francis's moral imagination is to be moved by mercy. Mercy is realized through concrete practices like taking time to bask in the tenderness of God, drawing near others and listening to their perspectives and experiences, exercising imagination through empathy in order to understand other people across differences, and accompanying and collaborating as coequals in cultivating inclusive relationships. These are all works of love, which Francis attests, are made possible by encountering God in love:

> Thanks solely to this encounter—or renewed encounter—with God's love, which blossoms into an enriching friendship, we are liberated from our narrowness and self-absorption. We become fully human when we become more than human, when we let God bring us beyond ourselves in order to attain the fullest truth of our being. . . . For if we have received the love which restores meaning to our lives, how can we fail to share that love with others?[57]

Francis's attunement to mercy is first and foremost about becoming more attentive and responsive to the presence and power of God at work in the world. Mercy (like grace) is a direct experience of the triune communion of love, making it possible to receive and share God's boundless love. Such an encounter that Francis describes "can be profoundly disconcerting" and also "quietly teaches us what it is to be real. It brings an intimate awareness of a tenderness within ourselves, a godly tenderness that we might not ordinarily understand that we possess . . . [so that we can] deliberately orient ourselves to becoming the kind of human community that God wants."[58] Tenderness reveals

---

56. In *Gaudete et exsultate*, Francis cites a line from the diary of Saint Faustina Kowalska, who envisioned Christ saying to her, "Mankind will not have peace until it turns with trust to my mercy" (*GE* 121).

57. *EG* 8.

58. Gillian Ahlgren, *The Tenderness of God: Reclaiming Our Humanity* (Minneapolis, MN: Fortress Press, 2017), 35.

the transparency and accountability that are needed in every level of the church, the strength to overcome complacency with the status quo and build relationships rooted in mutual respect and responsibility.

Mercy does not allow for bystanders; Francis calls Christians to "never remain on the sidelines of this march of living hope."[59] This encompassing communal enterprise will require a change in how Catholics understand their relationship to the local church. Instead of seeing the parish as the place where sacraments get dispensed, the site where optional services are offered,[60] the parish must be home to rituals and patterns of inclusive belonging and coresponsibility. Francis states, "The Eucharist, although it is the fullness of sacramental life, is not a prize for the perfect but a powerful medicine and nourishment for the weak."[61] These rituals put the faithful in touch with their weakness, serving as a reminder of our dependence on God and the community of faith. When it comes to moral formation, "communities of faith seem more important than faith itself," which means that personal belief is less impactful than shared experiences of belongingness.[62] For this reason, Francis's pedagogy of mercy will not translate to social or institutional transformation unless and until communities appropriate these words and actions by integrating them into their habits of belonging.

The Christian moral life leads to and flows from these rituals so that every encounter is an opportunity to witness mercy in our actions, just like the Samaritan on the road to Jericho (Luke 10:25–37). Francis appeals to the Samaritan's example as an ideal representation for

---

59. *EG* 278.

60. Sixty-eight percent of Catholics agree that "I can be a good Catholic without going to Mass," an indication of widespread ignorance or indifference regarding church teaching about the primacy of the sacramental life celebrated in community as well as the relationship between Eucharist and moral responsibility. Incidentally, 61 percent of Catholics agree that "Sacraments are essential to my faith," along with 66 percent who agree that "Helping the poor and needy is a moral obligation for Catholics." See Center for Applied Research in the Apostolate, "Sacraments Today: Belief and Practice among U.S. Catholics" (February 2008), http://cara.georgetown.edu.

61. *EG* 47.

62. Robert Putnam and David Campbell, *American Grace: How Religion Divides and Unites Us* (New York: Simon & Schuster, 2010), 444; see also 468–75. The authors discover that "Mobilization or exhortations by clergy seem not to be a major factor in explaining good neighborliness," whereas "friends in general have a powerful effect on civic involvement." They continue, "Having close friends at church, discussing religion frequently with your family and friends, and taking part in small groups at church are extremely powerful predictors of the range of generosity, good neighborliness, and civic engagement" (471–72).

building the "culture of encounter," as he discussed during his first travel as pope, celebrating Eucharist with refugees and migrants on the island of Lampedusa.[63] Mercy is also central for imitating Christ, who ate with sinners, Pharisees, and tax collectors—intimate actions with social outcasts, his own critics, and agents of the oppressive Roman Empire—and touched lepers, those who were thought to be punished by God, unworthy of mercy. The Samaritan and Jesus illustrate the geography of mercy, which involves going out of one's way to take up a vantage point from the margins and make it one's own.[64] These are the kinds of imaginative actions that make inclusive community possible, so that a "culture of encounter" yields a "culture of belonging." This personal orientation embraces human dignity so that no one is left out, showing the link between mercy and solidarity.[65] Solidarity relies on overcoming the fear of intimacy, being judged, or left out. It defies moral outrage, which feeds into categories of "us" and "them," the "superior" and "inferior." It replaces anxiety with awe and judgment with vulnerability. As Greg Boyle explains,

---

63. Francis's homily is inspired by the example of the Samaritan. He explains, "Today no one in our world feels responsible; we have lost a sense of responsibility for our brothers and sisters. We have fallen into the hypocrisy of the priest and the Levite whom Jesus described in the parable of the Good Samaritan: we see our brother half dead on the side of the road, and perhaps we say to ourselves: 'poor soul . . . !' and then go on our way. It's not our responsibility, and with that we feel reassured, assuaged. The culture of comfort, which makes us think only of ourselves, makes us insensitive to the cries of other people, makes us live in soap bubbles which, however lovely, are insubstantial; they offer a fleeting and empty illusion which results in indifference to others; indeed, it even leads to the globalization of indifference. We have become used to the suffering of others: it doesn't affect me; it doesn't concern me; it's none of my business!" See Pope Francis, "Homily," Mass at Lampedusa (July 8, 2013), https://w2.vatican.va.

64. Francis reflects, "At his own risk and danger, he goes up to the leper and he restores him, he heals him. In so doing, he shows us a new horizon, the logic of a God who is love, a God who desires the salvation of all. . . . Jesus touched the leper and brought him back into the community." See Pope Francis, *The Name of God Is Mercy*, 65.

65. As Greg Boyle proposes, "Soon we imagine, with God, this circle of compassion. Then we imagine no one standing outside of that circle, moving ourselves closer to the margins so that the margins themselves will be erased. We stand there with those whose dignity has been denied. We locate ourselves with the poor and the powerless and the voiceless. At the edges, we join the easily despised and the readily left out. We stand with the demonized so that the demonizing will stop. We situate ourselves right next to the disposable so that the day will come when we stop throwing people away." See Gregory Boyle, *Tattoos on the Heart: The Power of Boundless Compassion* (New York: Free Press, 2010), 190.

We are at our healthiest when we are most situated in awe, and at our least healthy when we engage in judgment. Judgment creates the distance that moves us away from each other. Judgment keeps us in the competitive game and is always self-aggrandizing. Standing at the margins with the broken reminds us not of our own superiority but of our own brokenness. Awe is the great leveler. The embrace of our own suffering helps us to land on a spiritual intimacy with ourselves and others. For if we don't welcome our wounds, we will be tempted to despise the wounded.[66]

Francis's embrace of mercy is an invitation to welcome our wounds. Mercy brings about healing through fidelity to God and one another, and fidelity is impossible without trust. Building trust lays the foundation for a more faithful church and a more just social order. It creates the conditions for inclusive participation and coresponsibility. It thrives in synodality, the commitment to accompany, consult, and to empower others to join in communal discernment. The 2014 and 2015 synods on marriage and the family, the 2018 synod on young people and vocation, and the 2019 synod for the Pan-Amazon region all signal Francis's desire to build a "listening church."[67] Synodality is an expression of the principle of subsidiarity in CST, first appearing in the 1931 encyclical *Quadragesimo anno* (no. 80). Subsidiarity points to the shared responsibility to work at the lowest effective levels and to participate in grass-roots organizing. As Francis remarked to a group of organizers, "You, the popular movements, are sowers of change, promoters of a process involving millions of actions, great and small, creatively intertwined like words in a poem; that is why I wanted to call you 'social poets.' . . . I congratulate you, I accompany you and I ask you to continue to blaze trails and to keep fighting."[68] This is more than a call to organize; it is a summons to find new ways to contemplate the world, communicate its beauty, truth, and goodness, and collaborate with others as bridge builders to make it easier for people to do justice and promote peace. This is the ground-up approach that is

---

66. Gregory Boyle, *Barking to the Choir: The Power of Radical Kinship* (New York: Simon & Schuster, 2017), 54.

67. Pope Francis states, "The journey of synodality is the journey that God wants from his church in the third millennium." The word "synod" means to "walk together." See Pope Francis, "A Listening Church," *America*, October 17, 2015, https://www.americamagazine.org.

68. Pope Francis, "Address to the Participants at the Second World Meeting of Popular Movements" (July 9, 2015), http://w2.vatican.va.

needed for more people to adopt the principles of CST into their specific social context.

While the primary documents in CST have not focused on mercy as a key resource for affirming human dignity, promoting human rights, or building a more just social order, Pope Francis has provided a blueprint for more robustly relying on mercy to foster communion and the common good. In *Laudato si'*, Francis accentuates how mercy is crucial for the kinds of relationships that generate justice and peace with all creation, human and nonhuman. He explains, "A sense of deep communion with the rest of nature cannot be real if our hearts lack tenderness, compassion and concern for our fellow human beings."[69] *Amoris laetitia* stands out as the most extensive appeal to the possibilities created by mercy. As the "building block" of society and the church, the "first and vital cell,"[70] the family is called to "be a sign of mercy and closeness" *ad intra* and *ad extra*.[71] As a communion of mercy, the family forms individuals who practice humility, fidelity, tenderness, fortitude, and solidarity. Families incarnate these virtues in the world, becoming "schools of solidarity"[72] and imagining new possibilities as a "factory of hope."[73] Francis also calls the church to adopt the "logic of pastoral mercy" in order to accompany and serve families who experience challenges and crises.[74] Francis explains:

> This is not sheer romanticism or a lukewarm response to God's love, which always seeks what is best for us, for "mercy is the very foundation of the Church's life. All of her pastoral activity should be caught up in the tenderness which she shows to believ-

---

69. *LS* 91. Francis also calls for environmental education that "seeks also to restore the various levels of ecological equilibrium, establishing harmony within ourselves, with others, with nature and other living creatures, and with God. Environmental education should facilitate making the leap towards the transcendent which gives ecological ethics its deepest meaning. It needs educators capable of developing an ethics of ecology, and helping people, through effective pedagogy, to grow in solidarity, responsibility and compassionate care" (*LS* 210).

70. *FC* 42.

71. *AL* 5.

72. Pope Francis used this phrase in an address on December 29, 2014. See also, Mary M. Doyle Roche, *Schools of Solidarity: Families and Catholic Social Teaching* (Collegeville, MN: Liturgical Press, 2015).

73. This phrase comes from an unscripted address at the Festival of Families in Philadelphia, whereas the official version released by the Vatican uses the phrase "workshop of hope." See Pope Francis, "Prayer Vigil for the Festival of Families" (September 26, 2015), w2.vatican.va.

74. *AL* 307–12.

ers; nothing in her preaching and her witness to the world can be lacking in mercy." It is true that at times "we act as arbiters of grace rather than its facilitators. But the Church is not a tollhouse; it is the house of the Father, where there is a place for everyone, with all their problems."[75]

To this, Francis adds a challenge to moral theologians to put an end to the "cold bureaucratic morality in dealing with more sensitive issues."[76] He laments the times when "We put so many conditions on mercy that we empty it of its concrete meaning and real significance. That is the worst way of watering down the Gospel." He immediately follows this with the following statement: "It is true, for example, that mercy does not exclude justice and truth, but first and foremost we have to say that mercy is the fullness of justice and the most radiant manifestation of God's truth."[77] This is the key development that Francis offers the church's social teachings: to move beyond trusting in God's mercy and justice to living in such a way as to embody mercy as the fullness of justice. Francis lifts up mercy as a unique theological, moral, and pastoral resource for meeting the needs of the church and world. Moreover, Francis underscores that mercy is more than a personal act of kindness, forgiveness, or generosity (which is more in line with charity than justice). Francis provides a framework for mercy—expressed through humility, fidelity, tenderness, fortitude, and solidarity—to inspire personal conversion and structural change.

No ecclesial or social movement succeeds because of a single person. For mercy and imagination to take hold, Christians need to interrupt the silence or the numbness that maintains the status quo. This is a time to be prophetic, to embrace the hope that not only is change possible, but trust that God, through experiences of mercifying, is transforming the church and world. This is the truth Francis aims to witness by speaking "the truth in love, calling us back to ourselves when we have lost our way" because "the holy person does not organize, dominate, or even interpret the signs of the times *for* us so much as he or she shows us *how to respond attentively* to every environment."[78] How should the church and its members respond attentively to every environment? With mercy.

---

75. *AL* 310.
76. *AL* 312.
77. *AL* 311.
78. Pramuk, *Hope Sings, So Beautiful*, 78.

CONCLUSION

Henry David Thoreau wrote, "This world is but a canvas to our imagination."[79] Pope Francis colors this canvas with his pedagogy of mercy, striving to inspire a commitment to practice humility, fidelity, tenderness, fortitude, and solidarity. He retrieves mercy as a central biblical theme and the core of the church's mission, since the church "is commissioned to proclaim the mercy of God, the beating heart of the Gospel, which in its own way must penetrate the mind and heart of every person."[80] Francis expands mercy beyond a personal gift from God so that it becomes the norm for relationships with God and others. Mercy bonds people together as loved sinners called and empowered to build up the reign of God. It unleashes a "revolution of tenderness" that aims to heal wounds left by the church and world. It creates the conditions for the vulnerability and trust necessary for the "culture of encounter" to unite people in overcoming separation and polarization. Mercy is the foundation for communion and solidarity so long as it is adopted on the personal, social, and institutional levels.

With mercy as the crux of his moral imagination, Francis calls Christians to live in an alert state of wonder, glimpsing and grasping new possibilities for practicing the principles of CST that map out a pathway toward a more faithful church and a more just ordering of society. Francis aims to inspire a curiosity that pushes the limits of what is possible as much as it activates social analysis to better understand the root causes of dehumanization, division, and deprivation. Francis calls us to integrate mercy into our moral imagination to correct our moral perception and keep it open to a continual need for conversion. It rejects rigidity, penetrates ambiguity, and embraces audacity.

Nothing happens in history unless it first happens in our imagination.[81] Francis imagines a church and world that orbit around mercy. For the "Francis moment" to become the "Francis movement," the church must be attuned to mercy. This means receiving mercy from God and extending mercy in a way that encounters the other with humility and tenderness. It involves building communities of inclusive belonging marked by mutual respect and responsibility. It requires practices and policies that witness fidelity by forging bonds of solidar-

---

79. Henry David Thoreau, "The Atlantides," in *A Week on the Concord and Merrimack Rivers* (1849), http://www.gutenberg.org.

80. *AL* 309.

81. This idea is inspired by a line from Gloria Anzaldúa, "Nothing happens in the 'real' world unless it first happens in the images in our heads," in her book *Borderlands/La Frontera: The New Mestiza* (San Francisco: Aunt Lute Books, 1987), 87. Thanks to Susan Reynolds for this insight and citation.

ity. It means building systems and structures that more overtly affirm human dignity and promote human rights, encourage participation and accountability, and build a commitment to the common good. As Pope Francis has shown through his words and actions, mercy is the "moral center" of the Christian tradition, the "beating heart" of the Christian moral life, and a visible discipline that witnesses the possibilities for transformation that result from experiencing God-who-is-mercifying.

9

"We Belong to a People"

Austen Ivereigh

One of the most significant language events at the Second Vatican Council was the disappearance of the description of the members of the church as *subditi,* or subjects, of a ruling monarch and priestly class. The Constitution on the Church, *Lumen gentium,* instead used the biblical term "People of God," associated originally with Israel, which became, thereafter, the favorite image of the church. With it came, in theory at least, the recovery of the early-church understanding of all the baptized faithful as disciples and an abandonment of the idea of first- and second-class citizenship implicit in the post-Constantinian monarchical ecclesiology that reached its apogee in the late nineteenth century.

Theologically, the People of God reflected the communion implicit in the inner life of the Blessed Trinity. *Lumen gentium* expressed the primary reality of the church as horizontal, consisting of all the baptized, without rank, with Christ at the head of the body: all are called equally and without distinction to holiness and the apostolate. Only secondarily did the vertical reality (hierarchy) come into play: the church is governed by the pope and the bishops in communion with him, but the pastors serve the faithful, encouraging their active engagement and cooperation in the mission of the church and their call to holiness.[1]

This shift relativized the institution, which now serves the People of God and its mission, not the other way round. Infallibility no longer rested with the hierarchy but the whole body, which "cannot err

---

1. John W. O'Malley, *What Happened at Vatican II?* (Cambridge, MA: Belknap Press, 2008), 73–74, 186; *GS* 9, 12.

in matters of belief," *Lumen gentium* claimed, when "by means of the whole peoples' supernatural discernment in matters of faith" there was agreement in matters of faith and morals "from the bishops down." For the task of evangelization and mission, the Holy Spirit showered gifts and graces "among the faithful of every rank."[2]

The reception and implementation of this vision in the decades after Vatican II were mixed, not least because of the notorious failure to recover the patristic tradition of councils and synods that were the corollary of a people-of-God ecclesiology. The revised *Code of Canon Law* of 1983 puts the rights and duties of all the People of God—at least on paper—prior to the hierarchy, but practically there have been few mechanisms to make this effective, such as local synods, by which the People of God could be listened to or could help discern decisions that affect the life of the church. Articulations of views by self-appointed lay groups—usually protesting or calling for governance reforms— have taken place at the fringes, but usually without or against the bishop. Where there has been a vigorous expression of lay missionary vitality—above all in the ecclesial movements, strongly promoted by St. John Paul II and Benedict XVI—it has largely bypassed the local churches or has been in tension with them. As Massimo Faggioli observes, the ecclesiological outlook of the movements themselves has often leaned toward "a modern or postmodern model of infallible one-man leadership much more than toward a first-millennium, ressourcement ecclesiology of collegiality."[3]

The lack of implementation of synodality reflected a suspicion on the part of St. John Paul II that increasing participation would bolster a hermeneutic of rupture, as well as antihierarchical liberation theologies and a false notion of democratization. The Polish pope's *Christifidelis laici* affirmed the notion of communion as "the central and fundamental idea" of Vatican II. At least in his papacy's theological articulation of that ecclesiology, communion tended to replace the council's understanding of the church as the People of God, and therefore to downplay the ecclesiological implications of *Lumen gentium*.[4]

The election of Pope Francis in 2013 marked a dramatic change of course: the People of God has replaced communion as the starting point of his ecclesiology, and he has proceeded with determination to create structures of collegiality and synodality. In this, he reflects

---

2. *LG* 12.

3. Massimo Faggioli, *The Rising Laity: Ecclesial Movements since Vatican II* (Mahwah, NJ: Paulist Press, 2016), 102.

4. Richard R. Gaillardetz, "The 'Francis Moment': A New Kairos for Catholic Ecclesiology," *CTSA Proceedings* 69 (2014): 63–80.

the Latin American church, which in four continent-wide general conferences from Medellín in 1968 to Aparecida in 2007 assumed and deepened the concept of church as *pueblo de Dios*. His first moments on the balcony of the loggia of St. Peter's, when he used a famous early-church formula in describing his new diocese as "the Church of Rome that presides in charity over all the Churches" and asked for the blessing of the people, sent a powerful signal of his determination to proceed "gently, but firmly and tenaciously" toward the goal of a "synodal" church. He told the Belgian newspaper *Tertio*: "Either there is a pyramidal church, in which what Peter says is done, or there is a synodal church, in which Peter is Peter but he accompanies the Church, he lets her grow, he listens to her, he learns from this reality and goes about harmonizing it, discerning what comes from the Church and restoring it to her." The secretary of Francis's C9 council of cardinal advisors, Bishop Marcello Semeraro, confirms that Francis is modeling the "synodal church" he wants to see, in which mutual listening allows for discernment.[5]

The heart of this reform has been the overhaul of the synod of bishops in Rome to create a mechanism of genuine discernment capable of addressing thorny pastoral questions such as the integration of the divorced and remarried (the topic of the synods of 2014 and 2015), or priestly celibacy in mission territories (set to be discussed at the synod on the Amazon in October 2019). Francis's synod reforms have been shaped by the Latin-American episcopal council (CELAM) meeting at Aparecida, arguably the only modern Catholic example of an authentically synodal process by a regional church. It was experienced by those present—including Cardinal Jorge Mario Bergoglio, who played a key role in it—as a Pentecostal event that allowed the whole church to look with the gaze of faith on the contemporary world and to speak freely about the reforms necessary to proclaim the gospel in new circumstances. One reason that Aparecida worked so well was that it was preceded by years of local and regional meetings, consultations, and studies, involving a culture of mutual listening and dialogue at all levels.[6]

---

5. Pope Francis, interview with *Tertio*, December 6, 2016. "Since the first centuries, the word synod has been applied, with a specific meaning, to the ecclesial assemblies convoked on various levels (diocesan, provincial, regional, patriarchal or universal) to discern, by the light of the Word of God and listening to the Holy Spirit, the doctrinal, liturgical, canonical and pastoral questions that arise as time goes by." See International Theological Commission, "Synodality in the Life and Mission of the Church," March 2, 2018, no. 4, http://www.vatican.va.

6. Cardinal Bergoglio, interview with *30 Días* ("Lo que hubiera dicho en el consistorio"), November 2007, and speech to CELAM's coordinating committee,

Francis painted a vivid picture of this "path of synodality" in his speech of October 2015 on the fiftieth anniversary of Paul VI's refounding of the synod during the final session of the Second Vatican Council, insisting to the bishops that it was what God was asking of the church in the third millennium. "Journeying together—laity, pastors, the Bishop of Rome—is an easy concept to put into words, but not so easy to put into practice," he noted, before outlining the core principles of efforts to do so. Because of the infallibility *in credendo* of "the whole people of God," it was vital not to separate the "learning" (*ecclesia docens*) from the "teaching" church (*ecclesia discens*)—those who teach must listen—and "since the flock likewise has an instinctive ability to discern the new ways that the Lord is revealing to the Church," there had to be a deep mutual listening at all levels, involving all the faithful, according to the ancient church principle that *quod omnes tangit ab omnibus tractari debet*: what affects all should be discussed by all. (As Pope Francis told Father Antonio Spadaro in 2013, "When the dialogue among the people and the bishops and the pope goes down this road and is genuine, then it is assisted by the Holy Spirit."[7])

What Francis in his speech called "a dynamism of communion which inspires all ecclesial decisions" meant opening up, listening, connecting with ordinary people's realities and concerns, through diocesan synods, priests' councils, and pastoral congresses of the sort that had long been on the wane in the 1980s and '90s. Such participation and engagement were a precondition of a "missionary" church, in which all took responsibility for evangelizing as missionary disciples, as well as acting as a sign in a world that too often "consigns the fate of entire peoples to the grasp of small but powerful groups."[8]

Francis announced reforms to the synod's method and structure in September 2018. *Episcopalis communio* preserved the idea of the synod as an essentially episcopal body in which bishop delegates (usually around 270) voted, but stressed that it should be at the same time "a suitable instrument for giving voice to the entire people of God, specifically via the Bishops, established by God as authentic guardians, interpreters and witnesses of the faith of the whole Church." The measures called for consultations before each Rome synod via local

---

Rio de Janeiro, July 28, 2013. On Aparecida as an "authentically synodal" process, see Diego Fares, "A 10 anni da Aparecida: alle fonti del pontificato di Francesco," *La Civiltà Cattolica* 2 (May 20–June 3, 2017): 338–52.

7. Antonio Spadaro, SJ, "A Big Heart Open to God: An interview with Pope Francis," *America*, September 30, 2013.

8. Pope Francis, "Address, Ceremony Commemorating the 50th Anniversary of the Institution of the Synod of Bishops," October 17, 2015, http://w2.vatican.va.

synods of priests, deacons, and lay faithful in local churches, and the presence in the synods themselves of auditors and special guests. At the October 2018 synod, on youth and vocation, thirty young adults each had an opportunity to address the assembly. Francis asked them to express any movements in their hearts in response to what they heard, which they did through applause and other gestures, acting as a kind of Greek chorus for the bishops.[9]

As vital as these structural reforms and innovations are to give life to the ecclesiology of *Lumen gentium*, however, they stand little chance of taking root unless the mentality and culture of the church develop alongside them. The pope's enrichment of the concept of the People of God that burst out at Vatican II has been arguably just as important as the structural reforms, as has been his sustained assault on clericalism, which in Francis's discourse is continually depicted both as the principal obstacle to missionary discipleship and as a form of nonbelonging that condemns the church to self-referentiality and sterility.

The clerical sex-abuse crisis, which has reappeared in 2018 in new scandals, offers, in Francis's discernment, a providential opportunity to accelerate the pastoral conversion to which he believes God is calling the church. In this chapter, we will consider Francis's rich and in many ways radical understanding of the church as a mythical anointed nation in which the faithful are called both to belong and to proclaim, and then describe his naming of various forms of nonbelonging (clericalism, elitism, authoritarianism) as a rejection of that calling. Finally, we will describe how the pope's guidance of the universal church through the global crises over clerical sex abuse in 2018 demonstrates his conviction that the tribulation is an unveiling, or revelation, of the corruption of clericalism, and a painful but necessary purgation which, if collectively embraced and assumed, offers a providential opportunity to move more rapidly toward the vision of the church as the anointed People of God.

THE POPE OF THE *PUEBLO*

Pope Francis's rich understanding of the concept of *el pueblo* cannot be separated from the "national-popular" current of Latin-American theology that flourished in Argentina above all in the 1970s and '80s. Although it was a movement of thinkers without an agreed-upon name—it was known variously as "the theology of the people," the

---

9. Pope Francis, apostolic constitution, *Episcopalis communio*, "on the synod of bishops," September 15, 2018.

La Plata School, and "theology of culture"—its main thinkers were easily identifiable from the pages of the journal *Nexo*, edited by the Uruguayan historian and thinker Alberto Methol Ferré. Along with Methol Ferré, the leading "people theologian," Father Lucio Gera, and others were key thinkers in CELAM, highly influential on the synod of 1974 and on Pope Paul VI's exhortation *Evangelii nuntiandi*, which in turn shaped the CELAM general conference of Puebla in 1979.[10]

Although they shared fundamental characteristics of post-Medellín Latin-American theology, not least the option for the poor, the *pueblo* theologians were critical of the Marxist and Hegelian elements in the liberationist hermeneutic, which in their view flattened the people into uniform, abstract sociological categories. For Gera and others, salvation history had to be understood from within the culture and experience of the People of God of a particular place. Francis has explained in a number of settings that the term *people* is not a logical or descriptive but a *mythical* category; to understand a people one has to enter into its spirit, heart, history, and *mythos*. This was the point at the heart of the theology of the people, Francis explained to Dominique Wolton: "to go to the people, see how it expresses itself."[11]

In this way, the La Plata School developed the concept of the People of God from its mystical, spiritual category in *Lumen gentium*, rooting it in culture and history, in what Bergoglio, following Romano Guardini, called the "concrete universal." A people is forged in a kind of "force field of divine action" in the concrete relationships in a given society. Guardini distinguishes this idea of people from an Enlightenment rationalism that only considers real what can be grasped through reason, and is therefore incapable of building a people, which comes about through an openness to the divine. As Francis put it at Easter 2019: "Only the anointing of culture, built up by the labor and the art of our forebears, can free our cities from these forms of slavery."[12]

---

10. See Juan Carlos Scannone, *La teología del pueblo: Raíces teológicas del papa Francisco* (Maliaño, Spain: Ed Sal Terrae, 2017); Emilce Cuda, *Para leer a Francisco: Teología, ética y política* (Buenos Aires: Manantial, 2016); Rafael Luciani, *El Papa Francisco y la teología del pueblo* (Madrid: PPC, 2016); Javier Restán Martínez, *Alberto Methol Ferré: Su pensamiento en Nexo* (Buenos Aires: Ed Dunken, 2010).

11. Pope Francis, with Dominique Wolton, *The Path to Change: Thoughts on Politics and Society*, trans. Shaun Whiteside (London: Pan MacMillan, 2017), 20.

12. Pope Francis, Udienza ai partecipanti alla conferenza promossa dalla "Fondazione Romano Guardini," November 13, 2015, discussed by Massimo Borghesi in *The Mind of Pope Francis: Jorge Mario Bergoglio's Intellectual Journey* (Collegeville, MN: Liturgical Press, 2018), 11–12; Pope Francis, Holy Thursday Chrism Mass, April 18, 2019, https://w2.vatican.va.

At a conference organized by Bergoglio in 1985 on the topic of "the evangelization of culture and the inculturation of the gospel," he spoke of the gospel revealing God's saving plan through Jesus Christ, while "the different cultures, fruit of the wisdom of the peoples" reflected "the creative and perfecting Wisdom of God."[13] The evangelization of culture can happen only through inculturation, just as the incarnation occurs within a people, transforming it. As Francis states it in *Gaudete et exsultate*, the Holy Spirit bestows holiness among God's holy faithful people, and in saving humanity enters into the life and history of a people.[14] Conversely, ideology flees fleshly reality; it remains as *gnosis*. Thus Bergoglio praised Methol's metaphysics as generative, for its subject "is the real being as such—determined and limited—who opens the door to the concrete universal" as opposed to the "imported ideologies that create abstract universals."[15]

For Francis, the great contribution of Vatican II was precisely its call on the church to be inculturated, entering into a people, helping it to grow and integrate its diverse elements against a shared horizon. When the church is "close" in this way—when it is inculturated, serving the people, rather than lording it over them—it creates culture; when it fails to be close, it inflicts damage.[16] When the church *qua* institution turns its back on the people, it is like an oligarchy that pursues its own interest rather than serves the common good. In this sense, *anti-pueblo* isn't so much a category of people as a mindset, which Bergoglio, in his Jesuit writings, refers to as an "isolated conscience."

In an address in Buenos Aires cathedral in 2002 before Argentina's political dignitaries, Cardinal Bergoglio pondered the Gospel story of Zacchaeus, the short-of-stature tax collector of Jericho who, after encountering Jesus, promises to give back to the people much more than he has taken. In calling Zacchaeus down from his sycamore tree, Bergoglio saw Jesus inviting him to come down from his self-sufficiency, the false personality he has constructed on the basis of his wealth, and to work now patiently and in solidarity alongside the mass of ordinary people. Zacchaeus, he explained, has become part of the people because he has renounced his arrogance and separateness. He remains a tax collector but one that serves, not exploits, for his heart has turned—Francis told young people in Santiago de

---

13. Austen Ivereigh, *The Great Reformer: Francis and the Making of a Radical Pope* (New York: Picador, 2015), 186.

14. *GE* 6.

15. Thomas R. Rourke, *The Roots of Pope Francis's Social and Political Thought: From Argentina to the Vatican* (London: Rowman & Littlefield, 2016), 85–87.

16. Pope Francis, *The Path to Change*, 22.

Chile—"from materialism to solidarity." He who was *anti-pueblo* is now *pueblo*.[17]

The pope's populism is theological and ecclesiological; it is the vision of *Lumen gentium*, not the political variety. Noting that, on Francis's trips in 2015, he had used the word "people" 356 times and "democracy" only ten, one liberal Italian historian claimed that Francis was a populist, nationalist authoritarian of the old school, "imbued with visceral anti-liberalism."[18] But Francis's invocation of the term "faithful people" is the very opposite of populism; it is a defense of the value and culture of a people from political instrumentalization.

Although *el pueblo* does not have the collectivist overtones of the Italian *il popolo* or German *das Volk*, it was common in the 1970s for both Peronists and the Marxist left to invoke the "people" as a justification for their politics, much as the French Revolution invoked the *volonté generale*. As a Jesuit, Father Bergoglio began to use the expression *el santo pueblo fiel de Dios* (God's holy, faithful people) in the 1970s to describe a form of belonging that resisted any such instrumentalization. In his talks as provincial of the Argentine Jesuits from 1973, he would portray this *pueblo fiel* as a distinctive body with its own culture, mindset, and hermeneutic, where God dwelt, and whom the church was called to serve and defend. "Our people has a soul," he said in 1998, "and because we can speak of a soul, we can speak of a hermeneutic, a way of seeing, an awareness." Thus, writing of Cuba that year—the year of John Paul II's visit to the island—he would describe how both Marxism and neoliberalism were alien to Cuba's "soul."[19]

For Bergoglio, the evangelized popular culture of the *pueblo fiel* was not just infallible in its believing but also the repository of a relationship with God. "When you want to know what the Church teaches, you go to the Magisterium," he told the Jesuits in 1978; "but when you want to know how the Church teaches, you go to the faithful people. The Magisterium will teach you who is Mary, but the faithful people will teach you how to love Mary." Where ideologies instrumentalized the poor, conceiving the "people" as a socioeconomic category or inert mass, Christian hope recognized that God was at work in the "special wisdom" of *el pueblo fiel* whom enlightened intellectuals failed to recognize. Whether left or right, revolutionaries or reactionaries, ideologues failed to see the "real movement going on among God's faithful people. . . . Thus they fail to join in the march of history where God is

---

17. Ivereigh, *The Great Reformer*, 270. Pope Francis, "Discurso del Santo Padre: Encuentro con los jóvenes," Shrine of Maipu, Santiago de Chile, January 17, 2018.

18. Loris Zanatta, "Un papa populista," *Criterio* 2424 (2016).

19. Ivereigh, *The Great Reformer,* 237, 250.

saving us, God is making us a body, an institution, God's power enters history so as to make of human beings a single body."[20]

This process of becoming a people is a key idea in Bergoglio's thought. To form part of a people is to form part of a common identity forged from social and cultural ties which come about not automatically but through a slow and difficult advance toward what Francis calls a "common project."[21] In *Evangelii gaudium*, Francis speaks of a slow and patient process of integration of disparate elements, in which responsible citizens act "in the heart of a people, not as a mob swayed by the powers that be."[22] The remainder of that section (nos. 221–37) offer Francis's four principles for "building a people in peace, justice, and fraternity."

For Francis, history offers a clear example of the church's action allowing God to create a people: the birth and development of Latin America's uniquely symbiotic culture in the years of the Spanish colony, above all in the Hapsburg era (from the early-seventeenth to the late-eighteenth centuries). The soul of the *pueblo nuevo* was forged, in Alberto Methol Ferré's famous reading, from actions of the missionary church following the Third Council of Lima in the 1580s. In opting for service and inculturation, and in making an option for the poor and the ordinary people, the church could become a *complexio oppositorum*, an agent of integration, creating a remarkable synthetic culture of pluriform yet separate elements precisely because it was attentive to God's presence in the *pueblo* and respectful of its traditions and culture, which carried the seeds of the gospel. To CELAM officials in Bogotá, Colombia, Francis in September 2017 praised "the popular piety of our people, which is part of its anthropological uniqueness and a gift by which God wants our people to come to know him," adding that "the most luminous pages of our Church's history were written precisely when she knew how to be nourished by this richness and to speak to this hidden heart."[23] In Paraguay in July 2015, for example, he described the Jesuit Reductions as "the most significant experiences of

---

20. Quotes are from various speeches and articles in the 1970s in Ivereigh, *The Great Reformer*, 110–16, 143.

21. Antonio Spadaro, SJ, ed., *En tus ojos está mi palabra: Homilías y discursos de Buenos Aires, 1999–2013* (Madrid: Claretianas, 2018), 25.

22. I'm translating literally from the Spanish ("ciudadanos responsables en el seno de un pueblo"), a text that the official English version of *EG* 220 ("committed and responsible citizens") fails to capture. Jorge Mario Bergoglio, *Nosotros como ciudadanos* (Buenos Aires: Archdiocese of Buenos Aires—Pastoral Social Buenos Aires, 2010–2016), 31.

23. Pope Francis, meeting with coordinating committee of CELAM, Bogotá, September 7, 2017.

evangelization and social organization in history," where "the Gospel was the soul and the life of communities which did not know hunger, unemployment, illiteracy or oppression," an experience that "shows us that, today too, a more humane society is possible. . . . Where there is love of people and a willingness to serve them, it is possible to create the conditions necessary for everyone to have access to basic goods, so that no one goes without."[24]

In Methol's reading, if the Hapsburg era allowed for the coming-into-being of a people, the emancipation era in the nineteenth century led to its disintegration. The turbulence of the independence wars introduced ruptures and cleavages within the body: between elite and *pueblo*, as creole leaders grabbed common and church lands, creating inequalities and impoverishment; and between priests and *pueblo*, as clergy became dependent on urban elites and bishops were appointed by the liberal state, such that the church became increasingly clerical and distant from the lived religiosity of the people. A third rupture was in the weakening of the bonds of civil society and between nations, which led to the fragmentation of Latin America into isolated, often feuding, nation-states, which in the nineteenth and early-twentieth centuries often went to war with one another with devastating consequences.

Methol saw in the Second Vatican Council the chance for the church to disentangle itself from the dead-end cycle of assimilation and rejection of modernity and to resume its colonial-era role as agent of reconciliation. The church's contemporary mission was now to heal the three ruptures of the national period. The first task of reform was to abandon clericalism and commit itself once again in humble service to the *pueblo*, to open up to the voice of the poor and the traditions of popular religiosity, which had developed outside clerical culture. The second was to promote a new popular-nationalist economics and politics—rooted in the values and interests of the *pueblo*—that sought to overcome gross economic inequalities and social exclusion, a true politics of the common good. Finally, and as a corollary of the first two, it meant resuming the frustrated journey to continental unity through dialogue and integration—*la patria grande*—which in turn implied a rejection of the "ideological colonization" of globalized technocracy.[25]

---

24. Pope Francis, "Meeting with Representatives of Civil Society: Address of the Holy Father," Léon Condou Stadium, Colegio San José, Asunción (Paraguay), July 11, 2015.

25. Austen Ivereigh, "The Pope and the *Patria Grande*: How Francis Is Promoting Latin America's Continental Destiny," in *The Search for God in America*, ed. Peter Casarella and Maria Clara Bingemer (Washington, DC: Catholic University of America Press, 2018). The key essay of Methol Ferré is "El resurgimiento católico

In Aparecida, this journey of change that the church was called on to make was described as a "pastoral and missionary conversion," in which all the baptized are called to take their place as "missionary disciples." That vision is the template for *Evangelii gaudium*, which sums up Francis's rich rethinking of the People of God in its third chapter on the proclamation of the gospel, which has two key elements.

First, *Evangelii gaudium* never stops to mention the hierarchy while painting the institution as secondary; its purpose is to awake the consciousness of the church as "first and foremost a people advancing on its pilgrim way towards God," which exists concretely in history as a body of "pilgrims and evangelizers, transcending any institutional expression, however necessary" (*EG* 111). The institution is relative to the church's core identity and mission: its law and authorities are necessary as bonds of communion and to assist the body to serve its purpose and mission, but God is already at work in his people, impelling them to evangelize. Thus, God has furnished the totality of the faithful with a *sensus fidei* that helps them discern what is truly of God; a missionary is anyone who has "truly experienced God's saving love," and all are called for an explicit witness in their lives to that experience (*EG* 120–21). These are not actions reserved to, or the prerogative of, the clergy, or the institution's authorities. As Archbishop Victor Manuel Fernández, commenting on this section, states, "Someone who receives a ministry in the church does not cease to be a people, and being a people is to live among others at their service."[26]

Second, the People of God is not just an amalgamation of individuals but a body called into being by God, who considers the complex interweaving of human relationships. As Cardinal Bergoglio stated in 2011, "God is present in, encourages, and is an active protagonist in the life of his people."[27] This process always takes place in a concrete people: "Grace supposes culture, and God's gift becomes flesh in the culture of those who receive it" (*EG* 115) Once the gospel has been inculturated in a people, it is then transmitted through popular religiosity, "a true expression of the spontaneous missionary activity of the people of God," in which "a people continually evangelizes itself," a

---

latinoamericano," in *Religión y cultura: Perspectivas de la evangelización de la cultura desde puebla.* Encuentro del equipo de reflexión del Celam y otros pensadores sobre el tema "Religión y cultura," Consejo Episcopal Latinoamericano 47 (Bogotá: Ed. CELAM, 1980).

26. Paolo Rodari and Victor Manuel Fernández, *La iglesia del Papa Francisco. Los desafíos desde Evangelii Gaudium* (Madrid: San Pablo, 2014), 126.

27. Jorge Mario Bergoglio, Prólogo, *Dios en la ciudad* (Buenos Aires: San Pablo, 2012), 5.

process in which the Holy Spirit is the principal agent. Francis's examples of expressions of popular piety and contagious holiness in *Evangelii gaudium* and *Gaudete et exsultate* do not involve a priest or church building, and feature many women: the faith of mothers tending their sick children saying the rosary or praying over a lit candle in a humble home; the men and women working hard to support their families; a woman going shopping who refuses to be drawn into gossip, and so on.[28] The examples reflect his conviction that popular religiosity is one area free from the virus of clericalism, which denies God's anointing.

CLERICALISM

Set against his rich People-of-God ecclesiology, Francis's sustained and vigorous assault on clericalism from the start of his pontificate becomes easier to understand. Clericalism is *anti-pueblo*: it is the refusal to belong to the People of God, a denial of the people's anointing. Francis describes clericalism as wanting to evangelize "for the people, but without the people; all for the people, but not with the people," as he put to the Jesuits in Colombia, adding that this "liberal, enlightened conception of evangelization" is a perversion of the life of the church that directly contradicts the vision of *Lumen gentium*.[29] Clericalism is not just a failure to evangelize; it is also an "oligarchic" form of corruption, one that uses the goods of the church to profit from the People of God. It is a *forma mentis*, and not just of clerics. Francis warns:

> You do not have to be a priest to be clerical. There is a clericalism that is manifest in people who live with a "segregated" attitude, with their noses in the air. They are those who live with an aristocratic attitude with respect to the rest. Clericalism is an aristocracy. You can be clerical even if you're a consecrated brother or a religious sister. You're not clerical because you celebrate Mass, but because you believe you belong to this aristocracy. This goes along with, in general, a way of living aristocratically which can be seen in attitudes that imply that one is beyond God's holy faithful people. Where there is clericalism, aristocratic mentality, elitism, the People of God are somewhere else. What locates you in the church is God's holy faithful people. It's the closeness with the people in the parish, the ones at school. . . . It's the *synkatábasis*

---

28. *EG* 125; *GE* 7, 16.

29. Pope Francis, Dialogue with Jesuits in Colombia: "La gracia de Dios no es una ideología," *La Civiltà Cattolica*, October 18, 2017.

of Jesus, who lowered himself to insert himself in the people. And clericalism is the opposite of insertion. The clericalist is part of an elite and does not see himself in the people. From there stem many consequences, above all when you get a bad use of power. Clericalism is at the root of many problems, as we are seeing.[30]

In his writings as a Jesuit and a cardinal, Bergoglio referred often to this attitude of self-withholding as an "isolated conscience." The isolation is twofold: both from God and from his people because, of course, God is present in his people. In his meditations on the *Spiritual Exercises* in the 1970s and '80s, for example, Bergoglio frequently linked this withdrawal to other attitudes he would later identify with clericalism: confusing dogmatism with doctrine, manipulating rather than shepherding, doting on one sheep and refusing to look for the missing ninety-nine, and so on. At the origin of this "isolated conscience" was "always something petty that we wish to keep for ourselves," a desire to seek comfort, or wealth, or tranquility—a rejection of poverty, a neglect of prayer, or a refusal of God's mission of service.[31] In an interview following Aparecida, Bergoglio described the prophet Jonah as an "isolated conscience" because "he did not know of God's capacity to lead his people with a Father's heart." Jonah preferred his own black-and-white schemes of righteousness to the mercy of God, and so refused the mission of evangelization God had entrusted to him.[32]

Having refused to serve God, the clericalist serves not God's people but himself. Francis regularly quotes Henri de Lubac's term "spiritual worldliness," in which the goods of religion and faith are used to enrich and benefit an elite at the expense of the people. Thus the priest (or wealthy lay patron) becomes an "intermediary" rather than a "mediator," one who benefits at the expense of the people rather than one who sacrifices himself for their sake.[33] In his addresses to clergy and bishops on ministry, Francis has often used these polar contrasts—closeness to/distance from the life of the People of God, pastoral/rigid,

---

30. Pope Francis, *La Fuerza de la Vocación: La Vida Consagrada Hoy. Una conversación con Fernando Prado CMF* (Madrid: Publicaciones Claretianas, 2018), 77–78.

31. Jorge Mario Bergoglio, "Tres Binarios," in *Meditaciones para religiosos* (Bilbao: Mensajero, 2014), 175–77.

32. Jorge Mario Bergoglio, interview with *30 Días* ("Lo que hubiera dicho en el consistorio"), November 2007.

33. In Spanish, Pope Francis plays with the verb *servir*, contrasting those who serve the people (*servir al pueblo*) with those who make use of the people (*servirse del pueblo*).

neighbor/bureaucrat, mother/policeman, self-giving/self-serving, and so on—to highlight the different attitudes toward the People of God. The pastor always belongs: "he feels himself a part of the church, of an actual community in whose journey he shares," he told the Italian bishops' conference, adding that "God's holy faithful people are the womb from which he is drawn, the family he has engaged with, the house he is invited to." This "common belonging" is what frees a priest from "an isolating and imprisoning self-referentiality."[34] The People of God are the ones who spot at once the difference between a "functionary of the sacred" and "a grateful servant," as he stated to the bishops in Chile.[35]

In his most important and detailed text on the topic of lay participation and clericalism, a letter addressed to Cardinal Marc Ouellet, president of the Pontifical Commission for Latin America, Francis spoke of the People of God as the horizon against which a pastor is measured. Clericalism "tends to diminish and undervalue the baptismal grace that the Holy Spirit has placed in the heart of our people" and "gradually extinguishes the prophetic flame to which the entire Church is called to bear witness in the heart of her peoples," he observed. "Lay people are part of the faithful Holy People of God and thus are the protagonists of the Church and of the world," he added, warning, "We are called to serve them, not to be served by them." Clericalism saw committed lay people solely in terms of those dedicated to the works of the church or the parish, creating a "lay elite" while forgetting "the believers who often burn out their hope in the daily struggle to live their faith."[36]

In his apostolic trips, the pope continually insisted on priests not leaving the People of God as they moved up the social ladder, above all in developing countries where priesthood was often an avenue of social mobility. It was sad, he said in Ecuador and Bolivia, to see "priests who are embarrassed to speak in the native language and so they forget their Quechua, Aymara, Guaraní." On the other hand, if patriarchalism in culture and customs led to clericalism, these had to be purified. Disturbed to discover during the charismatic priests' retreat in Rome that some of the African clergy had been upset at having to stand in a line with a tray to collect their food, Francis was

---

34. Pope Francis, "Opening of the 69th General Assembly of the Italian Episcopal Conference," May 16, 2016, http://w2.vatican.va.

35. Pope Francis, "Meeting with the Bishops," Santiago Cathedral Sacristy, January 16, 2018, http://w2.vatican.va.

36. Pope Francis, "Letter to Cardinal Marc Ouellet," March 19, 2016, http://w2.vatican.va.

appalled. "Please, let us never have any of this in the Church!" he told clergy in Nairobi, Kenya. "To serve! Not to be served or to use other people."[37]

In attacking the spiritually worldly, elitist, aristocratic, self-referential attitudes of clericalism, Francis had in mind the contrast between Jesus and the religious elites of his day, whom he bypassed. In his Jesuit writings, Bergoglio had observed how the Pharisees, Sadducees, the Zealots, and temple authorities had all turned the covenant faith of Judaism into a source of power or wealth or security for themselves, withdrawing from the People of God and ceasing to be a channel of grace and salvation for the poor. Their focus on maintaining and defending that which they sought to control and possess produced in them an envious ("not-seeing") blindness to the suffering of others. In challenging his disciples, Jesus was seeking to change their hermeneutic: to replace the narrow, myopic spectacles of the doctors of the law with the wide-angled lens of the heart of the Good Shepherd, a heart of openness and gratitude. That meant applying the law not as an instrument of control but of God's healing and grace. The core difference between discernment (the way of Jesus) and legalism (the way of the Pharisees)[38] was attentiveness to the grace present in concrete lives. In seeking to effect this shift in *Amoris laetitia*, Francis has faced the same accusations Jesus did: of undermining law and doctrine.

But the shift is not one of doctrine but of hermeneutics, as Francis showed in a homily at a Mass for new cardinals in February 2015, in which he reflected on Jesus's scandal-generating healing of the leper in the first chapter of Mark. Contrasting Jesus's concern for the unclean with the fear of the powerful religious who needed to keep the lepers at a distance, Francis observed how, in healing the lepers, Jesus had to stay outside the towns, and therefore to experience their point of view. From that perspective of the concrete lived experience of the lepers, it was obvious how Jewish cleanliness laws, geared to the protection of the healthy and the righteous, sacrificed the sick, whose plight was screened out of view by expulsion. Jesus overturned this "fearful, narrow and prejudiced mentality" not by abolishing or bypassing the law of Moses but by revolutionizing awareness, "opening new horizons for humanity and fully revealing God's 'logic,'" a logic that flowed from God's gaze of mercy and his desire to save and integrate. Hence, there

---

37. See Ivereigh, "The Pope and the *Patria Grande*." Also Pope Francis, "Address," Sports field of St. Mary's School, Nairobi (Kenya), November 26, 2015, https://w2.vatican.va.

38. Jorge Mario Bergoglio, "Formación permanente y reconciliación," in *Meditaciones para religiosos* (Bilbao: Mensajero, 2014), 80–92.

were "two ways of thinking and of having faith: We can fear to lose the saved or we can want to save the lost." Even today, he added, the same choice had to be made between "the thinking of the doctors of the law, which would remove the danger by casting out the diseased person, and the thinking of God, who in his mercy embraces and accepts by reinstating him and turning evil into good, condemnation into salvation and exclusion into proclamation."[39]

This pastoral conversion was only possible through immersion in the concrete lives of the People of God, especially on the margins of suffering and need, which meant leaving the fold and going out in search of those who were outside. Only through real-life contact with sin, poverty, and suffering could the church and its pastors be purged of pharisaism, self-referentiality, and clericalism. Because many of the Jewish laws, doctrines, and ritual practices of the time had given the disciples a sense of security, relieving them from asking what pleases God, Jesus purified his followers by leading them to lepers, paralytics, and sinners whose healing and integration called for rather more than the mere black-and-white application of norms. In contrast to the Pharisees, who were "paralyzed in an interpretation and rigorist practice of the law," Jesus's freedom in healing the outcast fulfilled God's purpose not by breaking the law or dispensing with it but by going beyond the mere observance of it to enable an encounter with God's mercy. In this way, Francis noted in a homily in Medellín, Colombia, Jesus could open up God to the people. "The Church does not belong to us, but to God. He is the owner of the temple and the field, and everyone has a place, everyone is invited to find here, and among us, his or her nourishment—everyone."[40]

For Francis, clericalism is thus far more than a vice or failing; it is a symptom of the persistence of a post-Constantinian ecclesiology that conceives of the institution as self-sufficient, superior to and separate from the outside world, and in which the security, reputation, and internal relationships of the clerical caste are the center of attention. Such a church tends by its nature to shrink by withdrawing from the people. It is a "Church of the ordained at the expense of the baptized," in which the interests and privileges of the elite caste are made coterminous with the mission of the church. In all these ways it rejects the new (yet old) paradigm of *Lumen gentium.* "What needs to be done today is to accompany the church in a deep spiritual renewal," Francis

---

39. Pope Francis, "Homily, Consistory to Create New Cardinals," February 15, 2015, https://w2.vatican.va.

40. Pope Francis, "Homily, Enrique Olaya Herrera airport, Medellín," September 9, 2017, https://zenit.org.

told the Jesuits in the Baltic States. "I believe the Lord wants a change in the church. I have said many times that a perversion of the church today is clericalism. But fifty years ago the Second Vatican Council said this clearly: the church is the People of God."[41]

With equal emphasis, Francis has said he believes the Lord today wants a church that evangelizes, and cites clericalism as its main obstacle. "Pick up again the Second Vatican Council, and read *Lumen gentium*," he told the Jesuits in Peru. "If there is something that is very clear, it is the awareness of the faithful holy people of God, infallible *in credendo*, as the Council teaches us. . . . We should never forget that evangelization is done by the Church as a people of God. The Lord wants an evangelizing Church, I see that clearly. This came from my heart, in simplicity, in the few minutes I spoke during the general congregations before the conclave. A Church that goes out, a Church that goes out proclaiming Jesus Christ."

That famous preconclave speech had a precedent in Cardinal Bergoglio's homily at Aparecida in 2007, in which he similarly depicted the church as worldly, fearful, self-referential, gnostic, living from its own light and incapable of evangelizing, in contrast to another vision of a church that was joyful, evangelizing, missionary, focused on the margins, and reflecting the light of Christ. In both Aparecida and Rome, he used the same image of the bent-over woman of the Gospels to describe the self-referential church, but in the former he spoke of the woman "who does nothing but look at herself, with the people of God somewhere else." It was a potent image of a church withdrawn from the People of God, and therefore incapable of evangelizing.[42]

THE ABUSE CRISIS

In what some have termed an *annus horribilis*, Francis in 2018 led the church through a year of crises and media scandals centered on its failures in past decades to put clerical abuse victims before the interests of the institution. In Australia, Germany, and the state of Pennsylvania in the United States, years-long inquiries published their findings, while in Chile, it was Pope Francis himself who ordered an investigation into abuse cover-up following a tumultuous visit in January 2018 in which he triggered a firestorm of criticism over his defense

---

41. Pope Francis, "Dialogue with the Jesuits in the Baltics," *La Civiltà Cattolica*, October 17, 2018.

42. Jorge Mario Bergoglio, "Homilía, celebración eucarística en Aparecida," May 16, 2007.

of a bishop accused of covering up for a priest abuser. The devastating report he commissioned from Archbishop Charles Scicluna led to Francis apologizing for his misjudgments and to a radical overhaul of the church hierarchy in the following months.[43]

The storm was at its most intense in the United States, where news broke in June 2018 that the former archbishop of Washington had abused a minor many years earlier. Soon afterward, it emerged that eighty-seven-year-old Cardinal "Ted" McCarrick had had a long history of predatory homosexual behavior in the 1980s and '90s that had been widely known, in spite of which he had been promoted to high ecclesiastical office. Into the febrile atmosphere of anger and shame provoked by the revelations dropped barely a fortnight later the results of a two-year probe by a Pennsylvania grand jury into the handling of decades of abuse allegations in eight dioceses over many decades. It painted a lurid picture of exploitation by priests of innocent young people while contending, in a wholly unnuanced way unsupported by the evidence itself, that bishops had wholly failed to act.[44]

During a late-August visit by Pope Francis to Ireland, the former nuncio to the United States, Archbishop Carlo Maria Viganò, claimed in an eleven-page "Testimony" that Francis had lifted restrictions imposed on McCarrick by Benedict XVI, and should resign. The letter had an incendiary effect on Francis's traditionalist and conservative critics in the United States, who saw in Viganò a moral crusader exposing moral corruption ("homosexual currents") at the highest levels of the church. In October 2019, 250 high net-worth conservative Catholics

---

43. Roberto Urbina Avendaño, "2018: 'annus horribilis' para los obispos chilenos," *Vida Nueva* (January 1, 2019). Australia's royal commission found that between 1980 and 2015, 4,444 people reported allegations of child sexual abuse to Catholic authorities: in total, 7 percent of Catholic priests in Australia between 1950 and 2010 were accused of child sexual abuse. The Pennsylvania report lists more than three hundred priests accused of abuse in six of the state's eight dioceses. When accused priests from the other two dioceses are added, it amounts to about 8 percent of the five thousand priests who served in Pennsylvania during the seventy-year period covered by the report. The German report published on September 12 recorded 3,700 cases of alleged sexual abuse of minors by Catholic priests, deacons, and clergy in Germany over a sixty-eight-year period, amounting to 4.4 percent of clergy, a figure close to that of the John Jay report in 2004.

44. On the Pennsylvania report, see Peter Steinfels, "The PA Grand-Jury Report: Not What It Seems," *Commonweal*, January 9, 2019. On McCarrick, see Laurie Goodstein, "He Preyed on Men Who Wanted to Be Priests. Then He Became a Cardinal," *New York Times*, July 16, 2018; and Boniface Ramsey, "The Case of Theodore McCarrick: A Failure of Fraternal Correction," *Commonweal*, October 29, 2018.

gathered in Washington, DC, for an "Authentic Reform" conference sponsored by a multimillionaire who called for a "cleansing" of the church, claiming, "Viganò has given us an agenda."[45]

Francis responded to the crisis in many ways: in letters, homilies, and interviews; in meetings with bishops and abuse victims; in specific juridical and pastoral actions such as prosecuting McCarrick, sending U.S. bishops on a retreat in January 2019, and organizing a key summit of the world's bishops in February 2019. At times, he also adopted a purposeful silence. The responses were both the fruit of his own discernment of the crisis, as well as a way of teaching the church how to discern. As he put it in October 2018 to some French priests in Rome, describing "a context in which the barque of the Church faces violent headwinds as the result of the serious failings of some of its members," the pastors were called "to witness to the strength of the Resurrection in the wounds of this world." The wounds were part of the witness; do not fear, he told them, to look on the wounds of our church, not in order to lament them but to be led to where Christ is.[46]

In this teaching, he drew on criteria for discernment in times of tribulation and persecution he had written about in a series of profound articles in the 1980s. There he identified, in principles deduced from St. Ignatius's guidance for retreatants, the temptations in such circumstances: an excessive ruminating on desolation, a defensive turning inward, a desire to blame and scapegoat and to divide the world into dualistic categories of good and bad, and to intellectualize. All these were ways of evading the spiritual task of discernment and reform, that is, prayerfully and humbly to face the questions: What is the Holy Spirit asking of us? How do we need to convert and change? Rather than lament and condemn, in short, Francis saw the church's task as to discern and reform. Embraced prayerfully and humbly, tribulation was a time of testing and purification, and an opportunity for conversion.[47]

---

45. The Viganò "testimony" can be found at https://assets.documentcloud.org/documents/4784141/TESTIMONYXCMVX-XENGLISH-CORRECTED-FINAL-VERSION.pdf (hereafter "Viganò testimony"). Christopher White, "Wealthy Catholics to Target Cardinals with 'Red Hat Report,'" *Crux*, October 1, 2018; Heidi Schlumpf, "At 'Authentic Reform,' Conservative Catholics Rally to 'Fix' Church Failures," *National Catholic Reporter*, October 5, 2018.

46. Pope Francis, "Discours du Pape François aux prêtres du diocèse de Créteil (France)," October 1, 2018, http://w2.vatican.va.

47. I summarize and analyze these writings in Austen Ivereigh, "To Discern and Reform: The 'Francis Option' for Evangelizing a World in Flux," *The Way* (October 2018); "Discernment in a Time of Tribulation: Pope Francis and the Church in Chile," *Thinking Faith* (May 8, 2018), www.thinking faith.org; and "A Time to Keep Silence," *Thinking Faith* (August 30, 2018), www.thinkingfaith.org.

A reading of his 2018 texts—letters to bishops and to the People of God, above all in Chile and the United States—shows how crucial was his People-of-God ecclesiology in leading the church through a process of conversion, in three main ways.

First, he showed that the acts of abuse and their cover-up were a product of clericalism (uprooting from the People of God) and spiritual corruption, and that the revelations of these offer the opportunity for repentance and conversion, a recentering on Christ and on the People of God.

Second, he argued that only such a profound spiritual conversion of hearts and minds was capable of bringing about necessary change. In this grace-filled process requiring repentance and humility, an exclusive focus on the juridical and institutional would not only distract from that task but risk accentuating the institutional idolatry at the origin of the crisis. For the same reason, the whole body of believers, not just bishops and clergy, needed to repent and adopt a stance of humble listening in order to allow the body as a whole to be transformed.

Third, he showed that in this process of conversion, it is God's holy faithful people that renews the institution, not the other way round. Only by recognizing God's presence and wisdom within the people, in a truly synodal church, will the equality as baptized be realized, and lasting conversion take root.[48]

REPENTANCE AND CHANGE

Francis was blunt about the extent and nature of the corruption that was being revealed, and his "pain and shame" at the "many crucified lives" that have resulted.[49] He continually identified the cause of

---

48. The documents are on the Vatican website (http://w2.vatican.va) unless otherwise stated. Francis wrote three letters to Chile: (1) To the bishops following Scicluna's report and summoning them to Rome (hereafter Chile First Letter): "Lettera del Santo Padre Francesco ai vescovi del Cile a seguito del report consegnato da S.E. Mons. Charles J. Scicluna," April 11, 2018. (2) To the bishops on their arrival in Rome (Chile Second Letter), dated May 15, 2018: the letter is untitled and not officially published, but leaked to www.t13.cl. (3) To the People of God in Chile (Chile Third Letter): "Carta del Santo Padre al Pueblo de Dios que peregrina en Chile," May 31, 2018. With respect to the U.S. crisis: (1) in the wake of the Pennsylvania report (Letter to People of God): "Letter of His Holiness Pope Francis to the People of God," August 20, 2018; and (2) a letter to the U.S. bishops (U.S. Bishops Letter): "A los obispos de la Conferencia Episcopal de los Estados Unidos de Norte América," January 1, 2019, available at www.usccb.org.

49. Pope Francis, Chile First Letter.

the crisis in the abuse of power of clericalism, which manifested in a threefold abuse: of power, of sex, and of conscience. In his Christmas 2018 greetings to the Roman Curia, he recalled the story of King David in 1 Sam 16:13 and 2 Sam 11–12, who was chosen and anointed by God. David took advantage of his position (abuse of power) to indulge his desire; forced Bathsheba to lie with him (sexual abuse plus abuse of power); and then sought to cover up his sin by disposing of her husband, Uriah (abuse of conscience plus abuse of power). "The chain of sin soon spreads and becomes a web of corruption," Francis observed, before noting how the king's moral decline produced no guilt but only a concern to preserve appearances. In the same way, consecrated men took advantage of their position to perform abominable acts yet carried on as if nothing had happened. Outwardly, they were perfect priests—with "boundless amiability, impeccable activity and angelic faces"—yet these "conceal a vicious wolf ready to devour innocent souls." They had no fear of God or his judgment, only of "being found out and unmasked."[50]

In his letters to Chile, he described the same descent into corruption of the institution as a whole, not just of individuals, in terms of a simultaneous turning away from Christ and his people. The church in Chile at one time used to put Christ in the center, and therefore defended the dignity of its people against the powerful; it was humble, prayerful, joyful, and evangelizing. But then came "a loss of prophetic power" and a "change in its center," with the result that the church called to show forth Christ "itself became the center of attention." Thus, "the painful and shameful revelation of sexual abuse of minors, of abuse of power and conscience on the part of ministers of the Church, and of how those situations were handled, are all clear evidence of this 'change of ecclesial center.'"[51]

At the same time, the church became "uprooted from the life of the People of God" which led to "desolation and the perversion of the nature of Church."[52] The result was "the loss of the healthy awareness of knowing that we belong to God's holy, faithful people which precedes us and—thank God—will succeed us."[53] Whenever the People of God has been reduced to "small elites," it leads to a "peculiar way of understanding the church's authority, one common in many communities where sexual abuse and the abuse of power and conscience

---

50. Pope Francis, Christmas greetings to the Roman Curia, December 21, 2018, http://w2.vatican.va.

51. Pope Francis, Chile Second Letter.

52. Pope Francis, Chile Third Letter.

53. Pope Francis, Chile Second Letter.

have occurred," he noted, adding that clericalism, "whether fostered by priests themselves or by lay persons," both enables and perpetuates abuse. "To say 'no' to abuse is to say an emphatic 'no' to all forms of clericalism."[54]

Francis likened the media's role in exposing the corruption to that of the prophet Nathan confronting David with the truth, and making him see the seriousness of his sin. Honest and objective reporters "sought to unmask these predators and to make their victims' voices heard."[55] The outcry of the victims, long ignored, proved more powerful than attempts to silence it, showing that "the Lord heard that cry and once again shows us on which side he stands."[56]

The crisis and the scandals, therefore, were a sign of God's coming, an opportunity for repentance and conversion, for the love of God to "come out to meet us and to purify our intentions" with "the forgiveness of our sins and the action of his grace."[57] A wounded church frees people from believing themselves superior, and that all depends on them.[58] "An awareness of sin helps us to acknowledge the errors, the crimes, and the wounds caused in the past and allows us, in the present, to be more open and committed along a journey of renewed conversion."[59]

CONVERSION OF HEARTS AND MINDS

Running through the 2018 texts on abuse is an insistence that the Church embrace this *kairós* and resist the temptations and distractions that would block it. A major temptation was to focus on protocols and legal instruments which in themselves are necessary but insufficient; the real task of the moment was a deeper conversion of hearts and minds, to accept the conversion God's grace was offering. A recurring phrase in the texts is that "ideas are discussed, situations are discerned": in other words, rather than argue about what to do, the task was to ask what God was asking of them.

Francis urged Chile's bishops to resist the "temptation of verbal diarrhea" or "taking refuge in 'universals'" (that is, abstractions) and instead allow themselves to be converted by truth and mercy.[60] It was

---

54. Pope Francis, Letter to People of God.
55. Pope Francis, Christmas greetings to the Roman Curia, December 21, 2018.
56. Pope Francis, Letter to People of God.
57. Pope Francis, Chile First Letter.
58. Pope Francis, Chile Second Letter.
59. Pope Francis, Letter to People of God.
60. Pope Francis, Chile First Letter.

vital not to try to turn the page too quickly, as politicians might, and so miss the deeper reckoning. Another evasion was to try to apportion blame on particular groups or individuals. In his second letter to Chile's bishops, Francis regretted the way some had tried to save their own skins, justifying themselves or accusing others, seeking scapegoats; it was vital to confess, as a body, the weaknesses and failures of that body, and "together to find humble and concrete responses in communion with the whole People of God."[61] In his letters to the People of God, Francis asked the whole body of faithful to do the same: only by moving forward together as a "synodal" church could Jesus be put back in the center. It wasn't a matter simply of replacing bishops; what the Holy Spirit was prompting was "an ecclesial transformation that involves us all."[62] He later expressed this in a global letter:

It is always helpful to remember that "in salvation history, the Lord saved one people. We are never completely ourselves unless we belong to a people. That is why no one is saved alone, as an isolated individual. Rather, God draws us to himself, taking into account the complex fabric of interpersonal relationships present in the human community. God wanted to enter into the life and history of a people" (*Gaudete et exsultate* 6). Consequently, the only way that we have to respond to this evil that has darkened so many lives is to experience it as a task regarding all of us as the People of God. This awareness of being part of a people and a shared history will enable us to acknowledge our past sins and mistakes with a penitential openness that can allow us to be renewed from within. Without the active participation of all the Church's members, everything being done to uproot the culture of abuse in our communities will not be successful in generating the necessary dynamics for sound and realistic change.[63]

He went on to ask the body of faithful to pray and fast, not because—as some angrily claimed—he was indicting the faithful for the sins of some clergy but because the People of God were anointed: as the agent of spiritual transformation, the channel of grace that the church so badly needed, their prayers and fasting would create space for God's mercy to act, allowing the whole body to "grow in the gift of compassion, in justice, prevention and reparation." As he told

---

61. Pope Francis, Chile Second Letter.
62. Pope Francis, Chile Third Letter.
63. Pope Francis, Letter to People of God.

Rome's clergy, the religiosity of the people was the "immune system of the Church."[64]

In his letter to the United States' bishops at the start of their January 2019 retreat at Mundelein, Illinois, Francis continually warned against trying to deal with their crisis of credibility by means of new norms or organigrams as if they were "a human resources agency" or "evangelization business." The conversion had to be a *metanoia*, a change in "our ways of praying, of managing power and money, of exercising authority and how we relate to each other and to our world." Only by entering into "affective communion with the feeling of our people" would the bishops avoid banality, defensiveness, and triumphalism, and the attempt to reduce everything to a matter of ethics and doctrine.[65]

The two temptations—scapegoating groups or individuals and focusing on ideas and doctrines rather than discerning the situation—were precisely those of Archbishop Carlo Maria Viganò and the more than dozen bishops who had come out in support of his crusade of purification. Viganò's specific charge against Francis for covering up McCarrick quickly collapsed, but his narrative that abuse was a matter of sexual laxity brought on by "pro-gay ideology" and that any attempt to blame clericalism was an attempt to divert attention from this blindingly obvious "fact" was appealing both to conservative bishops and media. The Viganò reform focused on restoring the prestige of the institution by scapegoating individuals and groups. It was essentially clericalist: the People of God's role was solely to be mobilized in indignation for the purpose of a campaign against the pope and the "homosexual current" of bishops.

From his daily homilies in the Santa Marta, Francis invited the People of God to discern the spirits behind Viganò's movement and its supporters, warning that "the father of lies, the accuser, the devil, acts to destroy the unity of a family, of a people." He spoke of the importance of accusing oneself rather than others, noting that "a sign that . . . a Christian does not know how to accuse himself is when he is accustomed to accusing others." Again at Christmas, he warned the curia that "the Tempter, the Great Accuser, is the one who brings division, sows discord, insinuates enmity, persuades God's children and

---

64. Pope Francis, Letter to People of God. Pope Francis, "Incontro . . . con il clero della diocesi di Roma," May 14, 2018, http://w2.vatican.va.

65. Pope Francis, U.S. Bishops Letter, January 1, 2019, and available in English and Spanish on the USCCB website. Quotes here are my own translations of the Spanish, which was the only official version.

causes them to doubt," and that "behind these sowers of weeds we always find the thirty pieces of silver."[66]

THE PEOPLE OF GOD AS AGENT
OF CONVERSION AND RENEWAL

Like Francis, Viganò called out moral depravity and corruption in the church. But the means to which he appealed was ultimately Pelagian, not depending on God's grace and mercy but on discipline and norms and a crusade of purification led by an imaginary new pope. Claiming to have stayed silent before hoping that "the hierarchy of the church could find within itself the spiritual resources and strength to tell the whole truth, to amend and to renew itself," he called for chastity in clergy and in seminaries and identified high-ranking bishops and cardinals as belonging to what he called "homosexual networks" promoting a gay ideology. The presumption was that the abuse crisis was the result of moral laxity of homosexuals and the collusion of leaders of loose doctrine who failed to act against them. Yet the most high-profile abusers were mostly conservative in doctrine, and not always gay.[67]

Francis had warned in *Guadete et exsultate* against the neo-Pelagian idea that "everything depends on human effort channeled by ecclesial rules and structures," leaving no room for God's grace.[68] For the pope, the crisis lay in a turning away from Christ, and renewal on turning back to the encounter with God's grace and mercy present in his people, the antidote to the ecclesial virus. He writes:

> The holy, patient, faithful people of God sustained and given life by the Holy Spirit is the best face of the prophetic Church that knows how each day to put the Lord at the center. Our attitude as pastors is to learn to trust in this ecclesial reality and reverence and recognize it in the ordinary people, who confess their faith in Jesus Christ, who love the Virgin, who earn their living from their work (so often poorly paid), who baptize their children and bury their dead; in this faithful people that knows itself to be sinner but believes in the mercy of the Father; in this silent, faithful people resides the immune system of the Church.[69]

66. Pope Francis, Christmas greetings to the Roman Curia, December 21, 2018.
67. Viganò testimony (see n. 45 above).
68. *GE* 59.
69. Pope Francis, Chile Second Letter.

Concretely, this meant bringing the People of God into the church's life and mission. He appealed directly to the faithful in Chile to be "protagonists of the transformation now called for" and to demand "renewed forms of participation" not as concessions but as the nature of the church itself calls for. "It is impossible to imagine the future with this anointing operating in each of you," he told them, before outlining that future as a new ecclesial culture in which the most vulnerable are listened to, criticism is not dismissed as treason, and an atmosphere of respect and care replaces an abusive culture.[70] As he put it in his global letter, "Without the active participation of all the Church's members, everything being done to uproot the culture of abuse in our communities will not be successful in generating the necessary dynamics for sound and realistic change."[71]

In other words, for the pope, change was a process that would be triggered by the church becoming what *Lumen gentium* imagined it to be. From the process of encounter and conversion as a body would flow the necessary moral transformation of both individuals and the institution. As he put it in *Gaudete et exsultate*, "In salvation history, the Lord saved one people. We are never completely ourselves unless we belong to a people" (no. 6).

CONCLUSION

Pope Francis has not just paid lip service to the People-of-God ecclesiology of *Lumen gentium*, but is seeking actively to bring it about, both through his vigorous opposition to clericalism as well as his encouragement of a discerning response to clerical sex abuse. In his invocation of the People of God, he has brought to bear on it the rich Latin American understanding of *pueblo*, which reflects the nationalist-popular political movements of the twentieth century and the theology of the *teología del pueblo*. His reading of Latin American colonial history via Alberto Methol Ferré has left him with a powerful conviction of God's presence in culture and the integrating impact of the missionary church as a *complexio oppositorum*. It is a reading that clearly starts from an ecclesiological notion of belonging first and primarily to an "anointed" people, and which understands the role of the institutional structures of the church and the clergy as being at the service of the ordinary people, the *santo pueblo fiel de Dios*. It is a reading that equally clearly sees a tragedy in the *embourgeoisement* and increasing remote-

---

70. Pope Francis, Chile Third Letter.
71. Pope Francis, Letter to People of God.

ness of the urban, privileged clergy, and the elitist mentalities that too often result.

At the heart of Francis's People-of-God ecclesiology is an understanding of the role of the clergy as pastors who belong to the holy people, are of the holy people, and who serve the holy people. Their leadership is exercised through service and discernment; their mission *ad gentes* starts from the recognition that God is already present within the life and experience of his people; the clergy help to build up the People of God by accompanying, discerning, and integrating from within that life and experience. Their assumption is that God has already anointed his people with charisms, and that the pastor's task is to encourage and guide them in their call to be missionary disciples.

Conversely, clericalism is a rejection of the ecclesiology of *Lumen gentium*. It makes the church coterminous with the institution, seeing the faithful as irrelevant or passive recipients. It claims to protect the priesthood but in reality instrumentalizes it for personal benefit. Rather than recognize and embrace God's presence in his people and his anointing of them, clericalism blocks that presence. Clericalism acts as an intermediary rather than a mediator; it seeks to build the priesthood at the expense of the People of God, and uses its power to exploit the faithful. It is an elitist mindset that can equally take over the nonordained. Rather than discerning and accompanying, it is legalistic and doctrinaire. It is not close and concrete but remote and abstract. It is concerned with not losing the saved rather than saving the lost. Clericalism withdraws the institution from the people.

Finally, Francis sees in clerical sex abuse the action of God, both intervening on behalf of victims and exposing the deep corruption and abusive culture that is the rotten fruit of clericalism. He is inviting the church to accept the process of conversion and purification that is made possible by scandal and failure, and is seeking to help the church to avoid the temptations that would undermine it. Given that the origin of the crisis is in the clerical institution turning its back on the People of God, only by allowing itself to receive the grace already present in the people can the church be restored and renewed. But that is a task that has to involve the whole body, so that, ecclesiologically, the process and its result are indistinguishable. Not without difficulty and in the face of vehement resistance, this is the spiritual strategy Pope Francis has adopted in the church's time of tribulation.

10

Francis's Leadership

Agbonkhianmeghe E. Orobator, SJ

A hunter who advances too far ahead of his fellow hunters ends up with an arrow in his behind.
—African proverb

At the outset, I wish to acknowledge two caveats. First, despite the somewhat suggestive opening proverb, this chapter is not a disquisition on papal anatomy. So, I request that you banish from your imagination any vision of a papal rear end riven with arrows. As a metaphorical device, the African proverb offers a salutary warning on the danger of leading change in "an ancient, complex and venerable institution made up of people of different cultures, languages and mindsets."[1]

Second, while not the only valid one, this chapter presents a view from the Global South. My perception of the first five years of Francis's papacy is unashamedly positive. Proof and justification for this bias should become evident further on. My primary purpose is twofold: to scrutinize the leadership style and agenda of Pope Francis and to examine some reactions and disputes that such leadership provokes. Rest assured, we set out to query Francis, not to glaze him with flattery or adulation.

At the completion of the fifth year of his pontificate, Francis has earned a global brand stature and distinction as an important staple of scholarship and debate. Columnists and scholars, commentators and

---

1. Christopher Lamb, "Reforming Vatican like 'cleaning the Egyptian sphinx with a toothbrush,'" *The Tablet*, December 21, 2017, http://www.thetablet.co.uk.

pundits, Vaticanologists and aficionados revel in the fecund pastime of decoding, deconstructing, and deciphering the 265th successor of Peter. Analysis of the foundation, intent, and direction of Francis's papacy has spawned an impressive collection of academic, popular, and devotional literature. The impact of his prophetic voice and compelling witness, variously rendered as "The Francis Effect"[2] or "The Francis Factor," influences and shapes multiple global discourses— from conversations about poverty, migration, and climate change to concerns about atrocities in South Sudan, Syria, and Congo. Ironically, even though students of Francis engage the enterprise with studied erudition, as we do presently, there is no mystery about Francis's leadership style and agenda. In many respects, Francis is anything but a revolutionary. Practically speaking, as a voice crying out in the world, the radicalness of his leadership is as unexceptional as the dogged perspicacity of a hunter is habitual. Yet, because he leads the way he does, Francis risks ending up with an arrow or more in his behind.

The most striking imagery of Francis's leadership evokes not the rather injurious intent of a hunter but the fulsome compassion of a pastoralist. In his oft-quoted phrase inspired by animal husbandry, Francis has advocated a leadership model of "shepherds with the smell of sheep" (*EG* 24). This ideal embodies a commonplace pastoral practice that is not realized simply by the pungency of one's body odor or the acuity of a person's olfactory senses. Leadership in such a pastoral manner summons practitioners to venture outside the cozy comfort of the sheepfold into the peripheral and precarious habitat of a wounded, marginalized, and impoverished humanity ("On the Call to Holiness in Today's World," *GE* 135).[3] Such leadership style doubles as a call to action that transforms the Christian church into a "bruised, hurting and dirty" community on account of its relentless pursuit of mercy, justice, love, and care for the Earth on the streets rather than ensconced in palatial episcopal ghettos (*EG* 49, 197–201).

Francis's professed preferential option for the periphery yields an alternate ecclesiology that is centrifugal by orientation and missionary

---

2. E. Maibach, A. Leiserowitz, C. Roser-Renouf, T. Myers, S. Rosenthal, and G. Feinberg, *The Francis Effect: How Pope Francis Changed the Conversation about Global Warming* (New Haven, CT: Yale Program on Climate Change Communication; Fairfax, VA: George Mason University Center for Climate Change Communication, 2015); John Gehring, *The Francis Effect: A Radical Pope's Challenge to the American Catholic Church* (Lanham, MD: Rowman & Littlefield, 2017); Agbonkhianmeghe E. Orobator, ed., *The Church We Want: African Catholics Look to Vatican III* (Maryknoll, NY: Orbis Books, 2016), 3–76.

3. Justin Welby, "Sheep," in *A Pope Francis Lexicon*, ed. Joshua J. McElwee and Cindy Wooden (Collegeville, MN: Liturgical Press, 2018), 179.

in nature, precisely because it draws the Christian community toward existential margins. By comparison, this outward-looking ecclesiology seems the polar opposite of a centripetal and self-referential ecclesiology preoccupied with self-preservation and self-aggrandizement. As Francis said to the Congregation of Bishops, leadership credentials in a missionary church are not fulfilled by "a manager, a chief executive officer of a company, nor one who remains at the level of our pettiness and little pretensions."[4] In reality, to take on the smell of the sheep, a leader must be prepared to live like one. Or, as a Rwandan proverb says, "If you want cows you must sleep like a cow."[5]

Understandably, for anyone in the church, especially self-appointed elites and power brokers, so inured to a life of leisure and ceremony, this kind of leadership presents a tough act to follow. Yet Francis has not invented a new teaching. If Vatican II is to be believed, "The joys and the hopes, the griefs and the anxieties of the people of this age, especially those who are poor or in any way afflicted, these are the joys and hopes, the griefs and anxieties of the followers of Christ" (*GS* 1). The novelty, however, resides in the fact that in summoning the church to live in solidarity and with compassion, in spirit and in truth, Francis personally embodies these values in his actions and deeds. Hence, Francis is not, as one African proverb puts it, a leader who is afraid to step on cow dung, preferring instead to lead from a sterile and safe distance.

And so, complementary to and in part illustrative of Francis's exercise of leadership is his personal integrity, which allows him to function as a leader, while consistently remaining himself irrespective of situations, contexts, or circumstances. Whether in Lampedusa or on a papal cortège, crouched at the feet of Muslim women refugees or shunning the ostentation of the papal dwelling, these images of commonplace pastoral service signal the authenticity and strength of Francis's character as a prophetic leader, not given to projecting expediently a public image while concealing a private persona that betrays a disconnect between personal life and professed convictions. His "feet-dirty, smell-of-the-sheep leadership style" challenges cardinals, bishops, priests, and the entire church with a tough leadership act.[6] As

---

4. Pope Francis, "Address to the Congregation of Bishops," February 27, 2014.

5. Antoine Kambanda, "'If You Want Cows You Must Sleep Like a Cow': The Bishop in the Church of Pope Francis," in *The Church We Want: African Catholics Look to Vatican III*, ed. Agbonkhianmeghe E. Orobator (Maryknoll, NY: Orbis Books, 2016), 65–76.

6. Chris Lowney, *Pope Francis: Why He Leads the Way He Leads: Lessons from the First Jesuit Pope* (Chicago: Loyola Press, 2013), 132.

noted earlier, some of us would repel this intrusion on our accustomed self-indulgence and fashion darts and arrows in self-defense.

Francis's practice of pastoral leadership has a more pertinent implication in that it exposes the abiding temptation of those in positions of authority to prey on the vulnerability of their communities. The putative shepherd could turn on the sheep. In Francis's own words, "bishops and priests who fall into the temptation of money and the vanity of careerism turn from shepherds into wolves, 'who eat the flesh of their own sheep.'"[7] Borrowing the words of Augustine, Francis argues that "when the bishop or priest takes advantage of the sheep for his own sake, things change: the priest, the bishop isn't for the people but a priest or bishop who takes from the people."[8] Hence, continues Francis, the lesson here is clear: "For a bishop isn't a bishop for his own sake but for the people's sake; and a priest isn't a priest for his own sake but for the people's sake."[9]

The preceding point suggests the vital importance of self-awareness in the measure of one's limitation and vulnerability in the exercise of leadership. A leader is prone to failure. Francis has demonstrated this self-awareness with humility and simplicity. His suppliant gesture on the night of his election was later followed by a candid self-disclosure in an interview with Antonio Spadaro in 2013: "I am a sinner," said Francis. "This is the most accurate definition. It is not a figure of speech, a literary genre. I am a sinner."[10] If that was 2013, consider Pope Francis's letter on April 8, 2018, to the Chilean bishops admitting his own "serious mistakes" in handling the clergy sex abuse scandal in Chile and, with "pain and shame," asking for forgiveness from all those he has offended.[11]

In Francis's leadership style, awareness, particularly of limitations and shortcomings, and the ability to learn from one's failure or to make amends for a mistake, represent an essential principle for everyone called to leadership and service in church and society. In the same interview with Spadaro, Francis admits, "Over time I learned many things. The Lord has allowed this growth in knowledge of government through my faults and my sins."[12] "We too," insists Francis, "are

7. Pope Francis, "Homily at *Domus Sanctae Martae*," May 15, 2013, http://w2.vatican.va.

8. Ibid.

9. Ibid.

10. Antonio Spadaro, "A Big Heart Open to God: An Interview with Pope Francis," *America*, September 30, 2013.

11. Pope Francis, Letter to Chilean Bishops, April 8, 2018, http://w2.vatican.va.

12. Spadaro, "A Big Heart Open to God."

human and are sinners"; "and we are also tempted."[13] Self-awareness as an aspect of the personal and leadership charisma of Francis is memorialized in his motto, *Miserando atque Eligendo* ("By Having Mercy and by Choosing Him"), borrowed from the homilies of Bede the Venerable, on Jesus's merciful and forgiving gaze on Matthew. As Pope Francis explains, "That finger of Jesus, pointing at Matthew. That's me. I feel like him. Like Matthew."[14]

Many studies attribute the origin and centrality of mercy in Francis's pontificate to the transformation that has characterized his personal journey. Mercy is not only the central message of Christianity but also a constitutive element of Francis's leadership vision and agenda for the church. As Cardinal Walter Kasper has noted, what "the church needs most today is the ability to heal wounds and to warm the hearts of the faithful; it needs nearness, proximity."[15] Francis renders this categorically in *Evangelii gaudium* as follows: "the church must be a place of mercy freely given, where everyone can feel welcomed, loved, forgiven and encouraged to live the good life of the Gospel" (*EG* 114). The well-documented narrative of Francis's character transformation offers a compelling case study in personal conversion achieved through grace and grit, humility and docility.[16]

Supposing the leadership portrait of Francis indicated here is accurate, the question arises: What is so challenging about following Francis's leadership style? What accounts for the suspicion that persists among pockets of resisters who have joined cause with formidable champions of discontent to stoke a backlash against Francis's leadership? There is no monocausal answer to these questions. On a cursory level, judging from the portrait that we have sketched, if Francis is a reformer or a prophet, his pedigree resides in his personal witness and his advocacy for openness to the possibility and necessity of renewal rather than an autocratic and mindless pursuit of doctrinal change. The *Irish Times* columnist Patsy McGarry is only half right in arguing that the change instigated by Francis is more a matter of leadership style than substantial change of doctrine.[17] Yet when critics attack the pope, it is for a perceived threat to the

---

13. Pope Francis, "Homily at *Domus Sanctae Martae*," May 15, 2013.

14. Ibid.

15. Walter Kasper, *Mercy: The Essence of the Gospel and the Key to Christian Life* (Mahwah, NJ: Paulist Press, 2013), x.

16. See Austen Ivereigh, *The Great Reformer: Francis and the Making of a Radical Pope* (New York: Henry Holt, 2014).

17. "Five years of Pope Francis: Lots of style, little substance," *Irish Times*, March 10, 2018, https://www.irishtimes.com.

security and self-sufficiency of venerable tradition and orthodoxy.

Examples of Francis's approaches that strain tradition and orthodoxy are not hard to find. They include his call for discernment of circumstances allowing communion for divorced and remarried Catholics; his invitation to priests to assume greater pastoral responsibility for sins, like abortion, previously deemed unforgivable; his suspension of judgment on the humanity of gay men and women, preferring instead to tread the path of mercy, compassion, and fellowship; the oft-forgotten papal reprieve for theologians considered delinquent and hitherto doggedly pursued by the Congregation for the Doctrine of the Faith; his singular ability to lend renewed urgency to the plight of the poor and marginalized (migrants, refugees, victims of human trafficking, and homeless persons); the recalibration of the center of ecclesiastical power in favor of the Global South; the study of the question of women deacons in the early church to inform conversation about contemporary roles of women in the church; the devolution of liturgical translations to the local church; and his checkered attempts at greater transparency, whether in financial accountability or the credibility of measures to address the clergy sex abuse scandal, and so on. Contrary to McGarry's position, for the coterie of discontents, these issues are more than just stylistics; they border on consequential questions. The contemporary assaults on Francis have intensified with respect to all these points. Furthermore, nor is reform in style an inconsequential undertaking in the charged atmosphere of ecclesiastical politics.

Whether we qualify it as a matter of style or of substance, or even "managerial reform,"[18] clearly, Francis's leadership has roused a phobia of change and a nostalgia for "a monolithic body of doctrine" (*GE* 43), as was recently epitomized by the *dubia* saga. Besides, to anathematize the phrase "It's always been done that way," as Francis so brazenly did, further provokes the ire of custodians of tradition who are unreceptive to change and wary of those who claim to bring it. Thus, as the *dubia* authors demonstrate, Francis's manner of leading change and the direction of change itself trigger with visceral intensity, albeit obliquely, the question: "Is Francis *still* Catholic?"

Under these circumstances, the barbs, arrows, and missiles aimed, so to speak, at Francis's rear end are particularly pointed. Openly excoriated for allegedly flirting with heresy, lambasted as agent provocateur of schism, and lampooned for seemingly harboring a denatured streak of Protestantism and pseudo-Anglicanism to the detriment of the doctrinal solidity of clearly defined Catholic teach-

---

18. Kerry Alys Robinson, "Leadership," in *A Pope Francis Lexicon*, ed. Joshua J. McElwee and Cindy Wooden (Collegeville, MN: Liturgical Press, 2018), 114.

ings, Francis—if we must believe his bitterest critics—represents a catalyst for the cataclysmic disintegration and destruction of the barque of St. Peter. Even while admitting to a scintilla of admiration for the pope's global public-relations prowess and charismatic appeal, doubters would dismiss as unconscionable the plausibility of a heretical pope being God's instrument for ecclesial reform like Cyrus of Persia of old. The stridency of opposition, such as is evident in "*Correctio filialis de haeresibus propagatis*" ("A filial correction concerning the propagation of heresies"),[19] generates a paroxysm of animosity, enough to prompt Andrew Brown of the *Guardian* to declare that among some of his own followers, "Pope Francis is one of the most hated men in the world today."[20] Although Brown overstates, even sensationalizes the situation, his statement does contain certain elements of reality. However, given such extreme perception of the man and his message, I am increasingly persuaded that Francis's greatest service to the church in the twenty-first century as its spiritual leader remains his singular, if somewhat contested, illuminating testimony that exposes with painful clarity the moral schizophrenia of a church where tangled political hypocrisy resents prophetic leadership and applauds doctrinal bigotry.

Over the last five years, the open polemics between Francis and some episcopal leaders have resulted in the negative portrayal of the pope as a weak protagonist of change who is incapable seemingly to make a concerted push for a radical transformation. However we assess the effectiveness of Francis's leadership and reform agenda, it bears noting that the struggle for influence and supremacy in the highest echelons of ecclesiastical power is neither new nor exceptional. Francis himself makes an incisive analysis of this tension by distinguishing two types of power struggle. Type One is an atavistic "struggle for power in the church" that has "existed since the time of Jesus himself"; it is sustained in the church by powerful networks vested in careerism, favored by social sycophants, and bolstered by "good-natured simony." Type Two, says Francis, is the "struggle for true power, which Jesus taught by his example of the power of service. True power is service." Using principles derived from the *Spiritual Exercises* of St. Ignatius of Loyola, Francis has this to say about the implications of the second type: to be a leader in the church is to be "promoted to the cross" and "promoted to humiliation." "That's true promotion." "Promotion that makes us more like Jesus. . . . That's love,

---

19. See http://www.correctiofilialis.org.
20. "The War against Pope Francis," *The Guardian*, October 27, 2017; https://www.theguardian.com.

that's the power of service in the church. And that's the way to serve others better who are on the way of Jesus."[21] Without ascribing any of these qualities to himself, Francis's leadership eminently embodies this principle of selfless and self-sacrificing service of the gospel.

Where does all this leave Pope Francis going forward in his Petrine ministry? Judging by a recently published survey of U.S. Catholics conducted by the Pew Research Center, Francis enjoys an approval rating that would make him the envy of political leaders.[22] But I prefer to treat such favorability rating with caution, because too often it amplifies the partisan view of things typified by so-called conservatives, traditionalists, or right-wing and their liberal, progressive, or left-wing adversaries. This binary taxonomy is not necessarily productive; it has the effect of simplifying a very complex situation. Besides, it represents a projection of a Western, mainly North American, hermeneutical framework that prioritizes a clash of ideas and generates heated single-issue debates as the dominant lens for reading everything from Pope Francis to Homer Simpson.[23] Although ideological tensions run deep in the short lifespan of this papacy, it would be wrong to reduce the claims to a simple either/or culture-war schema between a triumphalist left and a disaffected right. Weightier issues are at stake in church and society. And Francis knows it.

Behind the political tension and contention around Francis's leadership of the church lies the fundamental question of inclusion of women and men of various manners of life, orientation, and circumstance long-relegated to the margins of orthodoxy by zealous defenders of ecclesiastical privileges. From an African perspective, papal energy has never been so palpable, not in the manipulation or fabrication of doctrines but in the embodiment of the practice of mercy, justice, love, and care for God's creation—not forgetting the joyful spirit and sense of humor—especially in those places where humanity's brokenness confronts the healing message of the gospel with prophetic urgency. Francis's pastoral prioritization of these situations offers a more authentic benchmark for assessing his leadership credentials than do ideological antipathies.

Nonetheless, to be fair and balanced in our view of Francis's leadership, we have to admit that, perhaps, some of the arrows and missiles

---

21. Pope Francis, "Homily," May 21, 2013; cf. *GE* 118–120.

22. Pew Research Center, "Pope Francis Still Highly Regarded in U.S., but Signs of Disenchantment Emerge," March 6, 2018, http://assets.pewresearch.org; See also E. Maibach et al., "The Francis Effect."

23. See "Ted Cruz Thinks the Democrats Are the Party of Lisa Simpson; He's Dead Right," https://www.theguardian.com. See also *GE* 101.

are not entirely without justification, although some are misdirected and ill-timed. The words "struggling," "snail's pace," and "stalled" appear often in the appraisal of Francis's actions and motives. Joan Chittister, for example, has argued persuasively that "some things that must change clearly have not changed in these last five years. Instead, there is smoke without fire, commissions promised but not created, questions acceptable to ask, yes, but answers still scarce."[24] Granted, there is ample material to formulate a litany of unresolved issues under this pontiff, but the charge of "promise of action and the absence of results," "hollow leadership," and "unclear leadership" unfairly mischaracterizes Francis as a genial but unreliable double agent, who pays lip service to change while surreptitiously propping up the status quo. Besides, those who advance such criticism hastily obituarize Francis's reform agenda, as if it were already a finished business. Clearly, it isn't.

However the fact is to be understood, two points are noteworthy here. First, true, some steps are nearly not enough; and, while it is no doubt true that Francis has made some mistakes, much has changed in five years. As Martin Luther King Jr. once said, quoting another minister, "We ain't what we oughta be. We ain't what we want to be. We ain't what we gonna be. But, thank God, we ain't what we was." By his own leadership philosophy, Francis distinguishes the practiced political penchant of charlatans for occupying space, presuming to preserve authentic tradition, from the genuine desire to inspire and generate durable processes of change (*EG* 222–25). In my own judgment, Francis's fundamental agenda aims to create processes of renewal and reform. Like the parable of the sower, the seeds of change that he sows face multiple threats (Luke 8:4–15).

Second, Francis's struggles suggest the imperative of a corrective dose of realism to his initial and perhaps naïve underestimation of the formidable power, systemic intransigence, and instinctive rigidity of structures and protocols of the Roman Curia. Leading change in the hierarchical maze of the Vatican is an exercise beset with frustration and difficulties. Francis has vividly articulated this reality when, quoting nineteenth-century Belgian diplomat Archbishop Frédéric-François-Xavier de Mérode, he likened reforming the Curia to cleaning the Sphinx of Giza with a toothbrush. Nor, frankly, should it surprise anyone that rebuking members of his top leadership team as corrupt and cancerous bureaucrats, given to political intrigues, cliques, and complots; seduced by ambition and vainglory; and plagued by "spiri-

---

24. Joan Chittister, "Francis invites change, but we are the change," *National Catholic Reporter*, March 10, 2018.

tual Alzheimer's," "leprosy," and "emptiness" only escalates the frequency and intensity of arrows aimed at his rear end.

In the final analysis, if we may proffer a counsel to Pope Francis, it is this African proverb: "If you want to go fast, walk alone; if you want to go far, walk with others." Irish theologian and Scripture scholar Seán Freyne is quoted as saying that "it's a mistake to think that a pope has the power to do anything."[25] As a self-confessed reformed autocrat, Francis gets that message: "My style of government," he says, "as a Jesuit at the beginning had many faults. . . . It was my authoritarian way of making decisions that created problems."[26] This immensely contrite papal confession aside, not forgetting the botched Chilean abuse scandal, we possess no guarantee that Francis has overcome completely his proclivity for what papal biographer Austen Ivereigh describes as high-handed exercise of sovereign authority that manifests as "a highly personalistic government, which bypasses systems, depends on close relationships, works through people rather than documents, and keeps a tight control."[27] Be that as it may, such a candid admission of a propensity to err by the leader of a global organization, which has a legendary reputation of obsession with infallibility, deflates the moral victories and neutralizes the sabre rattling of conservative-leaning Catholics, who rail against Francis for egging the church too far away from their entrenched position, and liberal-leaning Catholics, who are exasperated that he is not moving fast enough to enact their agenda. Under these circumstances, the true test of leadership lies in the capacity to maintain a healthy process of consultation, encourage ongoing learning, remain unwavering in the pursuit of transparency and accountability; and persevere in humble listening.[28] Francis passes this test. And so, Seán Freyne is only partially right: the pope can do almost anything, *but never alone* (see *EG* 33).

Speaking of listening, we recall the Manja people of Central African Republic and the Bambara people of Mali in West Africa who maintain a rabbit as the totem of a leader.[29] This imagery prioritizes the arduous undertaking of listening over the authoritarian pronouncement of diktats. For our purposes, it also bears resemblance to three key principles that Francis has proposed to the church, namely, synodality,

25. Quoted in Chittister, "Francis invites change."

26. Spadaro, "A Big Heart Open to God."

27. Ivereigh, *The Great Reformer*, 384.

28. James Corkery, "Pope Francis and the Eight Cardinal Advisors," in *Thinking Faith* (September 30, 2013), http://www.thinkingfaith.org.

29. Elochukwu Uzukwu, *A Listening Church: Autonomy and Communion in African Churches* (Eugene, OR: Wipf & Stock, 2006).

subsidiarity, and collegiality. As Francis himself has argued, "We need to practice the art of listening, which is more than simply hearing," but entails "an openness of heart" that aims to include even those with whom we sharply disagree (*EG* 171).

Therefore, in conclusion, while Francis's leadership has delighted many and discomfited some, a renewed focus on inclusive dialogue and real consultation offers us an opportunity to beat the arrows of discord into common ground for conversation and "mutual listening in which everyone has something to learn."[30] As church, we need neither a hunter nor a maverick for pope—or, worse, a curator of "a museum of memories" (*GE* 139, 58; *EG* 95). What would suit us best is a leader with a big, humble, and contrite heart open to God and open to the world. And that leader, I submit, is Francis.

---

30. "Address of His Holiness Pope Francis, Ceremony Commemorating the 50th Anniversary of the Institution of the Synod of Bishops," October 17, 2015, http://w2.vatican.va.

11

African Wisdom in Dialogue
with *Laudato si'*

Christophère Ngolele

Pope Francis appeals to all humanity, requesting dialogue and reconciliation among all people, and between people and created nature. This appeal recognizes the role that everyone should play to recover our state as human beings created in the image of God together with other creatures. The recognition of our unique beauty as created by God reminds us of the beauty of all other creatures of God's creation and hence engages us to respect and protect all creatures. This chapter addresses the same concern for the recognition of and respect for the environment. It is a call for dialogue and reconciliation among human beings and with created nature from the African perspective in dialogue with the church's perspective as developed by *Laudato si'*.[1]

The environmental crisis raises a fundamental question of human identity as it portrays the prevailing conflictual context. The way we treat nature reveals something of our identity. This is very true from the perspective of African culture, where a person's entire identity is linked to the quality of one's relationships in a complex network of life. An African, traditionally speaking, qualifies for full human identity only insofar as he or she lives in harmonious relationships with fellow human beings, the ancestors, created nature, and God. Nature is as critical in this mixture of networks as the place of fellow humans.

The broken environment in which we live shows our broken humanity. The distorted relationships with nature that we are witnessing call

---

1. Pope Francis, *Laudato si'* (Vatican City: Libreria Editrice Vaticana, 2015).

us to revisit our identity, since our identity is determined by the quality of our relationships. The recognition of such disorder urges human beings to initiate a sincere dialogue with themselves and the created world to reach a full reconciliation. This is a condition for recovering our full identity. Here, the African identity stands as an appropriate partner to *Laudato si'*, since the African identity helps to recover relationality as an important dimension of human identity. The dialogue between *Laudato si'* and African identity is a major contribution of this work, as it leads to the proposition of an environmental ethics that is no longer based on the paradigm of dominion or stewardship. Rather, we consider an environmental ethics that is based on recognition and sacred care, one in which human beings are called to rediscover the right relationships that were intended by God, in whose image and likeness we are created.

This chapter considers three major observations: the presentation of African identity[2] in relation to the environment; the presentation of the church's contribution with an emphasis on *Laudato si'*; and the dialogue between these two.

AFRICAN PERSONHOOD RECONSTRUCTED

The first generation of African theologians mostly attempted to reconstruct African identity. This work of reconstructing one's identity is critical, as the Cameroonian Jesuit, theologian, and historian Engelbert Mveng observes: "If the creative genius of black people dies, it will be the end of our people. Our survival requires the restoration of our cultural sovereignty."[3] This section will deal with the new way some African scholars suggest looking at Africa and Africans. It is an attempt to correct biases that some Western missionaries and colonizers had about African people to the extent of misrepresenting them. One will notice, however, that in the attempt to reconstruct African identity, scholars have exaggerated and misrepresented the people and their culture.

In his book *African Religions and Philosophy*, John Samuel Mbiti, a Kenyan theologian, introduces a new dimension for understand-

---

2. In this chapter, *identity* will be used interchangeably with *personhood* and will carry the same meaning.

3. Engelbert Mveng, "Black African Art as Cosmic Liturgy and Religious Language," in *African Theology en Route*, ed. Kofi Appiah-Kubi and Sergio Torres (Maryknoll, NY: Orbis Books, 1979), 141.

ing African people. The complexity of their religious experiences is important for understanding who they are. For Mbiti, the encounter with several religious traditions in Africa in recent centuries has had a profound impact on life and identity. "It is religion, more than anything else, which colors their understanding of the universe and their empirical participation in that universe, making life a profoundly religious phenomenon."[4]

People in some African countries or communities celebrate life and events from a religious perspective that should capture our attention in defining African identity in this era. In acknowledging the complexities of the African identity, we should be able to read old practices with new eyes and draw meaning out of them. Such challenges are also raised by the Cameroonian priest, sociologist, anthropologist, and theologian Jean-Marc Ela. He observes that "the meaning of the festival, deeply rooted in the people's mentality and their socio-religious practices, forces us to reinterpret it as a response of faith to the message of the Beatitudes."[5]

Ela shares his strong awareness with the whole community in relation to the responsibility Africans should take to correct the injustices done to their identity. Here Ela addresses the issue of a serious evangelization of African culture, saying, "Today we need to reactualize the Christian mystery within a cultural structure, where 'symbolism expresses the destiny of humanity everywhere as a struggle between life and death.' Both the gospel and Africa require that of us."[6]

African identity is to be understood holistically, in all aspects. Congolese theologian Bénézet Bujo observes, "Africans are traditionally characterized by a holistic type of thinking and feeling. For them, there is no dichotomy between the sacred and the secular; they regard themselves in close relationship with the entire cosmos."[7]

The reconstruction of African identity should not be limited to duplicating African culture as it was ages before Christ. However, we should not speak of African culture by reducing Africa to the culture of today, as if Africa started with the modern age. We need to use the past, as well as consider the experiences of people living in Africa

---

4. John S. Mbiti, *African Religions and Philosophy*, 2nd ed. (Oxford: Heinemann, 1999), 256.

5. Jean-Marc Ela, *My Faith as an African* (Eugene, OR: Wipf & Stock, 2009), 6.

6. Ela, *My Faith as an African*, 43.

7. Bénézet Bujo, "Ecology and Ethical Responsibility from an African Perspective," in *African Ethics: An Anthology of Comparative and Applied Ethics*, ed. Munyaradzi Felix Murove (Scottsville: University of KwaZulu-Natal Press, 2009), 281.

today, to build a bright future for all. The exhortation of the Tanzanian priest and theologian Laurenti Magesa carries weight: "If we are to understand the deep meaning of spiritual identity and to come to terms with its implications for Christians in Africa, we might want to keep in mind the wisdom of maintaining the continuity between old and new realities in human life rather than succumbing to the temptation of creating a radical break between them."[8]

In fact, the concept of togetherness is so important in understanding the African personhood that South African Anglican Bishop Desmond Tutu says, "We are human because we belong. We are made for community, for togetherness, for family, to exist in a delicate network of interdependence."[9] This belonging has a tremendous implication for how we conduct our lives.

The pride of the African people should be visible in their actions and the way they apply the values they hold—from those of their ancestors to ones from their own lives. Environmental protection is one of the critical areas where these values are needed more urgently than ever. The environment becomes the place where African people should express their belonging together to the earth.

RECONCILIATION WITH THE ENVIRONMENT

African identity is only complete when all dimensions of an African person are safe. Bujo correctly observes that "experts now accept that Africans can only be understood in reference to their basic attitude towards life. Likewise, only from this standpoint can their relationship to the cosmos be explained."[10]

The connection between an African person and nature is deeply grounded; it responds to an existential necessity. There is an obligation embodied in the African faith. Nature is sacred. It is a place where their ancestors and other divine spirits dwell. Far from being a commodity to be used, nature is a mystery in the eyes of an African. For this reason, in many African cultures, people go into bushes for the initiation of the young ones; there, the secrets of life are revealed to them. From nature, elders and wise people collect leaves and roots to cure their sicknesses. In nature, they perform rituals. It is under the

---

8. Laurenti Magesa, *What Is Not Sacred? African Spirituality* (Maryknoll, NY: Orbis Books, 2013), 106.

9. Desmond Tutu, *No Future without Forgiveness* (New York: Random House, 1999), 196.

10. Bujo, "Ecology and Ethical Responsibility," 281.

trees that palavers bring about reconciliation. Nature becomes a privileged witness to reconciliation within the human community. Aware of these, Magesa asked the question that would become the title of his book *What Is Not Sacred?* According to Magesa, everything that exists carries spiritual meaning and weight.

In the context of African culture, every person aspires to become an ancestor one day. "The human community in Africa consists of the living, the unborn and the ancestors (the deceased)."[11] However, to become an ancestor, one must live an upright life, as measured by the way one respects the network of relationships one has. Morality is tested according to the way one relates to created nature with a sense of responsibility, recognition, care, and concern for the good of future generations. It is the way one cares about nature that qualifies one to be counted among the ancestors worthy of remembrance. Because nature is the place of an expression of human morality, one cannot mismanage created nature and still be respected by society in Africa. We cannot overlook the point that Francis makes in *Laudato si'* on the importance of the land for indigenous people. The "land is not a commodity but rather a gift from God and from their ancestors who rest there, a sacred space with which they need to interact if they are to maintain their identity and values" (*LS* 146).

Moreover, one should care for nature out of fear of the ancestors who are alive and active in human life and created nature. As Bujo states, "African ethics is based essentially on the community model that includes the living and the dead."[12] The communitarian aspect proves to be very helpful since it provides some influence on those who are morally weak and incapable of giving up some of their privileges to preserve the entirety of nature.

African culture and its religion have much to share with all of humanity. Because created nature is not something external to an African person, care for the environment ought not to be based on utilitarianism. Nature should be appreciated for itself and recognized as indispensable for all life. Wangari Maathai observes that "for many native peoples, such as the Aka of the Congo and other forest dwellers, the forests have not been fearful places that they must conquer or where they cannot go, but their entire world, the source of their food and medicine, clothing, shelter. To the Aka, the forest and indeed what

---

11. Chukwunyere Kamalu, *Person, Divinity & Nature: A Modern View of the Person and the Cosmos in African Thought* (London: Karnak House, 1998), 31.

12. Bénézet Bujo, "Is There a Specific African Ethic?" in *African Ethics: An Anthology of Comparative and Applied Ethics*, ed. Munyaradzi Felix Murove (Scottsville: University of KwaZulu-Natal Press, 2009), 117.

the world calls the 'environment' does not exist beyond or outside the human realm."[13]

African people are not linked to the environment by something of the past. Rather their connection to the environment is the condition necessary for recovering their African identity, surviving, and flourishing. Analyzing the eight United Nations Millennium Development Goals (MDGs) originally projected to be achieved in 2015 (to eradicate extreme poverty and hunger; achieve universal primary education; promote gender equality and empower women; reduce child mortality; improve maternal health; combat HIV/AIDS, malaria, and other diseases; ensure environmental sustainability; and develop a global partnership for development), Maathai calls for a new ordering of priorities. The environment ought to be one of the first priorities (it is now the seventh). According to Maathai, the MDGs cannot be realized if the environment does not sustain all our efforts.

> Achieving each of the eight MDGs depends heavily on healthy ecosystems; but this fact is often overlooked, and the seventh MDG has not received as much attention as the others. In my view, however, it is the most important, and all of the other goals should be organized around it. What happens to the ecosystem affects everything else.[14]

Maathai's writing is the fruit of her mature analysis of the MDGs. The invitation here commits everybody to actions that go far beyond the context of Africa, and echoes what Ela says: "We have not had the same past, but—unquestionably—we shall have the same future. The era of individual destinies is over. Thus, the end of the world has really arrived for each of us, for none can live any longer taking thought only for self-preservation."[15]

CATHOLIC SOCIAL TEACHING ON THE ENVIRONMENT

The church is committed to playing a significant role in whatever constitutes a significant part of human life and activity. According to *Gaudium et spes*, "The joys and the hopes, the griefs and the anxieties

---

13. Wangari Maathai, *Replenishing the Earth* (New York: Doubleday Religion, 2010), 93–94.

14. Wangari Maathai, *The Challenge for Africa* (New York: Anchor Books, 2010), 239–40.

15. Ela, *My Faith as an African*, 12.

of the men of this age, especially those who are poor or in any way afflicted, these too are the joys and hopes, the griefs and anxieties of the followers of Christ. Indeed, nothing genuinely human fails to raise an echo in their hearts."[16] In a very prophetic way, during the Second Vatican Council, the church made a clear turn in saying, "Through her work, whatever good is in the minds and hearts of men, whatever good lies latent in the religious practices and cultures of diverse peoples, is not only saved from destruction but is also cleansed, raised up and perfected unto the glory of God, the confusion of the devil and the happiness of man."[17] This very positive and receptive statement does not tolerate any justification for the church to close her eyes in the presence of challenges faced by human beings, such as the environmental crisis. What did Popes John Paul II and Benedict XVI do?

POPE JOHN PAUL II AND
THE ENVIRONMENTAL CRISIS

Throughout his ministry, John Paul II showed a strong awareness of the environmental crisis and a willingness to contribute to solving this crisis. An example can be seen in his message on the occasion of the celebration of the World Day of Peace, January 1, 1990. Here John Paul II clearly states that "faced with the widespread destruction of the environment, people everywhere are coming to understand that we cannot continue to use the goods of the earth as we have in the past. . . . A new ecological awareness is beginning to emerge which, rather than being downplayed, ought to be encouraged to develop into concrete programs and initiatives."[18] His May 1991 encyclical *Centesimus annus* also denounces human activities that do not bear a sense of responsibility. He saw that climate change is caused by the work of humans. "Instead of carrying out his role as a cooperator with God in the work of creation, man sets himself up in place of God and thus ends up provoking a rebellion on the part of nature, which is more tyrannized than governed by him."[19] Humans have forgotten that our

---

16. *GS* 1.

17. *LG* 17.

18. "Message of His Holiness Pope John Paul II for the Celebration of the World Day of Peace," January 1, 1990, http://w2.vatican.va, sec. 1.

19. John Paul II, *Centesimus annus*, in *Catholic Social Thought: The Documentary Heritage*, ed. David J. O'Brien and Thomas A. Shannon (Maryknoll, NY: Orbis Books, 1992), 37.

powers in created nature are "always based on God's prior and original gift of the things that are."[20]

BENEDICT XVI AND
THE CONCERN FOR ECOLOGY

Caritas in veritate is the first official document from the papal magisterium that contains a clear pronouncement on the issue of ecology. The context in which the encyclical was offered may have contributed to the particularity and clarity of its message on some issues, such as the necessity of caring for ecology. There was a desire to commemorate forty years of Pope Paul VI's great encyclical *Populorum progressio*, issued in 1967. This commemoration occurred amid an economic recession that forced the pope to wait and deepen his reflections on the issue. The recession was a serious crisis that would increase the gap between poor and rich countries. In this context, there was a need to clarify the issues and demand more equality in dealing with the issue of integral human development, which was so dear to Paul VI. Benedict XVI notes, "Integral human development is primarily a vocation, and therefore it involves a free assumption of responsibility in solidarity on the part of everyone."[21]

In *Caritas in veritate*, Benedict XVI returns us to the fundamental truth about ourselves and about our vocation. He specifies, "A vocation is a call that requires a free and responsible answer. Integral human development presupposes the responsible freedom of the individual and of peoples: no structure can guarantee this development over and above human responsibility" (*CV* 17). Responsibility is a very important dimension in human life, and it is only when we are able to live in a responsible manner that we can assume stewardship of the world.

Benedict XVI therefore calls upon each and every person of good will to take our duty of stewardship seriously and to live it in our relation to the created world. He invites us to live as stewards of the world, to wisely use the goods we find in our natural environments. The Roman pontiff states clearly, "Today the subject of development is also closely related to the duties arising from *our relationship to the natural environment*. The environment is God's gift to everyone, and in our use of it we have a responsibility towards the poor, towards future generations and towards humanity as a whole" (*CV* 48).

---

20. John Paul II, *Centesimus annus*.
21. *CV* 11.

Benedict XVI continues by using exegesis to convey the message about why humans must show responsibility in dealing with nature. He writes, *"Nature expresses a design of love and truth.* It is prior to us, and it has been given to us by God as the setting for our life. Nature speaks to us of the Creator (cf. Rom. 1:20) and his love for humanity. It is destined to be 'recapitulated' in Christ at the end of time (cf. Eph. 1:9–10; Col. 1:19–20)" (*CV* 48). This recognition has moral consequences. We must behave in a way that recognizes nature as a mirror of the Creator and permit it to speak God's message to all peoples, including coming generations.

It is in that view that the pope continues, "Human beings legitimately exercise a *responsible stewardship over nature*, in order to protect it, to enjoy its fruits and to cultivate it in new ways, with the assistance of advanced technologies, so that it can worthily accommodate and feed the world's population" (*CV* 50). The idea of stewardship is of utmost importance in the promotion of ecology, for it presents human beings not just as cohabitants of earth with nature but also as responsible for the protection and development of all created nature.

To accomplish his role and mission as the universal pastor, Benedict XVI draws some lessons from what he observes in human relationships with created nature. He notes, "The way humanity treats the environment influences the way it treats itself, and vice versa. This invites contemporary society to a serious review of its lifestyle which, in many parts of the world, is prone to hedonism and consumerism, regardless of their harmful consequences" (*CV* 51). Benedict XVI shares African wisdom and culture, expressed in the truly sacred link that binds together all that God has created, and the call to develop a more harmonious relationship with creation.

POPE FRANCIS AND *LAUDATO SI'*

In *Laudato si'*, Francis offers the most explicit pronouncement on the environmental crisis ever made by a Roman pontiff. This encyclical differs from the classical teachings of the church, and by that virtue, it is a kind of *Rerum novarum* of the twenty-first century. *Laudato si'* is not a doctrinal pronouncement; rather, it is a document that invites Christ's church to remain open to new calls from God in the situations of the world. In this encyclical, Francis expresses his conviction that "the urgent challenge to protect our common home includes a concern to bring the whole human family together to seek a sustainable and integral development, for we know that things can change" (*LS* 13).

The informational quality of this document makes it acceptable for people of good will beyond the boundaries of the church and engages them into action.

In *Laudato si'*, Pope Francis speaks of an "integral ecology" that envisions the environmental problem in a more holistic and integral manner. He acknowledges the fundamental links between the environment, human beings, and God. Francis relocates the environmental debate at the crossroad of every other discipline and dimension of human life. He prudently uses the information from many sciences concerned about environmental degradation, from physics and geology to environmental science.

Among the many key insights, *Laudato si'* appeals for a universal dialogue among all peoples. Francis has the courage to move from a church that has always considered itself as the center to a learning, or "listening," church. He appeals without fear "for a new dialogue about how we are shaping the future of our planet. We need a conversation which includes everyone, since the environmental challenge we are undergoing, and its human roots, concern and affect us all" (*LS* 14). He makes extensive references to other traditions' valuable contributions in the fight against environmental degradation. Francis's urgency comes from his conviction that this situation will not be resolved single-handedly. For the pope, "attempts to resolve all problems through uniform regulations or technical interventions can lead to overlooking the complexities of local problems which demand the active participation of all members of the community" (*LS* 144).

Another key aspect of this encyclical is the call for a change of attitude from dominion to stewardship or care for the environment. This is a huge shift in the well-established anthropocentrism of the church's teaching since its encounter with Greek philosophy. Francis argues that created nature—every single created element—has meaning in and of itself. Such an understanding brings an aspect of recognition that opposes the culture of dominion that human beings have over nature. Francis suggests, "Our insistence that each human being is an image of God should not make us overlook the fact that each creature has its own purpose. None is superfluous. The entire material universe speaks of God's love, his boundless affection for us" (*LS* 84).

Created nature should not be treated in a utilitarian manner. Francis clearly warns that "since the world has been given to us, we can no longer view reality in a purely utilitarian way, in which efficiency and productivity are entirely geared to our individual benefit. Intergenerational solidarity is not optional, but rather a basic question of justice, since the world we have received also belongs to those who will follow us" (*LS* 159). To emphasize his ideas, the Holy Father refers to the wisdom of the bishops of Portugal, for whom "the environment is part of a logic of receptivity. It is on loan to each generation, which must then hand it on to the next" (*LS* 159).

The approach developed by Francis is a holistic approach to created nature wherein Francis places everything in the context of a unique and shared universe created by God. *Laudato si'* urges us to depart from our anthropocentric approach to embrace an approach that recognizes the importance of each creature. The Bishop of Rome wants to develop an integral ecology that extends its horizon beyond traditional limits. According to him, "An integral ecology is marked by this broader vision" (*LS* 159).

Francis courageously abandons the scapegoat culture historically used by the majority of world leaders, who often place blame and responsibility on the poor, the weak, and those without a voice. The Roman pontiff denounces the culture of consumerism, which is promoted by superpowers who have a monopoly on the world economy. Prophetically, the pope remarks that "since the market tends to promote extreme consumerism in an effort to sell its products, people can easily get caught up in a whirlwind of needless buying and spending. Compulsive consumerism is one example of how the techno-economic paradigm affects individuals" (*LS* 203). Ultimately, for Francis, the ecological crisis is both a moral and a spiritual issue that should be dealt with through an attitude shift from the anthropocentric attitude toward created nature to one of awe and wonder. Through *Laudato si'*, he challenges the world's decision makers to face their own responsibilities.

Though the purpose of this short review of the encyclical is not to discuss all of its aspects (just as the purpose of the encyclical is not to resolve all problems), I should mention a few limitations. The pope does not mention the exclusion of women in social life as having an impact on the environmental imbalance. The way the church and the society at large have treated women is similar to the way they have treated the environment. Male domination has a great deal to do with the attitude human beings have toward the environment. Rita D. Sherma states that the pope "refrains from speaking of the injustice of androcentrism that is the cause of the near absence of one half of the human species from leadership in religion, politics, and economics."[22] These limitations should not overshadow the whole encyclical. As

---

22. Rita D. Sherma, "A Hindu Response," in *For Our Common Home: Process-Relational Responses to "Laudato si',"* ed. John B. Cobb, Ignacio Castuera, and Bill McKibben (Anoka, MN: Process Century, 2015), 360.

Sherma says, "*Laudato si'* is a commendable effort: it covers a lot of conceptual territory, it offers many valuable insights, and will, hopefully, bring faith back to the table in the search for ways and means of saving what remains of our natural world."[23]

AFRICAN WISDOM AND *LAUDATO SI'*

As noted earlier, Francis acknowledges the necessity of dialogue among cultures and different fields of science to overcome the environmental crisis that has become a tremendous concern of our time (*LS* 14). In response to this invitation, the African understanding of personhood stands as a valid and suitable partner for *Laudato si'* to contribute to the resolution of this crisis. A quick observation of various African communities, such as the San of South Africa, teaches us that elements of creation are recognized as holding divine attributes and, therefore, should be respected. For the San people, "some physical features of the environment are believed to be invested with supernatural power and are accorded due respect and awe."[24] This echoes the attitude of Francis, who invites us to look at the natural environment as capable of meaning something beyond what we can perceive or even suspect. He says, "Some less numerous species, although generally unseen, nonetheless play a critical role in maintaining the equilibrium of a particular place" (*LS* 34).

One can see in both viewpoints a consistent proposition regarding the kind of relationships human beings should have with created nature, inscribed in the reality of what Martin Buber describes in his book *I and Thou*. For Buber, "the aim of relation is relation's own being, that is, contact with the Thou. Through contact with every Thou, we are stirred with a breath of the Thou, that is, of eternal life."[25] Here we have an invitation to regain touch with created nature so that we can appreciate and listen to the environment—hear its songs of praise to God, as well as the cries of suffering at the abominable treatment by humans. In the same way, we cannot understand relationships outside of our will to see others as ourselves. Here, there is a need for reciprocity and mutual appreciation.

---

23. Sherma, "A Hindu Response," 360.

24. S. A. Thorpe, *African Traditional Religions: An Introduction* (Pretoria: University of South Africa, 1991), 28.

25. Martin Buber, *I and Thou*, trans. Ronald Gregor Smith (Edinburgh: T&T Clark, 1937), 63.

In keeping with this understanding, Francis eloquently reminds us that

a correct relationship with the created world demands that we not weaken this social dimension of openness to others, much less the transcendent dimension of our openness to the "Thou" of God. Our relationship with the environment can never be isolated from our relationship with others and with God. Otherwise, it would be nothing more than romantic individualism dressed up in ecological garb, locking us into a stifling immanence. (*LS* 119)

After a careful reading of the two sources, African personhood and *Laudato si'*, a new paradigm develops concerning the way a true and genuine relationship between humans and the rest of created nature should be enhanced from the human perspective. Inspired by these two perspectives, I suggest that human beings should move to a relationship with nature that is marked by recognition and sacred care. This is the attitude that comes from recognizing all created nature as Thou. Then, in accord with Buber's perception of Thou, human beings will recognize created nature as the Thou that both "makes its appearance as individuality" as well as the Thou that "makes its appearance as person and becomes conscious of itself as subjectivity."[26] This is important, because, in Buber's words, "the one is the spiritual form of natural detachment, the other the spiritual form of natural solidarity of connection."[27]

In both *Laudato si'* and African culture/religion, or ethics, the goal is the transmission of life. To be successful, an environmental ethic must promote life in all dimensions in every creature, including human beings. In keeping with this, Magesa affirms:

The foundation and purpose of the ethical perspective of African Religion is life, life in its fullness. Everything is perceived with reference to this. It is no wonder, then, Africans quickly draw ethical conclusions about thoughts, words, and actions of human beings, or even of "natural" cosmological events, by asking questions such as: does the particular happening promote life? If so, it is good, just, ethical, desirable, divine. Or, does it diminish life in any way? Then it is wrong, bad, unethical, unjust, detestable.[28]

---

26. Ibid., 62.

27. Ibid.

28. Laurenti Magesa, *African Religion: The Moral Traditions of Abundant Life* (Maryknoll, NY: Orbis Books, 1997), 77.

Similarly, in *Laudato si'*, Francis poses the question of life in relation to other beings that are still unknown to us. For him, our actions should respond to the question of whether they promote life in created beings as a whole. In this sense, the Holy Father invites us to a deep reflection on our relationship with the environment:

> It may well disturb us to learn of the extinction of mammals or birds, since they are more visible. But the good functioning of ecosystems also requires fungi, algae, worms, insects, reptiles and an innumerable variety of microorganisms. Some less numerous species, although generally unseen, nonetheless play a critical role in maintaining the equilibrium of a particular place. Human beings must intervene when a geosystem reaches a critical state. But nowadays, such intervention in nature has become more and more frequent. As a consequence, serious problems arise, leading to further interventions; human activity becomes ubiquitous, with all the risks which this entails. (*LS* 34)

The concept of life from the African perspective is not confined to human beings. Abundant life is the goal of African spirituality for everything that exists, including those parts of the natural environment that are not yet known to us. By embracing African understandings and incorporating them into its teachings on the environment, the Roman Catholic Church will be able to develop, with expanded language, a new paradigm of relationships between human beings and the created world, based on recognition and sacred care. This is the only condition under which we will recover our state of being human, as created in the image of God.

CONCLUSION

This chapter, hopefully, contributes to the development of a sound approach to the current environmental crisis. This investigation presents a few selected aspects of African wisdom and the church's teaching, with a particular interest in *Laudato si'*, the first encyclical dedicated to the issue of ecology. My intention is to first acknowledge the fact that something has gone wrong and then locate the origin of environmental degradation from the perspective of the Roman Catholic Church to suggest a possible way to dialogue with African wisdom. This acknowledgment is aimed at creating a new dynamic, a clear identification of actions needed to remedy what can be remedied. In this sense, drawing from his namesake, St. Francis, the pope presents the environmental challenges in the context of our own time to find the solutions.

We have also briefly considered developments in the teachings of recent popes on ecological concerns: John Paul II, Benedict XVI, and now Francis. This brief survey shows a clear move away from attitudes of dominion, in which humans have given themselves the right to use or abuse the natural environment, toward an attitude of recognition and sacred care, which can be drawn from the synthesis between Francis's *Laudato si'* and the understanding of personhood in the African cultural worldview. Francis shifts the paradigm in many ways and leads the Roman Catholic Church from the position of a knowing church to that of a more receptive, listening church.

Investigating this topic brings to the surface the awareness that we are still in the midst of this work. We have learned that, as human beings and as Christians, we have been a large part of the problem of our troubled environment. In the same way, we are invited to become a part of the solution to correct and overcome this disaster. The environmental crisis that was created by humans will not be resolved without great human effort and action. We must accept this reality, show our readiness to let go of our comfortable lifestyles, and protect within the natural environment what can still be protected. This is our sacred duty to God for his gift to us of life on earth.

12

The Concept of Nature from
Rerum novarum to *Laudato si'*

Barbara E. Wall

This chapter, from a philosopher, explores the treatment of the nature of the physical world in CST from *Rerum novarum* to *Laudato si'*. The concept of nature is not easy to understand. It is often identified with the physical world, which is ever changing. With regard to CST, the use of "nature," or *physis*, refers to the physical world. In Plato's *Timaeus*, we find that a craftsman creates the world according to the ideas, or universal forms,[1] which is a kind of internal organizational principle that one might refer to as "the structure of things."

Aristotle's view of nature and natural law provided a foundation for *Rerum novarum*'s retrieval of a Thomistic philosophical foundation for restoring order in the tumultuous, if not chaotic, social world of the late nineteenth century.[2] The language of CST uses the term "nature" to refer to the physical world—a world that has a relationship to God. It does not, however, use the language of "creation" to speak of this world until the CST documents of the late twentieth century.[3] Since

---

1. Plato, *Timaeus* 31b.

2. For treatment of the Neo-Thomistic influences on the early formation of natural law ethics, which provided a conceptual vehicle for exploring the moral guidance for understanding "natural law" as a mandate for the common good, see Stephen J. Pope, "Natural Law in Catholic Social Teachings," and Thomas A. Shannon, "Rerum Novarum," in *Modern Catholic Social Teaching: Commentaries and Interpretations*, ed. Kenneth Himes and Lisa Sowle Cahill (Washington, DC: Georgetown University Press, 2005), 41–71 and 127–50.

3. Cahill provides an important insight: "Since the Enlightenment, however, the rising ideal of human equality has helped theologians challenge received hierarchies. A salient example is patriarchy, supposedly licensed by the fact that woman was taken from man's rib (Gen 2:22), implying that she is inferior and

Vatican II, CST has placed greater emphasis on the role of the Christian in the world. The Second Vatican Council's Pastoral Constitution on the Church in the Modern World, *Gaudium et spes*, invited engagement in the world as co-creators of God's continued presence and life in the church.[4]

The next part deals with the relationship of the natural world to the treatment of women in CST. Several elements are interrelated in this analysis: the common good; the treatment of women as identified solely by their biological role in childbearing and child rearing, which can be perceived as a form of biological essentialism;[5] the relationship of CST to the world of nature; and the role of the church in the formation of all citizens, men and women, to act justly and promote the common good.

---

subordinate. . . . Similarly, the rights of humanity over the natural environment have been moderated in recent decades by theologies of reciprocity, if not equality, between humanity and non-human creation"; see Lisa Sowle Cahill, "Creation in Ethics," in *The Oxford Handbook of Theological Ethics*, ed. Gilbert Meilaender and William Werpehowski (New York: Oxford University Press, 2005), 13.

4. "The document makes a major new contribution to modern Catholic social teaching by presenting more explicitly developed theological grounds for the Church's social engagement than are found in the earlier social encyclicals. . . . These earlier social teachings were almost exclusively framed in concepts and language of the natural law ethic of Scholastic philosophy. One researches in vain the writings of the popes during the hundred years before the council for careful consideration of the biblical, Christological, eschatological, or ecclesiological basis of the Church's social role"; see David Hollenbach, SJ, "Commentary on *Gaudium et spes*," in Himes and Cahill, *Modern Catholic Social Teaching*, 226, 273.

5. In *The Reproduction of Mothering: Psychoanalysis and the Sociology of Gender* (Berkeley: University of California Press, 1978), Nancy Chodorow provides a feminist sociological argument against "biology is destiny" and challenges the prevailing theories of defining women by a sexual division of labor in which "mothering" is important for reproduction. See particularly "The Argument from Nature," 13–30. In "The Theological Study of Gender," a chapter in *The Oxford Handbook of Theology, Sexuality, and Gender*, ed. Adrian Thatcher (Oxford: Oxford University Press, 2015), Tina Beattie analyzes the influence of modern gender studies on Christian theology: "In its engagement with gender theory, theology must ask what is needed to repair the ruptured relationship between language and materiality, and between self and neighbour, without reinscribing bodies within the exhausted sexual essentialisms of modernity. Such questions must also be asked of our relationships with the non-human aspects of creation, for we are becoming aware of how interwoven our lives are with those of the rest of creation. . . . The quest for an incarnational, Trinitarian theology, deeply rooted in the goodness of creation, must attend to the significance of gender if it is to be faithful to the wisdom of its own tradition. Gender theory dissolves the moral certainties and sexual binaries of bourgeois Christian modernity and ushers in a new and as yet unknowable future" (46–47).

The treatment of women in CST follows the Greek philosophical understanding that women are inferior males and identified by their bodies as childbearers and nurturers. Throughout Western philosophical tradition, women have been viewed consistently with their bodies, whereas men are viewed more consistently with their minds.

Women's identification with biological reproduction associates them with the physical world solely based on biology. Such associations are reinforced by a sexual division of labor. In CST, women's "nature" is frequently referred to, if at all, as being different from that of men because of their social roles and biological differences. *Rerum novarum* states, "Women, again, are not suited to certain trades, for a woman is by nature fitted for home work."[6] And women are identified by their roles of childbearing and child rearing. Hence, there is a similarity in the treatment of the world of nature and women as identified with the physical world and biological determinism, which places both in a subordinate status.

This chapter explores the development of these concepts from *Rerum novarum* to *Laudato si'*, with an emphasis on retrieval, continuity, and development, with possibilities for future consideration, especially if a more egalitarian understanding of the integrity of women in their own right can be included as a more integral part of the flourishing of the church and the common good. The importance of Vatican II and its emphasis on an incarnational relationship to the world offers a new lens that affirms the dignity and integrity of all creation. Hopefully, such a lens will enable all to see beyond centuries-old social and cultural constructions, rooted in biological reductionism, of the nature and role of women, and affirm women as equal partners in the work of the church. Vatican II still needs further implementation, and this chapter presents how such inclusion is appropriate for a renewed Christian community that is about the promotion of the common good in all its potential.

THE COMMON GOOD

The common good is not a uniquely Christian concept. It is grounded in Greek philosophy; and, according to David Hollenbach, "for Aristotle in ancient Greece, the common good was the goal of the whole of public life. He conceived of the human being as a social or political

---

6. David J. O'Brien and Thomas A. Shannon, eds., *Catholic Social Thought: The Documentary Heritage* (Maryknoll, NY: Orbis Books, 1992), 30.

animal (*zoon politikon*) whose good is essentially bound up with the good of the *polis*."[7]

In *Rerum novarum*, Leo XIII, defining the end of society, stated, "Civil society exists for the common good and, therefore, is concerned with the interests of all in general, and with the individual interests in their due place and proportion."[8] In addition, references to the common good in *Quadragesimo anno* of Pope Pius XI in 1931 articulate the requirements of the common good.[9]

The most oft-cited text describing the demands of the common good can be found in *Gaudium et spes*: "As a result the common good, that is, the sum of those conditions of social life which allow social groups and their individual members relatively thorough and ready access to their own fulfillment, today takes an increasingly universal complexion and consequently involves rights and duties with respect to the whole human race."[10]

As one can see, the teaching of the common good is focused only on people at this stage of development. The more recent *Economic Justice for All: Pastoral Letter on Catholic Social Teaching and the U.S. Economy* addresses the global common good more specifically, even though the focus is still solely on people. It is understood that the fundamental

---

7. David Hollenbach, SJ, *The Common Good and Christian Ethics* (New York: Cambridge University Press, 2002), 11. Hollenbach explores the Aristotelian concept of the common good in *Nicomachean Ethics* 1169b, and *Politics* 1280b, 6–7, 1281a, 3–4. Jacques Maritain provides a rich analysis of the common good in *The Person and the Common Good* (New York: Charles Scribner's Sons, 1947): "There is a correlation between the notion of the *person* as a social unit and the notion of the *common good* as the end of the social whole. They imply one another. The common good is common because it is received in persons, each one of whom is as a mirror of the whole. . . . Let us note in passing that the common good is not only a system of advantages and utilities but also a rectitude of life, an end, good in itself or, as the Ancients expressed it, a *bonum honestum*. . . . The common good is something ethically good" (42–43). Maritain also implies that any consideration of the common good is concerned with the future.

8. O'Brien and Shannon, *Catholic Social Thought*, 33.

9. Ibid., 94. "Each class, then, must receive its due share, and the distribution of created goods must be brought into conformity with the demands of the common good and social justice. . . . This [common good] embraces the sum total of conditions of social living, whereby men are enabled more fully and more readily to achieve their own perfection." Could this understanding of the common good provide the kind of inclusion necessary to view women as having the same end?

10. Ibid., 181. Pope John Paul II referred to future generations as a justice concern with regard to the common good of the earth. See "Message of His Holiness Pope John Paul II for the Celebration of the World Day of Peace," no. 1, January 1, 1990, http://w2.vatican.va. Pope Benedict XVI referred to "*intergenerational justice*" (CV 48).

rights of each person to a life of dignity are the starting point for a new world order, and the common good is the concrete expression of that order. The common good is a moral good.[11]

On January 1, 1990, in his message for the celebration of the World Day of Peace, John Paul II, reading the signs of the times, addressed the world about the "lack of *due respect for nature*."[12] He also claimed that *"no peaceful society can afford to neglect either respect for life or the fact that there is an integrity to creation."*[13] Quoting the words of *Gaudium et spes*, he affirmed, "God destined the earth and all it contains for the use of every individual and all peoples."[14]

The understanding of the common good is expanded to include the respectful treatment of the integrity of the earth as a component of the common good for all people. The Catholic Bishops' Conference of England and Wales expands the understanding of the common good:

> The Church recognizes that care for the environment is part of care for the common good—the environment is one of the "common goods" which are the shared responsibility of the human race. . . . Those who feel moved to a loving care for the internal balances of nature are responding to a deep religious instinct implanted within them by God. . . . Our environmental "common goods" are not only available for careful use and enjoyment today, but are held in trust for the use and enjoyment of future generations. Public authorities must never treat them as having no intrinsic worth, nor commercial concerns see them merely as sources of profit or loss. . . . Because of this environmental mortgage that the future holds over the present, none of this natural wealth can be owned outright, as if nobody but the owner had any say in its disposal. Each generation takes the natural environment on loan, and must return it after use in as good or better condition as when it was first borrowed.
>
> In recent years one of the prime duties of public authorities has become the careful conservation of this environmental dimension of the "common good." Damage to the environment is no respecter of frontiers, and damage done by one generation has the capacity to damage future generations: these are among

---

11. National Conference of Catholic Bishops, *Economic Justice for All: Pastoral Letter on Catholic Social Teaching and the U.S. Economy* (Washington, DC: Office of Publishing and Promotion Services, US Catholic Conference, 1986), 58.

12. John Paul II, "World Day of Peace," (1990), no. 1.

13. Ibid., 7.

14. Ibid., 8.

the most powerful reasons for desiring the creation of effective global authorities responsible for the common good at international level.[15]

It is important to recognize the transformation of the concept of the common good in CST in the 1990s. However, the focus of the common good and the concern for the "common goods" are still rather anthropocentric in terms of the goods of the earth existing to serve humans. There is little recognition of the integrity of the physical world until *Laudato si'*. There are similarities with regard to the treatment of women in the tradition. In Greek philosophy, the treatment of the nature of women was one that assumed the inferiority of women, and it is not unrelated to our concerns about the created world and the ways we have been socialized to think about the created world in feminine language and categories. A patriarchal world reflects systemic relationships in which men are dominant and rule over subordinate women.[16]

WOMEN AND NATURE

When we explore the meaning of nature and creation, we need to understand the ways we have been socialized to think of the material world and the concomitant identification of women with the physical world. Much of Western philosophy and Christian thought relies

---

15. Catholic Bishops' Conference of England and Wales, *The Common Good and the Catholic Church's Social Teaching* (London: Catholic Bishops' Conference of England Wales, 1996), 25.

16. Sarah Coakley provides an interesting distinction between hierarchy and patriarchy. "'Hierarchy,' like 'power,' is a word much in need of nuanced and analytical reflection. . . . Where hierarchy simply means *order*, then, it is not at all clear that feminism should oppose it. . . . Patriarchy reflects a hierarchical world in which values and judgments are applied to establish relationships of superiority/inferiority." See Sarah Coakley, *God, Sexuality, and the Self: An Essay "on the Trinity"* (New York: Cambridge University Press, 2015), 319–20. Elizabeth Johnson provides a definition of patriarchy as well: "Women's theology uses technical terms to single out oppressive patterns of social and mental behavior. *Patriarchy*, or rule of the father, refers to social structures where power is always in the hands of the dominant man or men. Under patriarchy women never have equal access to power in the social sphere. *Androcentrism*, or male-centeredness, refers to ways of thinking that privilege men; it makes men's way of being human normative for all human beings. In androcentric thinking women are always derivative, off-center, less than human." See Elizabeth Johnson, *Quest for the Living God: Mapping Frontiers in the Theology of God* (New York: Continuum International, 2007), 95.

on the dominance of Platonic and Aristotelian thought. The physical world was bound by contingency and, often, seen as a world of chaos and change; hence, it was somewhat deceptive and unreliable with regard to the higher realms of value and knowing.

The focus of this part is the following: first, the conception of the nature of woman in the ancient world, which was a historical and social creation in which the basic unit was the patriarchal family; second, the views of Plato and Aristotle on the nature of women as inferior males; third, the medieval and Renaissance views of the nature of women and the physical world as a benevolent female occupying a subordinate position in a patriarchal relationship. Such patriarchal relationships of dominance and control were evidenced in how the earth could be plowed, cultivated, used as a commodity, and manipulated as a resource.[17] Such cultural constructs contributed to the establishment of hierarchical and patriarchal relationships that emphasized the superiority of men vis-à-vis women and the justification for a relationship of dominance and subordination of women, as well as the subordination of the physical world, nature, to domination by humans.

Rooted within the Christian tradition is the Greek conception of the nature of woman as inferior male, identified with the world of particular, physical existence and the realm of matter, whereas men are associated with the realm of ideas, or the forms, culture and the creators of history. The role of women is in the domestic realm, whereas the role of men is in the public world outside the home; hence, women in this worldview, along with the physical world of nature, were perceived as inferior and in need of being controlled.

The reason for women's inferiority lies in defect. Aristotle deduced the inferiority of women by referencing their biological differences. Since men are identified with the forms, women are identified with matter. "Women do not go bald because their nature is similar to that of children: both are incapable of producing seminal secretion." This is a deformity in the nature of the female.[18] According to Aristotle, "It

---

17. Celia E. Deane-Drummond, commenting on Aquinas's *Summa theologiae*, q. 92.1–q. 92.4, notes that Aquinas's position on the ontological status of women reflected the patriarchal culture of his time, "affording women a lower status than men" and that "Aquinas held that women were deficient in their reasoning powers." See Celia E. Deane-Drummond, *The Ethics of Nature* (New York: Blackwell, 2004), 186–87, 208. See also Jean Porter, *The Recovery of Virtue* (London: SPCK, 1994), 138–40.

18. Aristotle, *On the Generation of Animals* 784a5–12, quoted in Mary R. Lefkowitz and Maureen B. Fant, *Women in Greece and Rome* (Toronto: Samuel-Stevens, 1977), 6.

is best for all tame animals to be ruled by human beings. For this is how they are kept alive. In the same way, the relationship between the male and the female is by nature such that the male is higher, the female lower, that the male rules and the female is ruled."[19] Aristotle and people like St. Thomas Aquinas contributed to an understanding of rights as a reflection of the nature of things but lacked our understanding of the sacredness, integrity, and equality of women.[20]

The Greek identity of nature is understood as the physical world, the earth, and women. Women were perceived as identified with the physical world—not the rational world, as men were. Such images of women are of the nurturing, homebound mother. The identity of the earth as female also was central to many of the ancients. Women were seen as wholesome and life-giving. Ancient peoples viewed the earth as nurturing: "The female earth was central to the organic cosmology that was undermined by the Scientific Revolution and the rise of a market-oriented culture in early modern Europe. The ecology movement has reawakened interest in the values and concepts associated historically with the premodern organic world."[21]

Carolyn Merchant describes the transformation brought about by the Scientific Revolution. Francis Bacon, considered the "father of modern science," is perhaps a model of the kind of scientific and technological interests that reflect a patriarchal and hierarchical worldview. He claimed that the highest form of human ambition was "to renew and increase the empire of humanity itself over the whole universe of things."[22]

Merchant highlights the "Baconian fashion" of the Scientific Revolution's new method of interrogating nature:

---

19. Aristotle, *Politics* 1254b10–14.

20. See Matthew Scully, "Nature and Nature's God," in *Dominion: The Power of Man, the Suffering of Animals, and the Call to Mercy* (New York: St. Martin's Press, 2002), 287–350.

21. Carolyn Merchant, *The Death of Nature: Women, Ecology, and the Scientific Revolution* (New York: Harper & Row, 1983), xx–xxi. This book is an excellent treatment of dominion over nature from a philosophical and feminist perspective. Merchant continues, "In investigating the roots of our current environmental dilemma and its connections to science, technology, and the economy, we must reexamine the formation of a world view and a science that, by reconceptualizing reality as a machine rather than a living organism, sanctioned the domination of both nature and women. The contributions of such founding 'fathers' of modern science as Francis Bacon, William Harvey, René Descartes, Thomas Hobbes, and Isaac Newton must be reevaluated."

22. *The Oxford Francis Bacon*, ed. Graham Rees, vol. 11, *The "Instauratio magna." Part II: "Novum organum" and Associated Texts* (Oxford: Oxford University Press, 2004), 195.

Scientific method, combined with mechanical technology, would create a "new organon," a new system of investigation, that unified knowledge with material power. The technological discoveries of printing, gunpowder, and the magnet in the fields of learning, warfare and navigation "help us to think about the secrets still locked in nature's bosom." "They do not, like the old, merely exert a gentle guidance over nature's course; they have the power to conquer and subdue her, to shake her to her foundations." Under the mechanical arts, "nature betrays her secrets more fully . . . than when in enjoyment of her natural liberty."[23]

These excerpts from Bacon reflect a philosophical worldview of dominance that affects women and the earth. The use of sexual language employed under the protection and control of men is a paternalistic protection that keeps women in a childlike state of subordination and in need of protection. The use of the feminine references to the earth and the language of conquering and subduing earth/women are not atypical of the sixteenth century and still perdure today. Historically, in the seventeenth and eighteenth centuries, there was an absence of a tradition that affirmed the independence and autonomy of women, as well as any exploration of the integrity of nature and earth. The hegemony of men's control of women and nature decisively disadvantaged both. The androcentric fallacy that is built into all the mental constructs of Western civilization cannot be changed simply by "adding women." What is necessary is a restructuring of thought and analysis that accepts, once and for all, the fact that humanity consists in equal parts of men and women and that the experiences, thoughts, and insights of both sexes must be represented in every analysis that is made about human beings. Hence, if this could be achieved, then maybe we would be able to bring the common good to greater fruition for all creation.

The Greek philosophy that formed our social construction of gender and affirms that women are marginal to the creation of history and civilization has profoundly affected the relationships of mutuality and solidarity between men and women and the natural world. CST should be concerned about this issue at its core. This view has given some people in power a rather erroneous view of their place in civil society—a civil society that is ordained to the common good.

---

23. Francis Bacon, "Thoughts and Conclusions on the Interpretation of Nature, or A Science of Productive Works," in *The Philosophy of Francis Bacon*, ed. Benjamin Farrington (Liverpool: Liverpool University Press, 1964), 96, 93, 99, quoted in Merchant, *Death of Nature*, 172.

The domination of nature is linked to the domination of women. The treatment of the earth in the Baconian view is challenged by many today with regard to recognizing a world of sentient beings such as trees and their relational life.[24] Research on the life of the nonhuman world has called for consideration of our current use of language to describe the natural world. We can learn a great deal from our American Indian communities. Robin Wall Kimmerer provides insights from her Potawatonic tradition:

> I remember paging through the Ojibwe dictionary . . . trying to decipher the tiles. . . . The threads in my brain knotted and the harder I tried, the tighter they became. Pages blurred and my eyes settled on a word—a verb, of course: "to be a Saturday.". . . Since when is *Saturday* a verb? Everyone knows it's a noun. . . . And then I swear I heard the zap of synapses firing. . . . In that moment I could smell the water of the bay, watch it rock against the shore and hear it sift onto the sand. A bay is a noun only if water is *dead*. When *bay* is a noun, it is defined by humans, trapped between its shores and contained by the word. But the verb *wiikwegamaa*—to *be* a bay—releases the water from bondage and lets it live. "To be a bay" holds the wonder that, for this moment, the living water has decided to shelter itself between these shores, conversing with cedar roots. . . . To be a hill, to be a sandy beach, to be a Saturday, all are possible verbs in a world where everything is alive. Water, land, and even a day, the language a mirror for seeing the animacy of the world, the life that pulses through all things, through pines and nuthatches and mushrooms. . . . This is the grammar of animacy.[25]

---

24. Peter Wohlleben, *The Hidden Life of Trees: What They Feel, How They Communicate. Discoveries from a Secret World*, trans. Jane Billinghurst (Vancouver: Random House, 2015), 37–55. Wohlleben considers the forest a social network based on scientific evidence. Celia E. Deane-Drummond provides a helpful and cogent analysis of the relationship between women and nature. See Celia E. Deane-Drummond, "Feminism and the Ethics of Nature," in *The Ethics of Nature* (Oxford: Blackwell, 2004), 186–213. See also Deane-Drummond's "Pope Francis: Prophet and Priest in the Anthropocene," *Journal of Catholic Social Thought* 14, no. 2 (2017): 275–89: "While Charles Taylor confined his definition of social imaginary to the human sphere, the Anthropocene, in bringing the human into the biospheric and geological models of the earth, in effect creates a *bio*-social and *bio*-political imaginary where once held distinctions between humanity and the natural world no longer apply. This has crucial implications for defining moral action" (279).

25. Robin Wall Kimmerer, *Braiding Sweetgrass: Indigenous Wisdom, Scientific Knowledge and the Teachings of Plants* (Minneapolis, MN: Milkweed Editions, 2013), 54–55.

Perhaps we need to explore the possibility of moving beyond the language of a world of objects to be studied to a world of subjects that are all interconnected. The need to release our imaginations to see the world and wonder new possibilities and experiences. This is the call we hear in *Laudato si'*.

Looking at the CST of the nineteenth century and the wisdom it offers on the gifts and nature of women provides a context for understanding the social construction of gender, the similarity of the treatment of women and nature, and the subsequent transformation of women in the twenty-first century. CST's most essential affirmation of human dignity is threatened by a dualistic anthropology and lack of access in the decision making of church policies and traditions that affect all members of the church.[26] We need a new lens and language with which to view the world, and CST could provide this by its commitment to human dignity, solidarity, the common good, and the sacredness of all creation.

AN INCARNATIONAL APPROACH

In the late nineteenth century, the world's workers struggled with poor wages, working conditions that were harmful to the workers, and a worldview that accepted wealth and inequality as natural in society. *Rerum novarum* was a response to the desperate plight of many workers and the fear that workers might be lost to socialist institutions.

Rerum novarum addressed many important social issues, such as a just wage, distributive justice, and the common good. However, when it comes to relating to the created world, a hierarchy of being is reflected in such language that men rule over the earth "since he sees

---

26. In responding to CST's understanding of women's nature, Donal Dorr writes in *Option for the Poor and for the Earth: From Leo XIII to Pope Francis* (Maryknoll, NY: Orbis Books, 2016): "The objection to the position put forward in the various documents I have cited is twofold. First, it is seen as a priori rather than an approach that begins from a study of 'the facts on the ground.' Second, it is claimed that, despite his insistence on equality, [John Paul II's] approach is still shaped by a patriarchal and androcentric mentality. Those who are dissatisfied with the pope's approach hold that the issue of complementarity should be approached not in an a priori way with an assumption that one already knows what the 'ontological nature' of women is. It should rather be addressed in an a posteriori way by taking account of both what anthropology and sociology tell us about gender roles in different human cultures and what modern neuroscience has revealed about the development of sexual and gender differentiation" (300–301). This recommendation is consistent with the methodology of CST and the legitimacy of research from the disciplines cited above.

that things necessary for the future are furnished him out of the produce of the earth. . . . The soul bears the express image and likeness of
God, and there resides in it that sovereignty through the medium of
which man has been bidden to rule all created nature below him and
to make all lands and all seas serve his interests."[27] This is an anthropocentric focus. In addition, the world of the domination of nature is
the realm of men. Women are mentioned in the section on child labor.
Women "are intended by nature for work of the home—work indeed
which especially protects modesty in women and accords by nature
with the education of children and the well-being of the family."[28]

This is a form of dualistic anthropology. In the nineteenth century,
Rerum novarum was reflective of the norm—workers are men, and
women are not—that reflects the centuries-old dualism between the
public and private sectors of society. This ancient dualism is in large
part a product of biology. Women give birth to children; therefore, it is
assumed that women are the *natural* caregivers or child rearers. Such
acceptance is a product of a philosophical anthropology that relegates
wage labor as dignified work, which has rights associated with it.

Gaudium et spes did not emphasize that "women's place is in the
home" and recognized the role of women in the workplace. However, there is still a lingering dualistic understanding of the nature of
women as primarily mothers and responsible for the harmony of family life. "Women are now employed in almost every area of life. It is
appropriate that they should be able to assume their full proper role in
accordance with their nature. Everyone should acknowledge and favor
the proper and necessary participation of women in cultural life."[29]

Lisa Cahill addresses the issue of gender roles in her commentary
on John Paul II's *Familiaris consortio* and points to an ambiguity in his
treatment of trying to provide recognition of the greater independence
of women in the world, while continuing to espouse a role for women
that is predicated on their biology, which reflects a biological reductionism when it comes to understanding the advancement of women:

> Proceeding to the implications for women and society, the pope
> observes that historically "a widespread social and cultural tra-
> dition has considered women's role to be exclusively that of wife
> and mother, without adequate access to public functions which

---

27. Pope Leo XIII, On *the Condition of the Working Classes* (Boston: Daughters of
St. Paul, 1942), 10, 35.

28. Pope Leo XIII, On *the Condition of the Working Classes*, 37.

29. O'Brien and Shannon, *Catholic Social Thought*, 206. See also Dorr, *Option for
the Poor*, 287–308.

have generally been reserved for men." The pope seems to want it both ways, however, when he continues. "On the other hand the true advancement of women requires that clear recognition be given to the value of their maternal and family role, by comparison with all other public roles and all other professions." The pope cautions that women must not renounce their femininity to imitate the male role.[30]

The tradition of CST tends to identify the nature of woman with the activity of child rearing and homemaking. Even in *Laborem exercens*, a document dedicated to human work, John Paul II states, "It will redound to the credit of society to make it possible for a mother— without inhibiting her freedom, without psychological or practical discrimination, and without penalizing her as compared with other women—to devote herself to taking care of her children and educating them. . . . Having to abandon these tasks in order to take up paid work outside the home is wrong from the point of view of the good of society and of the family when it contradicts or hinders these primary goals of the mission of a mother."[31]

Today, the prevailing gender norm that recognizes men as "breadwinners" and women as "homemaker-wife" finds many challenges with the economic realities facing families and the need for both parents to share child-rearing tasks. This is not to diminish those women who choose to care for children and work in the home, as well as those men who take on these roles out of choice or necessity. The point here is a dualistic anthropology that identifies women with the work of the home and with "jobs that involve the sustenance and nurturing of vulnerable life"; in such work "the pope [John Paul II] writes, women 'exhibit a kind of *affective, cultural and spiritual motherhood* which has inestimable value for the development of individuals and the future of society.'"[32]

---

30. Lisa Sowle Cahill, "Familiaris Consortio," in Himes and Cahill, *Modern Catholic Social Teaching*, 374.

31. O'Brien and Shannon, *Catholic Social Thought*, 379. Christine Firer Hinze's "Women, Families, and the Legacy of *Laborem Exercens*: An Unfinished Agenda," in the *Journal of Catholic Social Thought* 6, no. 1 (2009): 63–92, brings much-needed attention to filling the gender gap in CST, which tends to identify the identity of woman with the activity of childrearing and homemaking. Hinze claims that "pragmatic-reconstructionist and liberationist . . . feminisms . . . offer resources for crafting an agenda in support of family and household work that is true to the impulses of Catholic social teaching and capable of upholding so-called 'feminine values,' but which steer around debates about gender" (66).

32. Hinze, "Women, Families, and the Legacy of *Laborem Exercens*," 76.

There is a major concern, here, if women are the repositories of the *affective life*. The affective life is an important ingredient in the spiritual life, especially enabling one to see things differently and enter into the experience of a world of wonder and beauty. The cultivation of the affective life is a human calling—not just a calling for women. The spiritual life is rooted in our affective ability to be open to the experience of God in our lives and to be affected by beauty in all its forms in such a way that enables us to be *touched* by them and respond. It can be a moment of profound transformation.

When *Rerum novarum* was written, nature's resources were seen as unlimited. They were there solely to serve humankind, which can nurture a one-dimensional response. Reading *Quadragesimo anno*, we find a first-time reference to social justice in the context of one class of humans excluding others in benefits (and the call to examine the issue of exclusion in social structures that benefit those in power). There is no specific reference to the world of nature; however, women are understood to be primarily mothers in this encyclical.[33]

Gaudium et spes still reflects a world of unlimited resources and the call to subdue the earth.

> For when, by the work of his hands or with the aid of technology, man develops the earth so that it can bear fruit and become a dwelling worthy of the whole human family, and he consciously takes part in the life of social groups, he carries out the design of God. Manifested at the beginning of time, the divine plan is that man should subdue the earth, bring creation to perfection, and develop himself.[34]

These earlier documents reflect a view of the world that in large measure no longer prevails with regard to the earth.[35] Francis's attempt to read the signs of the times is reflected in his pastoral and spiritual guidance to all. Everything in the world is connected, and he offers a

---

33. O'Brien and Shannon, *Catholic Social Thought*, 58.

34. Ibid., 203.

35. Marie I. George, "Aquinas and the General Precepts for Environmental Ethics," *Thomist* 76, no. 1 (January 2012): 73–123, points out in a lengthy article that Aquinas had no idea of modern science; however, "by caring for the integrity of earthly creation, we help insure that the earth serves its ultimate God-given purpose which is to bear witness to the goodness of God: thriving ecosystems and a greater number of species constitutes a more magnificent representation of God's goodness. By seeking to preserve creation's order and beauty we also help ensure that it serves its purposes of sustaining the human family and of leading the minds of human individuals to God" (123).

vision that reflects a view of creation as gift. We are merely tenants on the land rather than owners.

As we read the signs of the times today, there are many crises that could be raised. Let's just take one that has been significant in our liturgical life: water. Currently, the issue of clean, potable water exists on every continent in varying degrees. In the United Nations' Sustainable Development Goals (SDGs), the sixth goal is "clean water and sanitation." The seriousness of this goal is related to the lack of clean, potable water as a result of the growing salination of fresh water due to climate change, and wasteful and questionable uses of fresh water from streams, lakes, and ponds, which are routinely polluted by industrial dumping and fertilizers used on farms, which are washed away by storm water into local bodies of water.

Since water is a building block of all life, Christiana Peppard writes,

> our blue planet certainly seems watery, but of all the water in the world, 97.5 percent is saltwater, while only 2.5 percent is fresh water. Of the tiny proportion of fresh water, 70 percent is locked in ice caps and the polar regions. Nearly 30 percent is ground-water . . . and a mere 0.3 percent of all fresh water is surface water, or what we tend to think of as the "renewable" water supply.[36]

Surely global population continues to grow. However, John Paul II and Pope Francis frequently remind us of our consumerist way of life and the proliferation of plastic water bottles and wasteful models of consumption. Peppard points out that "affluence drives up consumption; leading the way 'with the largest water footprint' . . . is the United States. . . . Consider meat. . . . To produce a pound of beef

---

36. Christiana Peppard, *Just Water: Theology, Ethics, and the Global Water Crisis* (Maryknoll, NY: Orbis Books, 2014), 21–22. See also Gary L. Chamberlain's *Because Water Is Life: Catholic Social Teaching Confronts Earth's Water Crisis* (Winona, MN: Anselm Academic, 2018), where Chamberlain addresses six contemporary water crises. Also Ronald L. Sandler, *Character and Environment: A Virtue-Oriented Approach to Environmental Ethics* (New York: Columbia University Press, 2007), notes: "At present, people are using and polluting the accessible fresh water faster than it can be replenished or cleansed. Over one billion people lack access to safe drinking water, and over two billion people lack access to basic sanitation. The choices people make about consumption affect the availability of usable water. . . . For example, the Ogallala Aquifer, the largest in North America at around 190,000 square miles stretching from Texas to south Dakota and the source of irrigation for one-fifth of the farmland in the United States, is being depleted at 15 times the rate it is replenished. It has been dropping an average of 3 feet per year since 1991" (59–60).

requires approximately 1,799 gallons of water."[37] Clearly, there is a crisis here.

The relationship between humans and the environment is indisputable. This crisis affects all people and the planet. What recommendations can we find in CST to guide us to become co-creators of God's justice and peace in the world?

Laudato si' addresses the issue of water as one of primary importance.

> Water poverty especially affects Africa, where large sectors of the population have no access to safe drinking water or experience droughts which imperil agricultural production. . . . Even as the quality of water is constantly diminishing, in some places there is a growing tendency, despite its scarcity, to prioritize this resource, turning it into a commodity subject to the laws of the market. Yet *access to safe drinkable water is a basic and universal human right, since it is essential to human survival and, as such, is a condition for the exercise of other human rights.*[38]

Francis is calling all people to wake up from their focus on and infatuation with self to see the world relationally. He suggests that there is an intimate relationship with creation and that the redemption of the person and the universe are inextricably linked. All things are connected in a web of life. For the Lakota people, all things are related in a way that the individual has a kinship relationship to all creatures. Such humble recognition might diminish the widespread feeling of loneliness in the world. It is a spirituality of relationship that calls us to real human development.

Gaudium et spes provided a major paradigm shift in seeing the world as the *locus* for the discovery of God. Vatican II called for an engagement with the world, not a retreat from it. The call for systemic justice was equally important, and we continue to retrieve that commitment in *Laudato si'*. Vatican II reminded all Christians that they have an obligation to work for the transformation of the world, and at the same time, they have a destiny that transcends the political and social world. Such an obligation of justice can only be achieved in securing the common good, which includes all creation. This recognition of such inclusion is the work of *Laudato si'*.

Laudato si' grounds its environmental analysis in a critique of the soul, beginning with a recognition that the earth is suffering. Fran-

---

37. Peppard, *Just Water*, 22.
38. *LS* 15.

cis calls for a change in "lifestyles," which previous popes have also called for. He also calls for changes in "the established structures of power which today govern societies."[39]

Reading the signs of the times, Francis raises "global environmental deterioration" as a moral issue and an important ethical priority. He provides the example of St. Francis of Assisi as someone who

> shows us just how inseparable the bond is between concern for nature, justice for the poor, commitment to society, and interior peace. . . . If we approach nature and the environment without this openness to awe and wonder, if we no longer speak the language of fraternity and beauty in our relationship with the world, our attitude will be that of masters, consumers, ruthless exploiters, unable to set limits on their immediate needs. By contrast, if we feel intimately united with all that exists, then sobriety and care will well up spontaneously.[40]

Vatican II called us to engage the world. *Laudato si'* calls us to boldly love the world. To be open to wonder is an ancient call to allow the beauty of the world to enter not just our minds but our hearts as well. It is difficult for many of us to free up the capacity to see the beauty of the natural world, the beauty of the other, as we live harried lives; and our vision is often one-dimensional. We see, but really don't see. Even the conception of stewardship is a rather one-dimensional approach to the world.

In terms of a spirituality that is more incarnational, we need time for reflection and discernment of the ways we are caught up in a "throwaway culture."[41] Because we have so little time to reflect, we become numb, even to ourselves, and indifferent to the suffering of others.[42]

Four years ago, I was teaching ethics in a maximum-security state penitentiary. The men had all read *Laudato si'*, and I asked which part of it they found personal. A young man immediately answered, "When Pope Francis wrote about a disposable society, because I feel that is what I have become—someone disposable in the criminal justice system." There are many ways people are collateral damage in a society that Francis claims has deified the market. He calls us to see the world differently, which is a challenge, and echoes the words of Patriarch Bartholomew:

---

39. Ibid., 2.
40. Ibid., 5–6.
41. Ibid., 16.
42. Ibid., 25.

He asks us to replace consumption with sacrifice, greed with generosity, wastefulness with a spirit of sharing, an asceticism which "entails learning to give, and not simply to give up. It is a way of loving, of moving gradually away from what I want to what God's world needs. It is liberation from fear, greed and compulsion." As Christians, we are also called "to accept the world as a sacrament of communion, as a way of sharing with God and our neighbors on a global scale. It is our humble conviction that the divine and the human meet in the slightest detail in the seamless garment of God's creation, in the last speck of dust of our planet."[43]

In this one paragraph, we can find the vision for the completion of the call of Vatican II to engage with the world and be about the work of transforming the world in justice and love. It is a vision of hope—and the daily practice of the virtue of hope.

CONCLUSION

This chapter emphasizes the connectedness of everything, and the vision for a sacramental world must include a way of seeing women and the created world as having a sacredness and integrity that is part of the vision of integral human ecology and the further growth in our understanding of the common good. There is a vacancy if women are not included in the decision-making policies, along with the opportunity to share their experiences of living in a church that is slowly beginning to "see" them. So much more can happen if we take *Laudato si'* to heart and begin living it. The common good of all creation is dependent on our engagement and hope in a future for all creation.

The continued retrieval and renewal of Vatican II are implicitly and inextricably linked to the revision of the conceptualization of the earth and women as full participants in an incarnational world. We lost a sense of the earth as sacred with the introduction of dualistic thinking and a dualistic anthropology. Can we move beyond this divide? Do we have the imagination to connect these two realities, the earth and women, in the future of CST?

---

43. Ibid., 9.

13

The Story of a Small Charity for Resettlement of Trafficked People

Margaret S. Archer

Every parish, every religious Community, every Monastery, every sanctuary of Europe, take in one family.

—Pope Francis[1]

This is a simple short story written for those of goodwill who consider making a difference to the lives of those who have survived human trafficking. Motives will differ, but my primary concern is more "how" they go about starting up a charitable venture than "why" they do so. Each individual will have his or her narrative, but what they share is their need to work within the social context of any country, although this account is limited to England. Already, in writing "England," rather than "G.B." or the "U.K.," which are all different, I am signaling the importance of the legal context—however distinct it is— that Janus-like both recognizes the problem of human trafficking but also, paradoxically, both constrains *and* enables voluntary initiatives everywhere—though in different ways—and is particularly tricky in federal states and those with devolved powers of government.

Addressing the context is inescapable, because there is no such thing as "context-less action" in any society or part of it. Of course, sociologists and other social scientists will differ about the relative importance of different contextual elements—from international relations to the

---

1. Pope Francis, "Angelus Address on Restoring Communication," September 6, 2017, http://zenit.org.

unique characteristics of isolated communities; from ethnic relations to relatively homogeneous areas; from histories of internal antagonisms to those subjected to external conquest, subordination, or colonization, including postcolonialism. Those and many more shape the context and confront newly organized ventures with obstacles and challenges, but also with certain resources and a welcome in some quarters and opposition from others. Sometimes these three factors are recognized in advance, and sometimes they are encountered *en route*—or both.

The specific local context of this story is a small historic town in the Midlands, considered to be a "desirable" place to live, predominantly white, middle class, disproportionately elderly and tending to vote consistently center-right. Conversely, it has many community associations and more than a few charities, the gamut of English churches, a university on its doorstep, and a large lake, generous green spaces with playgrounds, and sporting facilities. Nearby is an "industrial" town with more than the national quota of unemployment, destitution, and refugees (given its multi-ethnic character). Whether this new small enterprise for the resettlement of survivors of human trafficking had been mooted in the historic or industrial town, it would necessarily have had to confront the same law of the land when seeking to answer the most immediate "how" question—namely how to get trafficked people to be referred to them?

CONFRONTING THE LEGAL CONTEXT

I wrongly believed that we (and who "we" are will be explained in the next section) would find this easy, given ownership of a terraced house in good condition and decorative order, with fitted appliances, including a wine fridge, a front and rear garden, and located on a street with a mix of young semiprofessionals, students, and retired people. The first bad surprise was the unhelpfulness of the internet websites. Googling "Housing for Trafficked People," or any permutations on this, yielded web pages promoting the good works of a variety of associations, which I had no reason to doubt, but they were not specifically concerned with "trafficking." The same can be said for asylum seekers. In other words, it was hard to find guidance and *one of my abiding criticisms is the absence of a "road map" indicating the procedure and points of contact.* This must present a major deterrent to those wishing to contribute, and who are not part of an almost underground network.

In search of advice, we contacted the Migrant and Refugee Centre in the adjacent town, which was helpful in terms of willingness to share their teaching and advisory facilities but referred only two indigenous cases of destitution. The local district council was also sympathetic, but tried to steer us toward asylum seekers as part of the government's none-too-generous undertaking over five years and without a definite schedule of arrivals. Thus, presenting myself as an ordinary person, offering an empty, rent-free house, and surrounded by a rising sea of need, was getting nowhere. The miniature experiment with "ordinariness" was abandoned.

From our PASS meeting of 2013,[2] we had some contacts. We knew the independent commissioner and some members of the Santa Marta Group, but we also knew of the National Referral Mechanism (NRM) for trafficked persons. Still trying to be an almost-ordinary citizen, I decided to tackle the latter, especially in the knowledge that the Salvation Army largely fulfilled this function. They could not have been more helpful and gave a crash course on "first responders" and the interface with the legal process that has been well summarized in a flowchart on a website for the film company Unchosen.[3] This clear information was publicly available, but not exactly prominent to the general public. What the flowchart makes clear is the tightly interwoven nature of relations between providers, provisions, and progress through the legal system once referral has taken place.

Supplemented by the publication from the Home Office[4] "for Home Office Staff" as "frontline staff guidance," it became clear that the "first responders," twelve of them, played a key role as gatekeepers.[5] Thanks to the Salvation Army having taken and circulated the details I gave to them, the Medaille Trust referred two trafficked Nigerian women, with a child each, and another on the way—somewhat diluting my guilt about having had empty accommodations for four months.

THE MODERN SLAVERY ACT 2015

The passage of this bill by the then-Home Secretary, Theresa May, was almost coterminous with our PASS plenary meeting "Human

---

2. PASS Workshop, 2013, "Trafficking in Human Beings: Modern Slavery," http://www.pass.va.

3. See https://www.humberantislave.com/uploads/8/0/9/0/80905500/nrm_fact sheet.pdf.

4. Home Office, *Victims of Modern Slavery* (Version 3), March 2016, https://assets.publishing.service.gov.uk/government/uploads/system/uploads/attachment_data/file/509326/victims-of-modern-slavery-frontline-staff-guidance-v3.pdf.

5. Ibid., 46.

Trafficking: Issues beyond Criminalization,"[6] and the leitmotif of our "Recommendations: 'Resettlement Not Repatriation.'" The strength and weakness of this act are well summarized by John McEldowney in that volume.[7] This act is hardly an inspirational text because many of its provisions, in fact, predated it (most importantly, the existence and appointment of the independent commissioner and the NRM, established in 2009).

One useful but difficult way to read the act is by looking for absences, and another is by searching for "token presences," such as the possibility of legal and financial initiatives not yet implemented, but which have not been taken up. Furthermore, mention of the prosecuted making compensation is contained in Clause 8(7), and Clause 9(1) clarifies that this would be payable to the victims. Whether or not this has ever been done remains unclear. Clause 41 may allow and support research to be undertaken, but we have no evidence of its initiation in the 2016 Review of the Act. Similarly, Clause 50(1) specifies that the "Secretary of State may make regulations providing for assistance and support to be provided to persons a) who there are reasonable [legal] grounds to believe may be victims of slavery or human trafficking." Beyond the forty-five days for "rest and reflection" with a "first responder," it is impossible for an academic to ascertain if such material assistance has regularly or ever been supplied. Finally, Clause 54(1) enjoins that (each and every?) commercial organization "must prepare a slavery and human trafficking statement for each financial year," covering its supply chains and its own business. Are these reports in the public domain? Transparency is not a prime objective in the implementation of the 2015 act.

Where absences are concerned, the task is easier. This is a bill for the *criminalization* of human trafficking and actually distances itself from the human question of *resettlement*. Indeed, Clause 41 specifies that the independent commissioner's duties *do not include "resettlement"* but are confined to (a) "prevention, detection, investigation and prosecution of offences" and (b) to the "identification of victims of those offenses." Although the term "repatriation" is not used, neither is it specified what happens to victims who might have made a sufficient case for their claims to having been trafficked to be deemed "reasonable" but who fail to sustain that these are "conclusive." They are granted the right to appeal, but the repetition of "assistance to

6. Margaret S. Archer and Marcelo Sánchez Sorondo, eds., *Human Trafficking: Issues beyond Criminalization* (Vatican City: Libreria Editrice Vaticana, 2016).

7. John McEldowney, "A UK Perspective on Human Trafficking: Aspects of the Modern Slavery Act 2015," in *Human Trafficking*, 191–212.

return home" and withdrawal of support imply that their days in Britain are numbered—to fourteen. Most of the text dwells on the definition of practices and on prosecution procedures that are addressed to the police and the legal profession respectively. The existence of bona fide victims of human trafficking and forced labor are the proximate causes of this act, but its provisions for them are confined to the forty-five-day period. There is no mention of further or onward referral, and the consideration of victims' rights is limited to the UN Convention. In all of this, the victims are reduced to objects of malfeasance by their traffickers, but not allowed the role of human subjects in need of resettlement.

If this seems a harsh evaluation of the act, the critical points made are reinforced by The Modern Slavery Act Review of 2016.[8] Produced one year later, it reads like a police and prosecutors manual. This is no accident if the scope of the review is assessed from the agencies consulted,[9] which include none concerned with victim care. There is a repetition of encouragement to the courts to apply reparation orders where assets are confiscated from perpetrators of trafficking to compensate victims. However, numbers of referrals to the NRM represented a 40 percent increase in 2014 with the Crown Prosecution Service supplying most.

It was in relation to the NRM that victim care was addressed at all, but it was concluded that "the support provided during the 45-day period appeared to be appropriate."[10] One police officer expressed his concern that "45 days within the NRM system is not sufficient time to decompress 10 years of incarceration." Another argued that this placed "officers in the invidious position of being able to do little more than recommend Charities to homeless victims for fear of being accused of incentivising the victim to give evidence at trial."[11] To these, the report responded that an extension of the forty-five-day time limit was possible (without giving the conditions to be met). Thus, securing convictions was clearly given priority over supplying care. Furthermore, a brief investigation of two geographical areas to which the review referred showed some enthusiasm in the police for reducing the forty-five days to forty-eight hours!

From the text, it emerges that the triangular relationship between the NRM (now dealing with rising numbers), the local authorities (operating without a clear financial brief), and the NGOs ("picking up the slack

---

8. Home Office, *The Modern Slavery Act Review*, July 31, 2016.
9. Ibid., 32.
10. Ibid., 25.
11. Ibid.

when a victim had been emancipated"[12]) fell well short of a smooth integration. As the independent commissioner stated to the Home Office in January 2017: "The NRM has become a cumbersome process with little coordination among the many stakeholders involved. . . . There is a univocal consensus that the current NRM is in need of reform and development." There is also the humane recognition that

> at present many victims who leave safe houses, after receiving a conclusive grounds decision, do not receive further support and thus disappear off the radar. If a potential victim receives a positive conclusive grounds decision they will be required to leave the safe house within 14 days, which is often not enough time to establish safe and secure pathways to mainstream services (where required). If a negative decision is received, that person will only be given 48 hours to leave safe accommodation. Supporting a potential victim until the conclusive decision is made and then ceasing to support so abruptly could be damaging for the victim and negatively affect their recovery.[13]

Thus, he concludes that a "move-on plan" should be developed by a multi-agency decision-making panel.

Lastly, the above improvements have been fleshed out in a House of Lords Modern Slavery (Victim Support) Bill.[14] It proposes extending "assistance and support" for twelve months after the forty-five days have expired and includes safe accommodation, material assistance, medical and counseling services, and a support worker. This could represent progress toward planned "resettlement," but for the legal confusion if not contradiction introduced by provisions for (successful) asylum seekers during the great wave of the latter seeking the Right to Remain in England as in most of Western Europe—a crucial conjunction to which I will return.

---

12. Ibid., 26.

13. All quotations are from a communication from the independent commissioner to the Home Office, January 10, 2017. Kevin Hyland, OBE, Letter to Sarah Newton, MP, "Identifying, Referring and Supporting Victims of Modern Slavery in the UK's National Referral Mechanism," January 10, 2017, https://www.antislaverycommissioner.co.uk/media/1114/letter-to-sarah-newton-mp-on-the-national-referral-mechanism.pdf.

14. Modern Slavery (Victim Support) Bill, House of Lords, June 26, 2017, https://hansard.parliament.uk/lords/2017-06-26/debates/4A04242D-D399-4CEE-9311-1DCBDC6BA28A/ModernSlavery(VictimSupport)Bill(HL).

THE EXPERIENCES OF "HOUSING, HELP AND HOSPITALITY" UNDER THE LAW

When Adunni and Yagazie[15] with their two young children came to live in our charity's house on November 3, 2016, both had already lodged their appeals with the Home Office against the negative decisions received about their Right to Remain in Britain, despite the acknowledgment that there were "reasonable grounds" for considering them to be trafficked persons. (Adunni had been in domestic servitude for sixteen years and Yagazie used in prostitution for a similar period). A year has passed, and their cases have not yet been resolved.

Adunni's case, for example, was under police investigation in London, where she had given interview evidence as had her trafficker. When I phoned the officer in charge about progress, she informed me that she was about to go on maternity leave and would hand over Adunni's appeal to a named colleague at the same police station. In any case, she added, she believed the trafficker's account of events. By going through Adunni's extensive documentation, I extracted hard evidence that the trafficker's statement was not veracious (for example, she was issued an NHS number in England when aged nine, while he maintained that she had not come to the country until four years later; date-stamped photos of her in his London house were found, providing additional confirmation, and details of parishioners willing to testify in her support had been supplied, but these witnesses had never been contacted). This was sent to the police station in question, but no reply was received. When Adunni telephoned them, they denied the existence of the officer who supposedly had taken over her appeal and also that anyone of her name had ever been on their books. Consequently, her new legal representative has initiated a prosecution against this station, but this cannot restore the years she has forfeited since 2012 when first lodging her case.

Considering the above, soon after she moved into our accommodation, we encouraged her to make use of the legal aid center in a nearby city. New documentation and the robust evidence that had emerged were submitted to the Home Office in relation to the Modern Slavery Act, 2015. A year later, her appeal is still being investigated by the Home Office, five years since she instigated legal action.

Meanwhile, the legal situation has become more complex, given the refugee crisis. Ironically, the treatment of asylum seekers and of trafficked persons is unequal in terms of the financial benefits received

---

15. For identity security, all names throughout the chapter are pseudonyms.

while their cases are under review as is the length of years accorded for the Right to Remain, if they are "successful." Both are less generous in relation to the trafficked! Consequently, Adunni's lawyer recommended that she now make new applications under both headings. This is said to be common practice on the grounds of "gaining the best for the client." An unintended consequence is that the number of live police investigations for trafficking are proportionately diminished (currently standing at a mere three hundred), while those for asylum seekers swell. For Adunni, now with two babies, this means that after five years of legal battles, she currently has three unresolved legal appeals on her hands, is still prevented from working, cannot enroll for accredited training courses with a fees' waiver or concessionary childcare, and has no idea of when this saga will end.

Furthermore, she has additional legal incongruities with which to contend. Counted as a single mother, she lived on £55 a week when she had only one child, compared with £73.90 a week for an asylum seeker in the same circumstances—even after Theresa May had reduced the benefits of the latter category.

But is Adunni a single mother? She had met a young Nigerian man at the evangelical church she attended with her trafficker's family. Once she escaped from their house, they married in a customary Yoruba ceremony. He acknowledges Adunni as his wife and himself as the father of her children, who are registered under his family name. The legal precedent for the validity of their marital status was a Yoruba case in 2015, deemed to be a valid marriage in English law by the Family Court of Law.[16] The paradox is that, although the Home Office has accepted in writing that his extradition is postponed until the outcome of his wife's appeal is conclusively determined, he has no Right to Work now that his student visa has expired and hence cannot support his wife and children. Thus, he is acknowledged as husband and father but denied the legal right to maintain his family.

The main fact toward which these and other circumstances[17] point is that prevailing legislation dovetails badly, and no efforts have been made to reconcile its disparate provisions in relation to trafficked per-

---

16. N v D (Customary Marriage) [2015] EWFC28; http://www.familylaw week.co.uk/site.aspx?i=ed144924.

17. For example, the local district council will neither grant nor deny the waiver of council tax upon the 3H house—whether Adunni is considered a trafficked person or an asylum seeker and legally she is both—even though a waiver would reduce council obligations to furnish scarce social housing for the five families of those coming from Syria, as recognized by the government flying them in as "successful" asylum seekers. We have now been waiting eighteen months for a decision on this matter.

sons and asylum seekers. Instead, the tendency is to pass both the burden and the bills to the voluntary sector. Adunni's £55 is paid by a women's aid charity and was arranged by the "safe house" they left, having been placed there by the NRM; so was the social worker who visits weekly; but Adunni has no statutory entitlements. Without such, she would fall into the category of the destitute and become reliant on housing and other provisions (if available) from a very different charity. The success of this confusing arrangement is dependent on the good interpersonal relations existing between Housing, Help and Hospitality (3H) and the social worker in question.

At the level of state regulatory, as opposed to legislative instruments, the density of prohibitions upon access to assistance for potential trafficked people also intensifies. First, provision is passed down to the local authorities, and when subjects are deemed ineligible by them for free accommodation, to the plethora of voluntary organizations, whose distribution varies from area to area. Thus, for example, we discovered that the government's "Healthy Eating" initiative is not a benefit for which victims of trafficking are eligible while their appeals are still outstanding. Consequently, 3H decided to make a contribution of £20 supermarket vouchers each to Adunni and Yagazie every two weeks. There is no control over what this is spent on, and sometimes the need for Pampers outweighs that for food. In this case, their only resort is to the food banks. The list of their "ineligibilities" is lengthy, and there is a consistent pattern to shift the task of providing something—always less and less—downward.

As a small charity, we are fortunate in having a generous church congregation and the Saint Vincent de Paul (SVP) society; the parish priest has offered a second collection in case of serious need and the SVP responds willingly, for instance, to the need for new school shoes. Nevertheless, we are acutely aware of the number of situations in which our residents are reduced to humiliating pleading (for bus passes, use of the public swimming pool, etc.). Doubtless, there are some who are even worse off that we see living homeless in the adjacent city, but it is unlikely that their experiences included a life of servitude or being sold as their preludes to destitution.

FORMING AND FORGING A SMALL CHARITY

Putting the infrastructure in place was not difficult. A notice in the church detailing furniture, bedding, and equipment that was required yielded more than enough for fully furnishing the house, and parishioners were thoughtful about the needs of babies and young children. Another notice generated a list of those interested in becoming active volunteers. This highlights the advantage of starting up from an established base whose existing network provides ready means of communication and is as close as one gets to a warranty for the personal integrity of the volunteers.

However, we were also aware that meeting the utility bills and, if necessary, paying council tax would be the largest expenditures. For these, we approached the parish finance committee, which "adopts" three charities annually for financial support. Here we met our first real obstacles. First, awareness of trafficking (as opposed to smuggling and asylum seeking) was hazy at best and, in 2016, was not helped by the xenophobia that the UK Independence Party (UKIP) intensified as part of its Brexit campaign. Second, church benevolence had assumed conventional forms: tolerant toward "second collections" for well-known causes; responsive to appeals from visiting priests from developing countries for school building and street children; but otherwise largely confining its activity to an annual cycle of bazaars and the sale of raffle tickets. Although Pope Francis consistently highlights the iniquities of trafficking for any purpose, his message had only penetrated dimly to most. Third, our start-up formula, which we hoped would spread to other denominations, faith groups, and humanist associations, was greeted as a novelty that generated suspicion among a few. One e-mail accused me of a personal "scam" to make money since the property and any equity remained in my name, although it was offered rent-free, insured, and structurally maintained by me as "landlord." I had adopted this approach, hoping that other organizations could find equivalent benefactors because we are not short on minor affluence in this small town. Many e-mails later, with the support of the parish priest, the parish finance committee agreed to our request for one year, and the utility bills were covered. It was hard to avoid the thought that to some the royal priesthood of the laity had been held premature in taking the initiative! The consoling counter-thought was that endless religious orders had met with similar resistance to humanitarian innovations over the centuries.

The volunteers posed a different problem because they were being asked to give something of themselves and their time rather than material contributions. Some were readily forthcoming; half of our trustees were or had been teachers and could envisage the roles they would perform. Others who were interested were frequently older, retired people deterred by thinking they had nothing to give, although it was stressed from the beginning that simple "befriending" was a great gift in itself. Yet others were much younger, well-educated mothers, keen to introduce Adunni and Yagazie to nutritional science, computerized budgeting, and advanced methods in childcare. How could such a disparate group become welded into a working team, one that was acceptable to our residents and could win their trust?

There is no easy answer. Gradually, we started to bed down together. The older and more reticent did seem to realize that a willingness, for example, to sit on the floor and absorb Yagazie's five-year-old boy in doing a jigsaw puzzle was a boon to her and that it could wean Robbie from watching endless television cartoons. The young mothers proved an asset in introducing Adunni's one-year-old to local "mother and toddler" groups and exploring free access to junior gymnastics, swimming, and out-of-school activities for Robbie. Nearly all were generous in using their cars to take whoever needed it into the bigger city for legal, hospital, and educational appointments as well as to the cheaper outdoor market. New exchanges grew organically, such as baking together and dressmaking. No, it was not perfect. There were the usual abrasions, personal preferences, and the reverse. An element I had not foreseen in advance was that in a terraced cottage, the visit of a single volunteer usually meant six people occupying the one sitting-room and quite a volume of noise and a variety of simultaneous demands for attention. Getting Robbie accustomed to turning off the television did help.

WHERE WE WENT WRONG

The first three months. From the start, our expectations were oversimplistic. Effectively, we assumed that, having a small house to themselves and the freedom of a safe (low-crime-rate) historic town, Adunni and Yagazie would grasp this new opportunity and want to explore. We took them on long walks to show them the facilities: the parks, playgrounds, lake, and ruined castle, as well as the charity shops, two supermarkets, a farmers' market, schools, the public library, health center, dentist, food bank, office bureau, and post office, with running commentaries on their accessibility, expense, and quality. Yet, day after day, in good weather for November, any volunteer who called found them huddled in the sitting room with lights on and blinds down.

It is correct to call the experiences they had been through ones of "domination," which characterizes modern as it did ancient slavery.[18]

---

18. Margaret S. Archer, "Being Trafficked to Work: How Can Human Trafficking Be Made Unsustainable?," in *Sustainable Humanity; Sustainable Nature: Our*

However, what we had not appreciated was that domination entails minute controls as well as brutal enforcement, and that control induces agential passivity. To be passive, to do nothing, is an ingrained attitude, and that not to initiate action(s) is to be innocent of infringing prohibitions, even those that had not been verbalized. Conversely, to be "active" was to display initiative, if not worse. On their part, we the volunteers were initially seen as replacement authority figures, and they awaited our instructions.

Equally, the parishioners had given them a warm welcome with a mountain of good quality (used) clothes and toys as well as useful gifts. My first surprise was that these young women did not scavenge this mountain for things needful or attractive, but mannerly took a few items that were readily observable. Repetitions of, "It's all for you— take what you want," merely resulted in multiple trips back for more. Equally, when Olubunmi's first birthday came several weeks later, her father arrived with a special cake, but so did several parishioners! We may have been the "new authorities," but we were also bearers of gifts—something that Christmas only exacerbated. Obliviously, we were intensifying their trafficked passivity, if in a kinder mode.

My own wake-up moment came over the issue of light bulbs! When one died, they simply told me so with the fairly obvious implication that I would supply replacements. I gave in the first time (it might have been an old bulb), but on the second occasion stated firmly that this was a normal event and normal families had to budget for it. However, a regular pattern soon emerged in which a request for something routine was the last question routinely asked as I was departing! They knew I owned the house, which could not be hidden (local council demands, etc.) and I was on the way to becoming "Big Boss," but now with role reversal; they requested, and I was supposed to respond appropriately.

It was the reality principle that rectified this situation. They needed food and baby items, for which they had to exit the house and make choices. Yet, we failed to understand the novelty to them of what we took for granted. A perverse effect of one volunteer's generosity was that she gave supermarket vouchers for £10 to a value of twenty times that. A frequent question on the doorstep became: "Has Anna left us any vouchers this week?" Vouchers had been reified into substitute purchasing power, divorced from earnings or benefits. It was necessary to tell them that when the magic vouchers had run out there was no "money tree."

Responsibility, ed. P. S. Dasgupta, V. Ramanathan, M. Sánchez Sorondo (Vatican City: Libreria Editrice Vaticana, 2015).

The second three months. As volunteers/trustees, we had monthly meetings where some of our younger members could present their strategy for combatting domestic passivity. Undoubtedly, they were correct, for example, in condemning the purchase of fizzy drinks on both dental and budgetary grounds. However, their production of a spreadsheet indicating spending priorities out of £55 a week was deemed too directive and patronizing to implement and contradicted our aim of encouraging them to assume personal autonomy. In any case, this proposal sailed too close to a domestic version of postcolonialism: What did we know about their eating preferences? Why did some volunteers talk about "African foods" as if there were not major variations within the British Isles? Why was a significant amount allocated for (nonprescribed) junior medication? This contributed to some rifts within the group. However, it also meant that some were being domineering and discounting that Adunni had cooked for a family of six for fifteen years. What we gradually learned was *how* to respond relationally to requests. Our "English" teacher, for example, replied to Yagazie's question, "How did you bake that cake?" by saying, "Let's make one together next time."

Meanwhile, their two legal appeals for the Right to Remain were slowly but imperceptibly moving through the Home Office system. Finally, I began phoning the London police station to discover where Adunni's case had reached. Realizing how important our intervention was, she voluntarily gave me her large file relating to her appeal over the last two years (the average waiting time for a decision is around eight months). This not only provided hard evidence but the realization that there is no neat division of labor between legal aid and its executors and resettlement and its volunteers. Not only may we be in for the long haul, but to be of help, we must be willing to move outside our zones of comfort, competence, and confidence to be of what aid we could.

WHAT PERHAPS WE GOT RIGHT

The last six months. Conversation analysts regularly reminded us that the central feature of dialogue is "turn taking." But that assumes many forms. Frequently, "question and answer" was necessary, as in "Is the central heating working properly?" or "Is the garden door still sticking?" But there is an equally crucial factor in developing human exchanges beyond the above necessities, and this is reciprocity (tempered by legitimate reticence). Without doubt, we volunteers were fascinated to know the histories of our survivors but, fortunately, our "middle-class" manners saved us all from blunt voyeurism. Interrogation was out; we all accepted this. But sometimes, questioning was unavoidable; for example, in completing a form for the local authority about the waiver of council charges, it was necessary to specify the duration and type of forced labor they had undergone. However, we need not be the questioners. In this instance, distancing was possible by encouraging them to fill in their own forms.[19] Then, it was easy enough to ask, "May I just check that we've covered everything?"

There were many lessons that carried over from interviewing techniques in social science. Personally, I had always found "ticking boxes" to be unrevealing. Instead, the lead given by Elizabeth Bott[20] and later, Doug Porpora[21] had been indispensable to my in-depth interviewing for my trilogy of books on personal reflexivity. The subjects were fellow human beings, and a fruitful dialogue ensued only if they were met as such. If the interviewees raised examples involving hair care, car maintenance, child birth, political demonstrations, or keeping a dog, I would share my stories on any and all such topics—with amusing anecdotes, if possible. The same applied here; our tenants had suffered enough from coercive hierarchical relations, and this was the time to meet them on the horizontal level of our common humanity. It is always amazing how much background information is conveyed through this "chatter." For instance, this is how I learned about the "loose" usages of the titles "Aunties" and "Uncles" by both Yoruba and Igbo, unconfined by genealogy, but playing a crucial part in the process of trafficking by means of "wooing" (convincing the victim's family that they had the young person's interests at heart). It also spills over into the terminology used by Nigerian traffickers, who differentiate the "Big Mama" from the "Little Mama" to designate different strata in the distribution of authority.

Nevertheless, it is sometimes unavoidable for volunteers to pass judgments, either individually or collectively. It has been mentioned that the parish finance committee initially paid for utility bills. When our treasurer noted that gas and electricity consumption went up month by month, without the usual summer reduction, and that sitting-room lights were on all the time, this could not go unmentioned;

---

19. We were greatly helped by their fluency in spoken and written English, given the length of time they had spent in England.

20. Elizabeth Bott, *Family and Social Network* (London: Tavistock, 1971).

21. Douglas V. Porpora, *Landscapes of the Soul* (Oxford: Oxford University Press, 2001).

it may cost our residents nothing, but this subtracted from the parish's generosity to other causes *inter alia*. In these circumstances, we presented the case straightforwardly, agreeing in advance that the newborn baby had required more warmth, but now that she was thriving at three months old, every effort should be made toward reductions. We mentioned our own attempts at home financing and that social housing often had coin-in-the-slot meters. The next bill is awaited, but no offense appeared to have been taken, perhaps attributable to the relationships already established and the tact of our treasurer.

The summer months were an opportunity to encourage them out of the house and to engage in virtually free outdoor activities as opposed to shopping. Sadly, neither was a nature lover nor fond of walking. Expeditions were limited because of the need for a car big enough to accommodate five people plus the driver (some were young children, which meant fitting baby seats) or driving in convoy. However, both were good mothers and would go more than an extra mile for their children. Our teachers came into their own with local knowledge of schools running summer activities for children with working parents; one volunteer (who had protested she had nothing to offer) turned out to know about activities (fairs and festivals) in local parks and took them there for picnics; the nearby swimming pool gave Robbie a week's crash course. Such was his enjoyment that we immediately enrolled him in weekly lessons after school this autumn term and put him on the list for junior gymnastics.

However, some of these were ambiguous experiences. One local school offered an occasional day trip to some attraction, but Yagazie was reluctant to let her son out of her sight. We had to disappoint him by appreciating that, with his mother forty years old and having been through the death of her daughter at three weeks old, Robbie possibly represented her one achievement in life. Yet Yagazie was more complex than we anticipated. She envisaged a future career as a trained care giver in a care home, for which she seemed very well suited. After offering herself as an unpaid auxiliary in the plentiful such homes within this small town, but without success, she took up voluntary work in a charity shop for the mentally handicapped during school hours, arranged on her own initiative. Thus, we learned to take joy in surprises. After all, we were there only to supply an open door to opportunity, not to take the credit for every use made of it.

Finally, we had to face the fact that we had two families living together in one small house. Prior to being referred to us, they knew one another only by sight and had occupied different buildings owned by the first-stage care givers. They are very different people, with different trafficking experiences, different Nigerian backgrounds, and different aspirations and needs. The children got on extremely well, and Robbie was very affectionate toward his young "sisters." However, what was fun to him—building vast structures from his presents of Legos—was a carpet covered with small pieces of plastic that Olubunmi could pick up and swallow. Domestic routines were and had to be gradually developed.

However, what Adunni and Yagazie shared in common was the black cloud of Home Office inertia and the constant awareness of being blocked by legal status or poverty from seizing opportunities. Not surprisingly, this resulted in constant anxiety, whose outlet was to quarrel frequently with each other over trivialities and then to retell everything to one or more of the volunteers. We recognized this as displacement activity but were relieved to find that such antagonism spiked after a few days and then disappeared—until the next time. The relief was that no lasting relational harm seemed to be accumulating, any more than with students who are sharing living quarters. Perhaps they will not remain as friends once they leave, but meanwhile, both reiterate how fortunate they are to have the house; they keep it immaculately clean and are acquiring the self-control not to take every feeling of depression out on the person with whom they temporarily live.

CONCLUSION

This has been a short story about Structure, Agency, and Culture (SAC), and every sociological account, even at the micro level, necessarily comes in a SAC if it is to aspire to adequacy.[22] To attempt a brief, honest summary of the complex relations between these three factors, two relationships stand out. On the one hand, the structural machinery put in place in Britain for dealing with trafficked persons is far from optimal and still overpreoccupied with criminalization rather than resettlement. The legal context is one that is dilatory, the solicitors representing victims are too few, and in our experience police investigations dovetail badly with court procedures and their need for accurate information. Finally, the burden is passed too readily to voluntary organizations that do not receive the necessary funding or clear guidelines about expectations or entitlements for the victims.

---

22. Margaret S. Archer, "Social Morphogenesis and the Prospects of Morphogenic Society," in Margaret S. Archer, ed., *Social Morphogenesis* (Dordrecht: Springer, 2013).

On the other hand, crude cultural differences did not play as big a part, especially in this white, middle-class small town, as we at 3H had feared possible. Despite the sociologists' (quite brief) affair with so-called identity politics, neither of our residents accentuated being African, Nigerian, or members of its main divisions into Yoruba or Igbo. Perhaps a perverse but positive effect of their long periods as trafficked people had been to give them a good command of English, the anticipation of remaining here, and the same basic conversancy with our institutions as most British citizens. As one of the few African members of our church congregation put it, "Thank God, for what you have done; I feared there would be more racism here." So did I after the Brexit vote, but when the three children were baptized during Sunday Mass, the faithful got to their feet and applauded.

That brings us to agency and the dependence of all things social on "activity dependence" and, often above all, on human relations. We at 3H had everything to learn and no personal experience on which to draw! First, we had to learn how to work together, and it took time to recognize that, genuinely, everyone did have something to contribute and to respect. Second, we had to learn to live with individuals' other commitments and accept that these were just as important as our own. Finally, we had to forge individual and collective relationships with Adunni and Yagazie, to take them where we found them, and to assist them in where they wanted to go. Most of us were somewhat disconcerted, for example, that they did not plan food shopping together, cook together, or eat at the table together (indeed, Robbie preferred the floor). However, our aim was never to impose ergonomic efficiency, and we all slowly learned to "live and let live." Now, despite our stumbling ineptitude, we hope that we can stimulate other churches and associations in our small town to join in similar initiatives, for which there is no blueprint and everyone has to learn as they move forward in goodwill.

But, for our first test, we were blessed with two young, resilient women, with a determination to forge a life of their own and for their children in this country. Trust is often misrepresented in the social sciences as a predicate for diverse groups working together, but first it has to be generated between them, and it can later degenerate among them. Our task, beginning from ground zero, was to put ourselves and our survivors together in a relationship that fostered the emergent property and power of trust and produced further relational goods. This is demanding on both parties—in both words and deeds—but without it, nothing constructive can get off the ground.

Lessons were learned or implicitly recognized from this small experience. There are powerful messages about the nature of law reform and the achingly slow process of making legal norms and rules address a pressing social problem. The policy making and legal frameworks matter and have direct impacts on trafficked individuals. Proposals contained in the Modern Slavery (Victim Support) Bill (HL Bill 4 2017–19), a private member's bill that received its second reading on September 8, 2018, and is now in committee, are worthwhile. The bill provides a statutory basis for support with a legal duty to ensure that any potential victim of modern slavery will be granted assistance and support, with temporary admission into the United Kingdom for a period of reflection and recovery of up to forty-five days. This would also provide a time frame for the status of a victim of slavery to be determined by the requisite authority, namely, the National Crime Agency's Modern Slavery Human Trafficking Unit and the Home Office Visas and Immigration departments. After the initial forty-five-day period, a "grant to remain" visa for a further twelve months would be available with further assistance and support provided. The terms of the bill include broadly defined support, such as safe and appropriate accommodation; material assistance, including finance; medical advice and treatment; counseling; a support worker; and translation services, as well as help with specialist legal advice and assistance including, where necessary and preferred, help with repatriation.

Such a range of support is all important and reflects the needs of the trafficked person. Unfortunately, progress is too often too little and too late. The Modern Slavery Act 2015 was a necessary first step, although with too much emphasis on criminal prosecutions. Lessons gained over the past two years have shown that, while prosecutions are desirable, they are rare. Despite the act, victims remain vulnerable and, in many cases, are left in a legal vacuum reliant on scarce resources and challenges to access specialist legal advice. This problem has been exacerbated by legal aid cuts. Voluntary organizations do their best but are under increasing pressures because of limited resources. Currently, the mechanisms for identifying victims and providing support leaves them with no formal legal immigration status or rights. Consequently, there are instances of victims reduced to destitution or continued enslavement. Authorities are perceived by victims as unhelpful and, at times, hostile. Finding a pathway to full participation in society is random and left to luck rather than sound procedures. The lack of support means that making ends meet can be a daily struggle, especially when confronted with a new language, domestic culture, and, in many cases, the lack of the necessary documentation to progress their lives and educate their children to their full potential.

Undoubtedly, at some stage in the future, the Modern Slavery Act should be the subject of postlegislative scrutiny to determine how it has worked. In the meantime, the needs of victims are critical, especially with increasing numbers being trafficked in what is now a lucrative trade. Ignoring victims comes at great cost, as properly protected, they may provide the necessary evidence to aid the detection of the planners and directors of human trafficking. Legislative solutions are important in taking matters forward, but no one should be in doubt that legislative quick fixes may salve the consciences of politicians and facilitate elections but rarely do they deliver all that is needed. The Modern Slavery Act has revealed the extent of the problem and unearthed the real human need for better protection for victims. It is our humanity that requires this need to be addressed. Individual efforts may make a difference, while accepting that there is no quick fix, but a full-scale consideration of the needs of the victims of human trafficking in the context of simplifying the law and providing trafficked victims with at least the same rights as asylum seekers is an urgent necessity.

14

The Lived Experience of the Faithful

*Annie Selak**

How might church teaching reflect the lived experience of the faithful? With the 2014 and 2015 synod on the family and the resultant apostolic exhortation, *Amoris laetitia*,[1] this question has gained new relevance and urgency. To address this question, we turn to what may be an unlikely source: American case law. The central role of narrative and experience in American case law provides an example of a system that straddles universal and particular demands, all while grounded in lived experience.

In describing the similarities between law and literature, Paul Gewirtz assesses that both "attempt to shape reality through language, use distinctive methods and forms to do so, and require interpretation."[2] The same can be said of church teaching, for it also shapes reality through language, uses distinctive methods and forms such as encyclicals and apostolic exhortations, and necessitates interpretation. This study puts church teaching in conversation with the examination of narrative and law. Might it be possible for church teaching to include narrative? The answer to this question is far from straightforward. This study illuminates the major contributions and limitations of this proposal, analyzing ways that church teaching might incorporate aspects of narrative that are central to law.

* The author acknowledges and is grateful to M. Cathleen Kaveny and Matthew A. Shadle for their helpful comments in the development of this chapter.

1. Pope Francis, *Amoris laetitia*, http://w2.vatican.va.

2. Paul Gewirtz, "Narrative and Rhetoric in the Law," in *Law's Stories: Narrative and Rhetoric in the Law*, ed. Peter Brooks and Paul Gewirtz (New Haven, CT: Yale University Press, 1996), 4.

To ground this examination in practice, this chapter uses *Amoris laetitia* as a case study. Its focus on the role of the family, as well as its recent issuance, makes it ripe for examination. Given this context, the study proceeds in five parts. First, we explore *Amoris laetitia* as the context for this study. Next, we examine law and narrative, seeking to define terms and trends in the American legal system. We give similar treatment to church teaching, examining what constitutes church teaching and significant theological themes. With this background established, we explore the benefits and liabilities of including narrative in church teaching. Finally, we assess the feasibility of this proposal through imagining methods for including narrative in the synodal process and *Amoris laetitia*, guided by a practical theology lens. Hopefully, this study will lift the multitude of voices in the church—voices that are currently missing from church teaching.

A CASE STUDY: *AMORIS LAETITIA*

Amoris laetitia was promulgated on March 19, 2016, and released on April 8, 2016. This apostolic exhortation came at the conclusion of the extraordinary synod of bishops on the pastoral challenges to the family in the context of evangelization, popularly known as the "synod on the family." Twice over two years, Octobers 2014 and 2015, the synod of bishops gathered to discuss issues related to challenges and graces of family life in the modern world. Five months after the conclusion of the synod, *Amoris laetitia* was promulgated, becoming the most recent document to contribute to church teaching on the topic of family life.

Of particular interest in this apostolic exhortation is the role of experience. Chapter 2, entitled "Experiences and Challenges of Family," opens with this paragraph:

> The welfare of the family is decisive for the future of the world and that of the Church. Countless studies have been made of marriage and the family, their current problems and challenges. We do well to focus on concrete realities, since "the call and the demands of the Spirit resound in the events of history," and through these "the Church can also be guided to a more profound understanding of the inexhaustible mystery of marriage and the family." I will not attempt here to present all that might be said about the family today. Nonetheless, because the Synod Fathers examined the situation of families worldwide, I consider

it fitting to take up some of their pastoral insights, along with concerns derived from my own experience. (*AL* 31)

In many ways, this opening paragraph affirms the role of experience. Referring explicitly to experience, as well as "concrete realities," Pope Francis affirms the need for church teaching to be grounded in reality. Yet, this paragraph also reveals pitfalls of the current approach. Francis draws on his own experience, a method that is natural and helpful, yet inherently limited. He also references the bishops' examining "the situation of families worldwide," but this examination was limited to surveys and unrepresentative speakers, aspects that will be examined in depth in the third and fourth sections of this chapter. What might it look like for a section on experience and challenges in the family to be grounded in the narrative of families throughout the world? How could real stories of the faithful be included in this document? This chapter addresses these questions, imagining possibilities for church teaching, such as an apostolic exhortation, to include narrative and evaluating the contributions and limitations of such a move.

LAW AND NARRATIVE

At the outset, it is helpful to define terms related to common law and narrative. Theologian and legal scholar M. Cathleen Kaveny defines common law as "a body of legal norms that is developed by judges over time, more or less organically, as individual judges decide the particular cases and controversies brought before them."[3] Beginning in England in the Middle Ages, King Henry II established a legal system with the aim of unification and integration. Itinerant judges traveled and decided cases based upon the king's law rather than local custom, giving rise to common law.[4] Through colonialism, common law spread throughout the empire. Kaveny emphasizes the important contribution of common law, stating, "The common law tradition is not only broadly influential, it is also conceptually rich. It offers a complex and multifaceted tradition of moral reflection in which norms of justice and norms of practical rationality are deeply intertwined."[5]

---

3. M. Cathleen Kaveny, "Law and Christian Ethics: Signposts for a Fruitful Conversation," *Journal of the Society of Christian Ethics* 35, no. 2 (Fall/Winter 2015): 5.

4. Thomas Alan Lund, *The Creation of the Common Law: The Medieval "Year Books" Deciphered* (Clark, NJ: Talbot, 2015).

5. Kaveny, "Law and Christian Ethics," 5.

Common law extends throughout the world, yet the focus of this study is secular law in the United States. In particular, this study considers the role of the judicial opinion. Gewirtz describes the three primary functions of a judicial opinion: "First, to give guidance to other judges, lawyers, and the general public about what the law is; second, to discipline the judge's deliberative process with a public account of his or her decision, thus deterring error and corruption; and third, to persuade the court's audiences that the court did the right thing."[6] Importantly, the judge explains the logic of the decision rather than simply issuing an answer. Gewirtz continues, "The opinion usually ends with the words 'It is so ordered,' emphasizing the coercive force that judges wield. But the written justification in the body of the judicial opinion is what gives the order its authority."[7] The source of authority comes through the entire opinion, including the attached narrative. This study focuses on two essential attributes of the judicial opinion: rhetoric of continuity and experience.

Judges often engage in rhetoric of continuity, seeking to place their opinion in line with the larger tradition. Gewirtz explains, "In their dominant rhetoric, judges typically try to root a new decision in some text that precedes the decision of the case at hand—the text of the Constitution or a statute or a prior judicial ruling. In this rhetorical mode, courts justify their actions as compelled by preexisting law, or at least closely continuous with it, even when a break is occurring."[8] Further, an important feature of judicial rhetoric is a sense of cohesiveness matched with inevitability. Peter Brooks explains, "Courts must attempt to present their opinions as seamless webs of argument and narrative. The story of the case at hand must be interwoven with the story of precedent and rule, reaching back to the constitutional origin, so that the desired result is made to seem an inevitable entailment."[9] This rhetorical style signals the importance of continuity and tradition in American law.

Given that cases are based on stories and not abstract rules, the judicial opinions serve as pivotal contributions to tracing continuity. Kaveny explains, "It would be fair to say that the narratives incarnate the law—the legal tradition has its life in the movement from case to case. When asked to reflect on the state of the law on a current topic, lawyers and laypeople alike tend to think of the 'rule' articulated

---

6. Gewirtz, "Narrative and Rhetoric in the Law," 10.

7. Ibid.

8. Ibid.

9. Peter Brooks, "The Law as Narrative and Rhetoric," in Brooks and Gewirtz, eds., *Law's Stories*, 21.

across cases. But it is just as important to think in terms of 'characters' and 'roles.' It is people who are incarnate—not rules."[10] Narratives, despite being particular, are woven together with other narratives to connect and deepen the tradition, illustrating the ability of narrative to advance a universal claim. This quality will become very important in evaluating the benefits of including narrative in church teaching. The particularity of people, characters, and roles is a central attribute of law, to which we now turn.

Cases are not hypothetical but, rather, real accounts of the lived experience of persons. Kaveny explains the importance of this attribute:

> The crucial features of that accountability follow from the fact that law's narrativity is not realistic narrative (pace Hans Frei); rather, it is real narrative. No hypothetical situation imagined in a seminar room can match the three-dimensional texture of an actual case, nor replicate the multitude of overlapping connections between the general and the specific, the traditional and the innovative. Precisely because the narratives of the common law are real and not merely realistic, the situations these narratives grapple with reveal the strengths and weaknesses of human nature as manifested in actual human beings living in particular times and places.[11]

The connection of law with lived experience extends beyond the case to become part of the tradition. The names that populate the American legal system—Dred Scott, Jonas Yoder, Al Smith, Mildred and Richard Loving, Ernesto Miranda—are rooted in the lives of real, actual people. Kaveny underscores the beneficial aspects of the particularity of narrative, explaining, "By attaching names to cases, the common law tacitly presupposes that particular human persons stand at the center of the relevant moral and social analysis. As the Dred Scott case suggests, the institution of slavery is not understandable apart from its effects on the lives of unique individuals, people like Mr. Scott and his family."[12] In addition, the narrative is attached to the case and follows the case, allowing future generations to read the narrative in ways that may not be apparent to modern eyes.

This brief overview of the role of narrative in American case law highlights many of its benefits. The particularity of narrative,

---

10. Kaveny, "Law and Christian Ethics," 9.
11. Ibid., 6.
12. Ibid., 11.

grounded in the actual experience of persons, is woven together with other concrete situations to create an overarching legal system. This relationship between the particular and universal is a major contribution of the American legal system to the examination of using narrative in church teaching.

CHURCH TEACHING, TRADITION, AND THEOLOGY

It is helpful to begin a discussion on church teaching with defining precisely what is meant by this term, for it is often misunderstood. Ecclesiologist Richard Gaillardetz succinctly states, "There is no definitive listing of Catholic Church teachings."[13] This does not mean that there is no church teaching; rather, there are a multitude of different types of teaching. Church teaching can be a nebulous category, given that many different sources and forms constitute this category, including doctrine, catechism, creeds, and ecclesiastical documents. The lack of authoritative listing moves away from the impression that revelation is a collection of propositional truths to the more expansive view of revelation put forth in *Dei verbum*.[14]

United in God's word, church teaching can be thought of in four categories: definitive dogma, definitive doctrine, nondefinitive authoritative doctrine, and prudential admonitions and provisional applications of church doctrine.[15] Advanced discussion of these categories is beyond the scope of this study, though basic definitions are helpful. Definitive dogma comprise doctrinal teachings that "directly mediate divine revelation."[16] Dogma is the most central of church teaching and was affirmed by both Vatican I and II as irreformable. Definitive doctrine includes teachings that are "thought to be necessary for preserving divine revelation but that are not themselves divinely

---

13. Richard Gaillardetz, *Teaching with Authority: A Theology of the Magisterium in the Church* (Collegeville, MN: Liturgical Press, 1997), 69.

14. Vatican Council II, *Dei verbum*, http://w2.vatican.va. For an extensive study of *Dei verbum*, consult Herbert Vorgrimler, ed., *Commentary on the Documents of Vatican II*, vol. 3 (New York: Crossroad, 1989); and Gerald O'Collins, *The Second Vatican Council: Message and Meaning* (Collegeville, MN: Liturgical Press, 2014).

15. Congregation for the Doctrine of the Faith, "Declaration in Defense of the Catholic Doctrine on the Church against Certain Errors of the Present Day," *Origins* 3 (July 19, 1973): 97–112; Congregation for the Doctrine of the Faith, "The Ecclesial Vocation of the Theologian," *Origins* 20 (July 5, 1990): 118–26; Gaillardetz, *Teaching with Authority*, chap. 4.

16. Gaillardetz, *Teaching with Authority*, 102.

revealed."[17] Nondefinitive authoritative doctrine refers to teachings that are related to divine revelation and can help the faithful understand God's word, yet are nondefinitive and reversible.[18] Gaillardetz clarifies that "many, perhaps most Church teaching belongs in the category of authoritative, nondefinitive doctrine."[19] Many moral norms and teaching related to ethics fall within this category. Finally, there is the category of prudential admonitions and provisional applications of church doctrine. As the name suggests, these are distinguished from the other three categories by their provisional character. These teachings are "concerned not so much with the proclamation of God's word as with offering prudential judgments regarding the soundness of theological and ecclesiological developments in the Church."[20] In discussing the possibility of including narrative in church teaching, we are referring primarily to the categories of nondefinitive authoritative doctrine and of prudential admonitions and provisional applications of church doctrine. Currently, these do not include narrative, though the remainder of this chapter will explore the possibility of incorporating narrative into documents such as apostolic exhortations.

A potential entry for narrative comes through the role of listening in revelation. *Dei verbum* affirms the role of listening in divine revelation, for the opening sentence proclaims, "Hearing the word of God with reverence and proclaiming it with faith, the sacred synod takes its direction from these words of St. John: 'We announce to you the eternal life which dwelt with the Father and was made visible to us. What we have seen and heard we announce to you, so that you may have fellowship with us and our common fellowship be with the Father and His Son Jesus Christ (1 John 1:2–3).'"[21] Gaillardetz interprets this introductory passage as an affirmation of the centrality of listening, stating, "This suggests that the great attention that the Roman Catholic tradition has given to the *teaching* acts of the bishops needs to be matched by equal attention to the *listening* process of the bishops. If the bishops are authoritative *teachers* of the apostolic faith, it is only because they are first *hearers*."[22] The bishops teach through listening to the faithful, in whose lives God is revealed. The centrality of listening can be a connection to the role of experience and narrativ-

17. Ibid., 117.
18. Ibid., 120–21.
19. Ibid., 122.
20. Ibid., 123.
21. *DV* 1.
22. Gaillardetz, *Teaching with Authority*, 85.

ity. Through listening to the lives of the faithful, narrative may organically begin to be included in church teaching.

An interesting point of examination regarding narrative and church teaching is the role of experience in Christian ethics. Narrative is not explicitly named, yet experience is highlighted as a source of ethics. Lisa Cahill describes the four sources of Christian ethics: "the foundational texts or 'scriptures' of the faith community—the Bible; the community's 'tradition' of faith, theology, and practice; philosophical accounts of essential or ideal humanity ('normative' accounts of the human); and descriptions of what actually is and has been the case in human lives and societies ('descriptive' accounts of the human)."[23] These sources should not be separated out and pitted against one another but, rather, must be held together. In this study, we understand narrative as a subset of experience, referring to a particular type of experience.

An example of the use of experience in an ethical examination is Margaret Farley's book *Personal Commitments: Beginning, Keeping, Changing*.[24] Rather than discussing commitments on strictly an abstract level, Farley uses experience and narrative. She explains her method: "I will begin, then, not with a definition of commitment (although I will eventually come to that), but with examples of the kinds of experiences I am attempting to understand."[25] Farley goes on to use examples of the lived experience of commitment in people's lives, illustrating the complexities of commitments given different experiences. She highlights commonalities of experience, for although the experiences vary, the underlying questions evoke similar meaning. In analyzing the value of naming persons and experience, Farley states: "The name is less important than the reality named, but a name helps us to attend to the reality."[26] Farley captures a fundamental reality of narrative: names draw our attention to important realities. Though this reality may be accessible in the abstract, the very act of naming signifies greater importance. Naming evokes realities that often go unnoticed, calling attention to central themes of the human experience.

Farley's approach helps to connect experience to narrative. By drawing on experience as a source of Christian ethics and illustrating

---

23. Lisa Sowle Cahill, *Between the Sexes: Foundations for a Christian Ethics of Sexuality* (Philadelphia: Fortress, 1985), 5.

24. Margaret A. Farley, *Personal Commitments: Beginning, Keeping, Changing*, rev. ed. (Maryknoll, NY: Orbis Books, 2013).

25. Ibid., 12.

26. Ibid., 14.

examples with narrative, Farley bridges the gap between experience and narrative. Through this move, we are able to see the merits of narrative as an illustration of experience. Narrative builds on experience, allowing experience to be captured in theological examination. Farley's examination not only provides an example of the contributions of experience to theology, but also displays the possibilities for further incorporation of narrative into theology. From this, we can imagine what it might look like to include narrative in Church teaching.

It is helpful to address narrative theology briefly. There is a robust movement in narrative theology, which gained significant momentum in the 1970s and 1980s.[27] Alexander Lucie-Smith articulates the method of narrative theology as "one that starts not with abstract first principles, but with a particular story; it is inductive rather than deductive. The story it examines is found, or 'embodied,' in a community's tradition and is usually taken to sum up or encapsulate the community's beliefs about itself, the world and God."[28] Elements of narrative theology, such as its foundation in a particular story and connection to experience, enhance the method of this study. For example, in his landmark article "The Narrative Quality of Experience," Stephen Crites argues that "the formal quality of experience through time is inherently narrative."[29] Thus, Crites's argument affirms the movement of the previous examination of Farley's use of experience as analogous to narrative.

In addition, it is interesting to examine the role of narrative in Scrip-

---

27. My approach in this paper is indebted to narrative theology, yet ultimately this study is asking a different question. This study is examining the inclusion of lived experience through narrative, whereas narrative theology often looks to the metanarratives that govern society and may or may not be true. There is a greater acceptance of myths and fictional stories in narrative theology. It does not conflict with the questions of this study but, rather, proceeds in a different direction. For an in-depth analysis of narrative theology, see H. Richard Niebuhr, *The Meaning of Revelation* (New York: Macmillan, 1960); Hans W. Frei, *The Eclipse of Biblical Narrative: A Study in Eighteenth and Nineteenth Century Hermeneutics* (New Haven, CT: Yale University Press, 1974); Stanley Hauerwas and L. Gregory Jones, eds., *Why Narrative? Readings in Narrative Theology* (Grand Rapids, MI: Eerdmans, 1989); Alasdair C. MacIntyre, *After Virtue: A Study in Moral Theory*, 3rd ed. (Notre Dame, IN: University of Notre Dame Press, 2007); Paul Nelson, *Narrative and Morality: A Theological Inquiry* (University Park: Pennsylvania State University Press, 1987).

28. Alexander Lucie-Smith, *Narrative Theology and Moral Theology* (Hampshire, England: Ashgate, 2007), 1.

29. Stephen Crites, "The Narrative Quality of Experience," *Journal of the American Academy of Religion* 39, no. 3 (September 1971): 291.

ture.[30] The Old and New Testaments alike are filled with narrative. Paul Nelson affirms that the narrative dimension of Scripture contributes to our theological understanding of Scripture and increases accessibility to the laity.[31] Scripture also affirms the connection of narrative and revelation. The story of creation is told through two narrative accounts of the formation of the earth, creation, and humanity. Covenant comes to us through narratives of the exodus. Jesus's mercy is told through stories of miracles and signs. This displays that narrative is not extrinsic to theology and discipleship, but, rather, narrative is central. Exploring the addition of narrative to church teaching is not taking a tool used in law and imposing it on theology. Rather, narrative is a central revelatory form used to mediate God's revelation in Scripture. Lucie-Smith argues, "It is precisely through narrative that God reveals himself to us, and narrative is his chosen means of communication."[32] Using narrative in regard to conveying human experience in church teaching is new, though the role of narrative in Scripture is foundational.

BENEFITS AND LIABILITIES

How might church teaching incorporate experience and narrative? This section explores the benefits and liabilities of including narrative in church teaching, specifically in an apostolic exhortation. Imagine if *Amoris laetitia* included narratives of experience of the faithful. Sections on newly married couples would include narrative of the lived experience of the challenges and joys of adjusting to married life. Discussions on homosexuality would be founded on narratives of same-sex couples and coming-out accounts of families. This is not an "add narrative and stir" approach but, rather, a way of reworking the entire process to include narrative from the beginning.

The inclusion of narrative is rooted in an understanding of revelation. If we take seriously that God continues to reveal Godself to us, then we must recognize that God is present in the stories of the People of God. Opponents to the inclusion of narrative might critique the fact that church teaching conveys divine revelation. While this is certainly true of dogma, it is a limited view of revelation. The inclusion of narrative does not mitigate the view of church teaching as divine revelation.

---

30. A high point of narrative theology and scripture is Frei, *The Eclipse of Biblical Narrative*.

31. Nelson, *Narrative and Morality*, chap. 5.

32. Lucie-Smith, *Narrative Theology and Moral Theology*, 2.

Rather, it asserts that divine revelation can and does occur within the lived experience of the faithful. Including narrative in church teaching is predicated on a robust understanding of God's continued revelation in the lives of the faithful.

From this, we can see that narrative captures something new. Ecclesial documents are a familiar genre, making it predictable in format. When reading a document promulgated by the pope, one can expect a certain rhythm, use of sources, and even syntax. References to Scripture and previous church teaching root the new teaching in tradition. The tone is often formal. Long paragraphs are in succession, grouped under large categories. God is referred to in masculine language. These similarities, and countless others, all create a genre of church teaching. Including narrative not only expands what is classified in this genre, but also expands the type of knowledge that is conveyed. In discussing narrative and law, Daniel Farber and Suzanna Sherry comment, "The new storytellers believe that stories have a persuasive power that transcends rational argument. Indeed, one of the standard claims about stories is that 'there are some things that just cannot be said using the legal voice.'"[33] This points to the addition of something new, something that cannot be captured with a strictly ecclesial voice. Narrative taps into this "something more."

Theopoetics is at the cutting edge of discussions surrounding form and content in theology.[34] In her book *Poetics of the Flesh*, Mayra Rivera discusses the necessity of poetics to point to themes and experiences that cannot be captured by traditional theological approaches. More than just a writing style, poetics gestures to larger themes, such as "a recognition of the limits of our knowledge and appreciation for the imaginative dimensions of thought."[35] Poetics not only expands imagination but is also "indispensable for addressing histories marked by disruption, displacement, and irrecoverable loss."[36] Analogously, narrative introduces not only new content but, more importantly, new ways of thinking and being. It expands the content of church teaching, yet it also expands the approach and location of church teaching in the lives of the faithful. Narrative taps into a part of the person that is not accessible by constitutions, letters, and apostolic exhortations. Given

---

33. Daniel A. Farber and Suzanna Sherry, "Legal Storytelling and Constitutional Law: The Medium and the Message," in Brooks and Gewirtz, *Law's Stories*, 42.

34. For an overview of theopoetics, see L. Callid Keefe-Perry, *Way to Water: A Theopoetics Primer* (Eugene, OR: Cascade Books, 2014).

35. Mayra Rivera, *Poetics of the Flesh* (Durham, NC: Duke University Press, 2015), 158.

36. Ibid., 2–3.

that God is present in all things and cannot be fully captured, it is only fitting that church teaching expand to new forms.

An area in which church teaching, especially in the form of an apostolic exhortation issued after a synod, could be informed by judicial opinions is the presence of dissent. For example, let us look to Supreme Court decisions. The majority opinion is written by a justice and signed by concurring justices. Concurring opinions can also be written, in which a justice agrees with the ruling but relies on different reasoning. The dissenting justices are not excluded but can write dissenting opinions that are preserved with the case. "In a case where there are multiple opinions, there is a debate occurring within the text itself."[37] The narrative in the law is inherently multifaceted, enriching the reception of a diverse document. It goes without saying that this process cannot and should not be transplanted into the formation of church teaching. However, interesting considerations arise from this. Could narrative from a variety of experiences be included in an apostolic exhortation to show the diversity of the lived experience of this teaching? For example, in discussing divorce and remarriage, both positive and negative experiences of the annulment process could be included to convey the range of experiences. This presents a multifaceted and dynamic vision of the church, incarnated in the lives of the faithful and sometimes marred by the presence of sin in the church.

The presence of dissent in the narrative in the law also brings to the surface questions about truth. Gewirtz states, "The existence of multiple opinions defeats the ability of any single opinion to enshrine any particular version of reality as the undoubted truth."[38] When one is thinking about truth as related to church teaching, there is a particular need for nuance. One might think that the presence of conflicting opinions negates any truth claim of the teaching. However, this view is predicated on a narrow understanding of truth as a zero-sum game. Narrative and experience expand our understanding of truth, making it possible to see that there are many truths. While dogma is considered divine revelation, the categories of definitive doctrine, nondefinitive authoritative doctrine, and prudential admonitions and provisional applications of church doctrine have a possibility for error, even if remote. More than just a possibility of error, there is a possibility of many truths. Experience highlights that many accounts that may seemingly conflict can be held as true given different experiences. Again, the example of positive and negative experiences of a diocesan annulment process illustrates this point. A positive experience of an

---

37. Gewirtz, "Narrative and Rhetoric in the Law," 12.
38. Ibid., 11.

annulment does not invalidate a negative experience; both can be held together as true. This expands our view of truth and revelation positively, once again expressing an expansive view of revelation.

Similarly, narrative moves us beyond an impression that a single form of reality exists. Catherine MacKinnon explains, "Much of the contemporary storytelling impulse has sprung from resistance to the claim of exclusivity of the single dominant version of social reality."[39] Narrative forces an encounter with the "other," opening us up to experiences that we may not know, whether due to social location, ability, or ignorance. This is especially important in a global church. It is tempting to think that one's own experience of church is the only experience of church. Narrative moves us beyond this temptation.

Narrative and experience can address the tension between universal and particular that often arises in Catholic ecclesiology. In an attempt to speak to the universal nature of the church, the particular experience can be rendered invisible within the whole. Likewise, attention to the particular can come at the expense of the universal, attending to one specific instance rather than the greater whole. The universal dimension of narrative addresses this tension. Hayden White refers to the "metacode" of narrative, which highlights the ability of narrative to convey and connect "messages about a shared reality."[40] The universal dimension of narrative operates through the particular experience, thus giving language to the connection between universal and particular. Narrative does not quickly solve this problem, for it is not a problem with a solution but rather a relationship that is always in the midst of negotiation. Narrative enters a particular experience, yet does so through the unifying element of story. As such, it can help the church enter more deeply into the relationship between universal and particular.

Another benefit of the narrative dimension of law is the need for interpretation. As mentioned in the introduction of this paper, Gewirtz contends that law requires interpretation, such as "how we should think about the 'original intent' of the authority, what the role of the reader is in creating the meaning of a legal text, and whether texts change meaning over time, how that occurs, and what that means."[41] This type of interpretation necessarily happens with church teaching

---

39. Catherine A. MacKinnon, "Law's Stories as Reality and Politics," in Brooks and Gewirtz, *Law's Stories*, 234.

40. Hayden V. White, *Metahistory: The Historical Imagination in Nineteenth-Century Europe* (Baltimore, MD: Johns Hopkins University Press, 1975), 66.

41. Gewirtz, "Narrative and Rhetoric in the Law," 4.

but is often ignored. It is frequently assumed that church teaching is one-dimensional and straightforward, as countless examples from the Catholic blogosphere reveal. The narrative dimension of law necessitates interpretation, and highlighting this aspect of church teaching is a helpful addition that moves us beyond a propositional model of revelation. Further, including narrative in church teaching would bring the need for interpretation to the foreground, for narrative lends itself to interpretation.

The inclusion of narrative also advances ecclesial identity, reminding the church that we are a people of narrative. Stanley Hauerwas underscores the importance of narrative in ecclesial identity, stating, "The primary social task of the church is to be itself—that is, a people who have been formed by a story that provides them with the skills for negotiating the danger of this existence, trusting in God's promise of redemption."[42] By including narrative, the church is reminded that we are a people constituted by narrative. Controversial issues become secondary to the greater narrative of the church founded on the gospel and living out the paschal mystery. In this sense, our own narratives of experience root us in the greater narrative of the church and enrich our ecclesial identity.

The inclusion of narrative in church teaching opens the door to reform. Farber and Sherry argue, "Advocates of storytelling believe that stories can play a fundamental role in advancing social reform. Only through stories, they contend, can the fundamental racist, sexist, and homophobic structures of our society be confronted and changed."[43] For example, Nancy Pineda-Madrid uses narratives of "feminicide" in Ciudad Juárez to ground discussions of sexism and feminist movements in the concrete. As a result, the reader resists tendencies to ignore or, worse, demonize these movements in the abstract and instead is confronted with the human dimension of feminicide.[44] When the concrete, lived experience of the impact of racist, sexist, and homophobic structures is shown, there is a common impulse to respond with reform.

While narrative has the potential to contribute positive ways of thinking about church teaching, there are also limitations. The overarching problem stems from the practical: How would narratives be

---

42. Stanley Hauerwas, *A Community of Character: Toward a Constructive Christian Social Ethic* (Notre Dame, IN: University of Notre Dame Press, 1981), 10.

43. Farber and Sherry, "Legal Storytelling and Constitutional Law," 37.

44. Nancy Pineda-Madrid, *Suffering and Salvation in Ciudad Juárez* (Minneapolis, MN: Fortress Press, 2011).

included? Related to this are issues connected to culture, privilege, and marginalization. It is necessary to address these problems in assessing narrative.

The practical question of how to include narrative in church teaching is substantial. Though narrative has the power to unite, selecting a handful of stories from the 1.2 billion[45] Catholics in the world is problematic at best. Whose stories would be privileged? In a world marked by consistent devaluing of certain lives based on race, ethnicity, gender, age, sexual orientation, and socioeconomic status, the question of whose story counts is equally essential and complicated.

For an answer to this question, it is helpful to turn to the larger question of process surrounding the apostolic exhortation. The first place to look in analyzing the inclusion of voices is the synodal structure itself. The 2014 and 2015 synods were marked by an inclusion of many voices beyond the participating bishops. At the 2014 synod, there were thirty-eight auditors and sixteen experts present, of which twenty-four persons total were married.[46] While the inclusion of married couples in a synod on the family is to be commended, the implementation was not without problems. Though the married couples spanned nationalities, they each were affiliated with a movement, such as the Natural Family Planning Advisory Board of the United States Conference of Catholic Bishops, the Focolare movement in Africa, and the organization Couples for Christ in the Philippines.[47] While it is impossible to have fully representative auditors address the synod, it is striking that the married couples appear to be unrepresentative of mainstream Catholics, given their affiliation with these largely conservative movements. For example, the experience of the couple affiliated with the Natural Family Planning Advisory Board is not representative of the 77 percent of Catholics in the United States who support the use of birth control[48] and the 98 percent of U.S. Catholic women who use a method

45. David Johnson, "See the Growth in Catholics around the World since 1900," Time Labs, September 21, 2015, http://labs.time.com.

46. The delegates included sixty-one cardinals, one cardinal patriarch, seven patriarchs, one major archbishop, sixty-seven metropolitan archbishops, forty-seven bishops, one auxiliary bishop, one priest, and six religious. In addition to the experts and auditors, there were eight fraternal delegates. See Vatican Information Service, "Cardinal Baldisseri on the Synod on the Family," Criterion Online Edition, October 3, 2014; http://www.archindy.org/Criterion/vatican/2014/vis 1003.html#ebf36e56-c196-2616-09c7-542ea0e6ce73.

47. Massimo Faggioli, "The Synod without a Script," *The Tablet*, October 2, 2014, http://www.thetablet.co.uk.

48. "U.S. Catholics View Pope Francis as a Change for the Better," Pew Research Center's Religion & Public Life, March 6, 2014, http://www.pewforum.org.

of birth control other than natural family planning.[49] Affiliation with specific movements took precedence over mainstream experience, resulting in the bishops hearing a limited experience unrepresentative of the overwhelming majority of the Catholic faithful.

This example illustrates the difficulty with selecting narratives to be included. The story of the Natural Family Planning Advisory Board conveys a truth, yet it is not representative of the majority experience. However, how can a representative experience be defined? There is a need for a diverse set of voices, yet also a need to balance this with representation. It is important to note that being representative extends beyond reflecting data surrounding averages. I propose that if the inclusion of narrative is pursued, careful attention must be given to including diverse experiences that represent a range of experience, being sure to focus on those experiences that appear to be at the center of gravity of the faithful. Data can assist in this endeavor, but it is not the only answer. Every attempt must be made to bypass political connections governing the selection of voices.

In addition, it must be noted that we inherit a tradition that is marked by racism and sexism, resulting in the privileging of certain narratives over others. MacKinnon describes the tendency to marginalize women's contributions related to law and narrative: "Women's accounts have been more commonly called anecdotes, impressions, although they are at the very least testimony and, as such, evidence."[50] Church teaching inherits a tradition of relegating women's experiences to the margins, and one can assume that a similar tendency to minimize women's contributions would be present in the inclusion of narrative in church teaching.

Furthermore, there are cultural differences surrounding story. MacKinnon notes this in legal writing: "Judicial authorship, too, varies in voice, including across cultures. In Canada, even judges writing for the majority will use 'I'; the first-person singular never appears in majority opinions in the power-obsessed, objectivity-sensitive United States."[51] The focus on objectivity in the United States would almost certainly apply to narrative in church teaching as well. This is an example of where the history of law and narrative can serve as an example of potential hazards. It is essential that any attempt at inclusion of narrative take into account cultural differences, especially given the

---

49. Rachel K. Jones and Joerg Dreweke, "Countering Conventional Wisdom: New Evidence on Religion and Contraceptive Use," Guttmacher Institute, April 2011, https://www.guttmacher.org.

50. MacKinnon, "Law's Stories as Reality and Politics," 234.

51. Ibid., 236.

context of Western theology, which claims that its approach is universal and free of cultural differences.[52] This is a significant liability of the inclusion of narrative, and a culturally competent response is essential in further examination.

These examples of sexism and racism also demonstrate why narrative has the potential to expand our thinking about church teaching. Given that story and narrative are often associated with feminine attributes and non-Western cultures, narrative has the potential to include these sources that are too often relegated to the margins of the church. Narrative lifts up other sources of knowledge and power. By looking to narrative, we are also affirming experiences that are ignored or belittled. Thus, if carried out with an eye to the oppressive forces at work in the world, narrative has the potential to subvert oppression and lift up those excluded and marginalized.

EVALUATION AND REVISITING *AMORIS LAETITIA*

This final section imagines how narrative might be included in *Amoris laetitia*. Now that the potential contributions and limitations of the inclusion of narrative as a form of experience in church teaching have been examined, it is necessary to evaluate the overall merit of this proposal. Broadly speaking, the benefits surround diversity and experience. Narrative grounds teaching in real life. This affirms that God is active in experience and that revelation is ongoing. The liabilities surround issues of implementation and feasibility.

Diversity of experience must be represented in narrative. This could happen through the inclusion of several narratives in the document. Including narrative of diverse experience when introducing and discussing a new topic, such as adjusting to marriage, women's roles in society, and the daily experience of marriage, would result in a robust, engaging document grounded in the lives of the faithful. Given the variety of experiences based on factors such as socioeconomic status, gender, continent, race, and sexual orientation, it is essential that narratives come from a diverse range of experience. National and regional bishops' conferences could play a large role in surfacing and submitting these narratives. Ideally, the narrative would not come at the end stage of the process and simply be inserted into the final document

---

52. For a genealogy of whiteness and theology, see Willie James Jennings, *The Christian Imagination: Theology and the Origins of Race* (New Haven, CT: Yale University Press, 2010); J. Kameron Carter, *Race: A Theological Account* (New York: Oxford University Press, 2008).

but, rather, would be heard throughout the synodal process, thereby shaping the entire process.

In the previous section, we addressed many of the problems related to the lay auditors at the 2014 synod. It is worthwhile to consider how to include lay auditors positively. While the synod is not a gathering of the entire church, but rather a gathering of bishops, it remains an important body that discusses issues that reach into the lives of the faithful. What might it look like to engage with the conversation partners beyond their remarks to the synodal assembly? One suggestion is that observers should issue an observers' report at the conclusion of the synod. This would allow for a response from a distinct point of view and would also deepen the bishops' own experience. An observers' report would also be of great service to the pope in creating and issuing the apostolic exhortation. It would serve to amplify and perhaps critique the bishops' recommendations and, in turn, provide a broader view of the topic in service to the pope.

The inclusion of lay auditors and narrative within the synod is essential, yet there is also more possibility for inclusion in the preparation process. For example, diocesan pastoral councils are ideal venues for discussion prior to the synod. Bishops could meet with their pastoral council and hear their own experience. With this preparation, bishops could arrive at the synod already grounded in the narrative of their diocese. These narratives may never make it to the synod floor or the apostolic exhortation, yet they would influence the discussion in untold ways.

Another aspect of preparation includes the surveys that were sent prior to the 2014 synod. While the surveys were a step in the right direction, they were far from perfect. The synod secretariat sent a thirty-nine-question document to the bishops and asked for it to be distributed widely and immediately in preparation for the synod. There was significant confusion surrounding the distribution of the questionnaire, for it was handled differently in many countries, and even handled differently within dioceses of the same country. The bishops were specifically asked by the synod secretariat to engage with the members of the church on the topic of the family, thereby broadening the conversation and grounding it in the lived experience of the faithful. "Engagement," however, became equated with "distributing a questionnaire." Polling, rather than dialogue and conversation, is indicative of a view of the faithful that sees them more as survey subjects and less as conversation partners. The opportunity to include narrative took a backseat to quantifiable data. While the questionnaires were an important step, the overall engagement remains flawed. Furthermore, the survey process remains several steps removed from a robust inclusion of voices in the document itself. If narrative is to be truly included in the synodal process, it must be based on bishops listening to narrative rather than reading data.

Given the diversity of the church throughout the world, a variety of approaches for conversation would be necessary. Thankfully, the church has a rich tradition of theological reflection that has been bolstered by praxis-based, theological-method inquiries. This is especially rich in the fields of theological education and practical theology. In the United States, a method such as Don Browning's practical method of theological reflection would fit especially well with synod preparation, for the problem-oriented approach is in harmony with the selection of a synod topic that is a problem or particularly relevant issue.[53] Each region could engage a method of dialogue that fits the cultural context.

These proposals do not exhaust the possibilities for narrative in church teaching. Rather, they illustrate concrete examples of methods to include narrative. They are incomplete but, ultimately, feasible. The possibility of including narrative in church teaching may initially appear to be overwhelming or outlandish, yet small procedural changes could open doors to this inclusion.

It is probable that a critic would respond to the proposal of narrative by noting that the church is not a democracy, and, therefore, the inclusion of other voices is unnecessary or inappropriate. Gaillardetz notes, "One often hears the slogan, 'the Church is not a democracy,' yet almost never does one hear its necessary ecclesiological correlate, 'neither is the Church a monarchy or an oligarchy.'"[54] The same sentiment can be applied to the synod of bishops, for this is the process from which the apostolic exhortation arises. Though the synod is not the parliament of the church, it is also not an oligarchy. As a distinct form of leadership in the church, it is necessary that the synod function as a gathering of bishops while also fostering a relationship between the synod and the People of God. From this, an apostolic exhortation such as *Amoris laetitia* might capture the richness of the church through the inclusion of diverse voices, more fully embodying the Body of Christ.

---

53. For an overview of Browning's method, see Robert Kinast, *What Are They Saying about Theological Reflection?* (Mahwah, NJ: Paulist Press, 2000), chap. 6; Don S. Browning, *A Fundamental Practical Theology: Descriptive and Strategic Proposals* (Minneapolis: Fortress Press, 1991).

54. Richard Gaillardetz, "Ecclesiological Perspectives on Church Reform," in *Church Ethics and Its Organizational Context*, ed. Jean Bartunek, Mary Ann Hinsdale, and James Keenan (Lanham, MD: Rowman & Littlefield, 2006), 67.

Narrative grounds church teaching in the lived experience of the faithful. Moreover, it takes seriously a theology of revelation, looking to the many ways that God continues to reveal Godself through personal experience. While including narrative in church teaching, such as an apostolic exhortation, is not an easy endeavor, it would enhance our understanding of the connection between experience and revelation. The problems related to logistical efforts, most especially cultural considerations, are important and should not be minimized. At the same time, narrative has the potential to expand our understanding of the church and revelation. Including narrative in church teaching may not be the perfect solution, yet the process of imagining this opens up possibilities for expanding our understanding of church teaching and its connection to lived experience.

15

Alternative Economic Visions

John Sniegocki

A central theme of the papacy of Pope Francis has been critique of the inequities and destructiveness of our world's prevailing economic system. This system, according to Francis, "has imposed the mentality of profit at any price, with no concern for social exclusion or the destruction of nature."[1] Francis argues that the existing economic order is "intolerable," "runs counter to the plan of Jesus," and must undergo profound structural transformation.[2] In articulating this critique of existing forms of capitalism, Francis emphasizes that he is reaffirming and building on earlier papal teachings, especially those of Pope Paul VI and Pope John Paul II. In this chapter, we will highlight these papal critiques of capitalism and the empirical evidence that supports them. We will also explore the nature of the alternative that CST proposes. This alternative can be best described by the term "economic democracy." Finally, in the concluding sections, we will highlight the work of some key figures in the fields of political economy and social analysis whose proposals could further enhance CST, and we will explore the central role of grass-roots social movements in bringing economic alternatives into being.

THE CRITIQUE OF EXISTING CAPITALISM

Pope Francis's critique of existing forms of capitalism is articulated very powerfully in a talk that he gave to a worldwide gathering of

---

1. Pope Francis, "Address to Second World Meeting of Popular Movements," July 9, 2015, http://w2.vatican.va.
2. Ibid.

grass-roots social movements in Bolivia in 2015. In this talk, Francis states:

> Do we realize that something is wrong in a world where there are so many farmworkers without land, so many families without a home, so many laborers without rights, so many persons whose dignity is not respected? Do we realize that something is wrong where so many senseless wars are being fought and acts of fratricidal violence are taking place on our very doorstep? Do we realize something is wrong when the soil, water, air and living creatures of our world are under constant threat? . . . These are not isolated issues. . . . I wonder whether we can see that these destructive realities are part of a system which has become global. Do we realize that that system has imposed the mentality of profit at any price, with no concern for social exclusion or the destruction of nature? If such is the case, I would insist, let us not be afraid to say it: we want change, real change, structural change. This system is by now intolerable: farmworkers find it intolerable, laborers find it intolerable, communities find it intolerable, peoples find it intolerable. . . . The earth itself—our sister, Mother Earth, as Saint Francis would say—also finds it intolerable.[3]

There are at least eight main criticisms that Francis makes of the prevailing global economic order.

Excessive Inequality

Francis strongly critiques the high levels of inequality that the dominant economic order is generating and the free market and deregulatory policies that facilitate this. "As long as the problems of the poor are not radically resolved by rejecting the absolute autonomy of markets and financial speculation and by attacking the structural causes of inequality," says Francis, "no solution will be found for the world's problems." "Inequality," he stresses, "is the root of social ills."[4] This inequality, Francis suggests, derives from an idolatrous pursuit of profit at the expense of all other values: "We have created new idols. The worship of the ancient golden calf has returned in a new and ruthless guise in the idolatry of money and the dictatorship of an

---

3. Ibid.
4. *EG* 202.

impersonal economy lacking a truly human purpose."[5] Echoing earlier statements of Paul VI, Francis warns that current forms of capitalism have generated economic domination: "A new tyranny is thus born which unilaterally and relentlessly imposes its own laws and rules. . . . In this system, which tends to devour everything that stands in the way of increased profits, whatever is fragile, like the environment, is defenseless before the interests of a deified market, which becomes the only rule."[6]

The evidence in support of Pope Francis's claims concerning rising inequality is abundant. For example, it was recently estimated in a report by Oxfam International that the richest forty-two people in the world now possess as much wealth as the poorest 3.7 billion people combined, about half of the world's population.[7] With regard to consumption, it is estimated that the wealthiest 20 percent in the world are responsible for nearly 80 percent of private consumption. The poorest 20 percent are responsible for only around 1.5 percent. In other words, a person in the top 20 percent consumes on average about fifty times as much as those in the bottom 20 percent.[8] More broadly, it is estimated that seven out of ten people live in countries where inequality has widened in the past thirty years.[9] In the United States, inequality is at or near its highest levels since before the Great Depression.[10]

Creation of the "Excluded"

As part of the escalation of inequality, Francis argues that a permanent undercaste of the excluded is being created around the world. These are people who are permanently unemployed and marginalized, not needed by the economic system. "Masses of people," he says, "find themselves excluded and marginalized: without work, without possibilities, without any means of escape."[11] "The principal ethical dilemma of this capitalism," Francis declares, "is the creation of discarded people, then trying to hide them or make sure they are no lon-

---

5. *EG* 55.

6. *EG* 56.

7. Larry Elliott, "Inequality Gap Widens as 42 People Hold Same Wealth as 3.7bn Poorest," https://www.theguardian.com.

8. World Bank figures cited in Anup Shah, "Consumption and Consumerism," January 5, 2014, http://www.globalissues.org/issue/235/consumption-and-consumerism.

9. Oxfam International, "An Economy for the 99%," January 2017, https://www.oxfam.org.

10. Journalist's Resource, "U.S. Income Inequality Highest since the Great Depression," March 30, 2016, https://journalistsresource.org.

11. *EG* 53.

ger seen."[12] In 2017, the number of unemployed persons globally rose to more than two hundred million, a new record high. In addition, 1.4 billion people experience employment that is classified by the International Labour Organization as highly "vulnerable," lacking the most basic employment security.[13]

Exploitation of Workers

Along with expressing concern for those who are excluded from employment, Francis also critiques the widespread violation of workers' rights in the existing global economic order. He laments the existence of "so many laborers without rights" and expresses his deep support for those who are fighting to obtain these rights.[14]

In the 2017 International Trade Union Confederation (ITUC) Global Rights Index, one of the major sources of data on violations of workers' rights, only 12 of the 139 countries investigated (mostly Western European/Scandinavian countries) were classified as experiencing no regular violations of workers' rights. The majority of the countries studied were placed in the worst two classifications—"no guarantee of rights" (46 countries) and "systematic violation of rights" (33 countries, including the United States).[15]

Throughout the world, many workers are forced to work for less than a living wage. Half of the workers in South Asia and two-thirds of the workers in sub-Saharan Africa, for example, are classified as living in extreme or moderate poverty, according to the International Labour Organization.[16]

Conflict and War

Francis sees a strong connection between inequality, exclusion, and violence. "Until exclusion and inequality in society and between peoples are reversed," he states, "it will be impossible to end violence."[17] Moreover, Francis argues that major parties in our economic system in fact profit from violence and war:

---

12. Pope Francis, "Address to 'Economy and Communion' Movement," February 4, 2017, https://w2.vatican.va.

13. International Labour Organization, *World Employment and Social Outlook: Trends 2017*, 1–2.

14. Pope Francis, "Address to Second World Meeting of Popular Movements."

15. International Trade Union Confederation, *2017 ITUC Global Rights Index: The World's Worst Countries for Workers*, https://www.ituc-csi.org.

16. Ivana Kottasova, "Global Unemployment to Hit 200 Million as Wages Stagnate," January 13, 2017, http://money.cnn.com.

17. *EG* 59.

There are economic systems that must make war in order to survive. Accordingly, arms are manufactured and sold and, with that, the balance sheets of economies that sacrifice man at the feet of the idol of money are clearly rendered healthy. And no thought is given to hungry children in refugee camps; no thought is given to the forcibly displaced; no thought is given to destroyed homes; no thought is given, finally, to so many destroyed lives.[18]

Arms sales in 2016 by the top one hundred weapons producers totaled an estimated $375 billion, with U.S. companies accounting for 58 percent of sales.[19] Arms sales by the U.S. government to foreign armed actors rose 25 percent in FY 2017.[20] These arms sales helped to fuel twenty-eight armed conflicts worldwide. Overall, global military spending in 2016, the last year for which full data are currently available, totaled around $1.5 trillion.[21] To put this spending into perspective, this is over fifteen times the amount of funds that Oxfam International estimates is needed annually to end global extreme poverty.[22]

Consumerism and the "Globalization of Indifference"

Pope Francis also critiques the dominant capitalist economic system for fostering many harmful values such as consumerism, "rampant individualism," and a desire for instant gratification.[23] He suggests that these values are linked to a "throwaway culture," a decline in empathy (part of what is thrown away are people), and what he terms a "globalization of indifference."[24] We end up, he claims, "being incapable of feeling compassion at the outcry of the poor, weeping for other people's pain, and feeling a need to help them."[25]

---

18. Pope Francis, "Address to First World Meeting of Popular Movements," October 28, 2014, https://w2.vatican.va.

19. Vera Kern, "SIPRI: Weapons Sales up Again Worldwide," December 11, 2017, http://www.dw.com/en/sipri-weapons-sales-up-again-worldwide/a-41735391.

20. "US Arms Sales Jump 25 percent in FY 2017," December 19, 2017, https://www.reuters.com.

21. Project Ploughshares, "Armed Conflicts Report 2017," http://ploughshares.ca.

22. Oxfam International, "Reward Work, Not Wealth," January 2018, https://www.oxfam.org/sites/www.oxfam.org.

23. *LS* 162.

24. *LS* 43; *EG* 54.

25. *EG* 54.

Destruction of the Planet

At the core of Francis's critique of the world's prevailing economic system is the fact that it is destroying our planet, our "common home." "An economic system centered on the god of money," says Francis, "also needs to plunder nature, to plunder nature to sustain the frenetic rhythm of consumption that is inherent to it. Climate change, the loss of bio-diversity, deforestation are already showing their devastating effects in the great cataclysms we witness."[26] Francis understands well the enormous depth of the problems and gives voice to a compelling sense of urgency:

> Doomsday predictions can no longer be met with irony or disdain. We may well be leaving to coming generations debris, desolation and filth. The pace of consumption, waste and environmental change has so stretched the planet's capacity that our contemporary lifestyle, unsustainable as it is, can only precipitate catastrophes.[27]

Speaking specifically of climate change, Francis states: "It is either now or never. . . . Every year the problems get worse. We are on the verge of suicide."[28] The world's leading climate scientists agree. Joseph Romm, a prominent U.S. climate scientist, issued this strong warning following a survey of recent climate change developments: "Unrestricted emissions of greenhouse gases threaten multiple catastrophes, any one of which justifies action. Together, they represent the gravest threat to humanity imaginable."[29]

Undermining of Democracy

Francis is highly critical of the ways that the concentrated wealth translates into concentrated control of the political system, undermining authentic democracy. "The breach between the peoples and our current forms of democracy is growing ever greater," says Francis,

---

26. Pope Francis, "Address to First World Meeting of Popular Movements."

27. *LS* 161.

28. Pope Francis, comments to media aboard papal plane during return from Africa, November 30, 2015, https://www.romereports.com/en/2015/11/30/full-text-of-the-pope-s-press-conference-aboard-the-papal-plane.

29. Joseph Romm, "A Stunning Year in Climate Science Reveals that Human Civilization Is on the Precipice," November 15, 2010, https://thinkprogress.org/a-stunning-year-in-climate-science-reveals-that-human-civilization-is-on-the-precipice-1df7316f3232/. For a compilation of the latest news concerning climate change realities, see http://www.heatisonline.org.

"due to the enormous power of the financial and media sectors that would seem to dominate them." He speaks of the need for grass-roots movements to "revitalize and recast the democracies, which are experiencing a genuine crisis."[30] Again, the data is strongly supportive of Francis's assertions. The *Economist* magazine's annual Democracy Index, for example, found that a majority of the 167 countries included in their rankings experienced a decline in democracy in 2017 and that the percentage of the world's population living in a democracy of any sort (they use the language of "full democracies" and "flawed democracies") fell to below 50 percent.[31]

The Promotion of a Culture of Fear and Scapegoating

As inequality widens and conditions for many become more insecure, Francis warns that politicians may arise who will seek to exploit this fear and try to scapegoat marginalized groups. Sooner or later, he says, the problems of the current system come to light:

> The wounds are there, they are a reality. The unemployment is real, the violence is real, the corruption is real, the identity crisis is real, the gutting of democracies is real. The system's gangrene cannot be whitewashed forever because sooner or later the stench becomes too strong; and when it can no longer be denied, the same power that spawned this state of affairs sets about manipulating fear, insecurity, quarrels, and even people's justified indignation, in order to shift the responsibility for all these ills onto a "non-neighbor."[32]

Clearly, such scapegoating (against immigrants, ethnic and religious minorities, etc.) is prevalent in many parts of the world today, including the United States. Francis warns against seeking "the false security of physical and social walls." He speaks instead of the need to "build bridges between peoples, bridges which enable us to break down the walls of exclusion and exploitation."[33]

---

30. Pope Francis, "Address to Third World Meeting of Popular Movements," November 5, 2016, http://w2.vatican.va.

31. Scotty Hendricks, "New report shows democracy is in decline everywhere — including the United States," February 5, 2018, http://bigthink.com/scotty-hendricks/a-new-report-shows-democracy-is-in-decline-everywhere-including-the-united-states.

32. Pope Francis, "Message to Meeting of Popular Movements in California," February 17, 2017, https://w2.vatican.va.

33. Pope Francis, "Address to Third World Meeting of Popular Movements."

POPE FRANCIS AND CATHOLIC SOCIAL TEACHING

In presenting these critiques of global capitalism, Francis emphasizes that such criticisms are deeply rooted in the tradition of CST. Pope Paul VI, in his landmark 1968 encyclical *Populorum progressio*, for example, articulated similar concerns about existing forms of capitalism:

> It is unfortunate that . . . a system has been constructed which considers profit as the key motive for economic progress, competition as the supreme law of economics, and private ownership of the means of production as an absolute right that has no limits and carries no corresponding social obligation. This unchecked liberalism leads to dictatorship rightly denounced by Pius XI as producing "the international imperialism of money." One cannot condemn such abuses too strongly. . . . A type of capitalism has been the source of excessive suffering, injustices, and fratricidal conflicts whose effects still persist.[34]

In a later document, *Octogesima adveniens*, Pope Paul VI raises particular concern about the negative impacts of large corporations:

> We can see new economic powers emerging, the multinational enterprises . . . which are largely independent of the national political powers and therefore not subject to control from the point of view of the common good. By extending their activities, these private organizations can lead to a new and abusive form of economic domination on the social, cultural, and even political level.[35]

In response to these injustices and inadequacies of existing forms of capitalism, which he describes as a "woeful system,"[36] Pope Paul calls for far-reaching reforms. The nature of these reforms called for by Paul VI and other popes are highlighted later in this chapter.

Critical views of capitalism were also strongly expressed by Pope John Paul II. While many people are more familiar with John Paul's opposition to existing forms of "communism," he also raised profound concerns about capitalism and, in doing so, emphasized his continuity with earlier CST:

---

34. *PP* 26.
35. *OA* 44.
36. *PP* 26.

The Church, since Leo XIII's *Rerum Novarum*, has always dis-
tanced herself from capitalist ideology, holding it responsible
for grave social injustices. I myself, after the historical failure of
communism, did not hesitate to raise serious doubts on the validity of capitalism.[37]

Reflecting on John Paul's views, Pope Francis states:

Saint John Paul II . . . warned of the risk that an ideology of capitalism would become widespread. This would entail little or no
interest for the realities of marginalization, exploitation, and
human alienation, a lack of concern for the great numbers of people still living in conditions of grave material and moral poverty,
and a blind faith in the unbridled development of market forces
alone. . . . Sadly, the dangers that troubled Saint John Paul II have
largely come to pass.[38]

Highlighting the warnings of Paul VI and Pius XI against the "international imperialism of money" and "global economic dictatorship,"
Francis states:

They are harsh yet accurate words spoken by my predecessors,
who warned us about what was to come. The Church and the
prophets for millennia have been saying things that we find
scandalous when the Pope repeats them today, in a time when
the phenomenon has reached unprecedented proportions. The
entire social doctrine of the Church and the magisterium of my
predecessors rejects the idolatry of money that reigns rather than
serves, that tyrannizes and terrorizes humanity.[39]

The terrorism of global capitalism, says Francis (manifested, he
argues, through the acts of "corporations, loan agencies, certain 'free
trade treaties,' and the imposition of measures of 'austerity' which

---

37. Pope John Paul II, "What Catholic Social Teaching Is and Is Not," *Origins* 23
(1993): 256–58. The quote is from a speech delivered by John Paul during a trip to
Latvia in 1993. For extended discussion of Pope John Paul II's views on capitalism
and related issues and the distortion of his thought by Catholic neo-conservatives
such as Michael Novak and George Weigel, see John Sniegocki, "The Social Ethics
of Pope John Paul II: A Critique of Neoconservative Interpretations," *Horizons: The
Journal of the College Theology Society* 33, no. 1 (Spring 2006): 7–32.

38. Pope Francis, "Address to the Roman Roundtable of the Global Foundation," January 14, 2017, https://w2.vatican.va.

39. Pope Francis, "Address to Third World Meeting of Popular Movements."

always tighten the belt of workers and the poor"[40]), is the most basic and fundamental form of terrorism in the world today. "That basic terrorism," says Francis, "feeds derivative forms of terrorism like narcoterrorism, state terrorism, and what some wrongly term ethnic or religious terrorism."[41] For terrorism in its various forms to be overcome, says Francis, there needs to be far-reaching structural change.

Economic Democracy, Solidarity, and Ecological Conversion

Being highly critical of both Soviet-style economics and the existing dominant forms of capitalism, what then does CST suggest as an alternative? The popes have emphasized that there is no single model that should be implemented, but rather that there are certain fundamental principles that must be respected for any economic system to be judged morally acceptable. These principles include what CST terms a "universal destination of goods," which asserts that primacy must be given to meeting the basic needs of all over an unbridled right to accumulation for a few.[42] Theologically, this claim is grounded in an understanding that all ultimately belongs to God and that God wants the goods of creation to be equitably shared. This principle is understood to place certain limits on the right to private property.[43] Other principles include the importance of participation, respect for the dignity of workers, respect for creation, and the fostering of solidarity.

In broad terms, the principles of CST outline a vision of what can be called "economic democracy." Though the term is only used explicitly a few times in the tradition (by John Paul II, for example, as noted below), it summarizes well the overall trajectory of papal thought on economics in the past century. What is meant by economic democracy? In brief, economic democracy refers to a much more equitable, though not strictly equal, distribution of wealth, along with significantly increased worker and community participation in economic

---

40. Pope Francis, "Address to Second World Meeting of Popular Movements."
41. Pope Francis, "Address to Third World Meeting of Popular Movements."
42. See, for example, *LS* 93.
43. For example, Paul VI states: "To quote St. Ambrose: 'You are not making a gift of your possessions to the poor person. You are handing over to him what is his. For what has been given in common for the use of all, you have arrogated to yourself. The world is given to all, and not only to the rich.' That is, private property does not constitute for anyone an absolute and unconditioned right. No one is justified in keeping for his exclusive use what he does not need, when others lack necessities"; *PP* 23.

decision making and adequate governmental regulations to protect workers, consumers, and the environment.

Significantly, CST views political democracy and economic democracy as complementary and dependent on each other. Repeatedly, CST has argued that concentrated economic power runs the grave danger of being translated into concentrated political power. We saw above, for example, Pope Paul VI's concern that multinational corporations "can lead to a new and abusive form of economic domination on the social, cultural, and even political level."[44]

In its most concentrated form, economic democracy is present in worker-owned cooperatives, member-owned credit unions, and similar enterprises. Support for worker- and member-owned cooperatives has deep roots in CST, going back to some of the first modern CST documents. This support was strongly reaffirmed by Pope John Paul II, who spoke of cooperatives as an integral part of direly needed efforts to "promote real economic democracy."[45] This support has been affirmed as well by Pope Benedict XVI and by Pope Francis. "The Church," Francis says, "has always recognized, encouraged, and appreciated cooperatives." The work of cooperatives, he adds, "is not only positive and vital, but also continues to be prophetic."[46]

The vision of economic democracy that CST sets forth recognizes the value of markets, as opposed to Soviet-style central planning, but it stresses the need for extensive regulation of markets on behalf of the common good. "The market," Pope John Paul II argues, "[must] be appropriately controlled by the forces of society and by the state, so that the basic needs of the whole of society are satisfied."[47] Furthermore, in order for markets to be effective in meeting true needs, wealth must be widely dispersed. "It is the task of nations, their leaders, their economic powers and all people of goodwill," John Paul II declares, "to seek every opportunity for a more equitable sharing of resources."[48] Similarly, criticizing what he terms "the scandal of glar-

44. *OA* 44.

45. Pope John Paul II, "Promote Real Economic Democracy, Address to the Central Institute of Cooperative Credit Banks of Italy," June 26, 1998, https://w2.vatican.va.

46. Pope Francis, "Address to Representatives of the Confederation of Italian Cooperatives," February 28, 2015, https://w2.vatican.va. For Pope Benedict XVI's discussion of cooperatives, see *CV* 65–66, and his "Address to Members of the Confederation of Italian Cooperatives," December 10, 2011, https://w2.vatican.va.

47. *CA* 35.

48. Pope John Paul II, "Message to the World Food Summit," November 13, 1996, https://www.ewtn.com/library/PAPALDOC/JPSUMMIT.HTM.

ing inequalities," Pope Benedict XVI highlights the crucial importance of "pursuing justice through redistribution."[49] He suggests that in order to properly protect the common good "the State's role seems destined to grow, as it regains many of its competences."[50] Thus, Popes John Paul II and Benedict, like Pope Francis, are highly critical of more libertarian free-market policies. A key claim of CST from its inception is that the state has a vital role to play, especially in providing protection and support to those who are most vulnerable and marginalized in society.

As part of this overall vision of economic democracy, other specifics that are called for in CST include:

- a critique of "free trade" and emphasis on well-regulated, fairer terms of trade;[51]
- debt relief for the world's poorer nations;[52]
- greater investment in areas such as health and education and significantly reduced levels of military spending;[53]
- land redistribution;[54]
- truly progressive systems of taxation, in which the wealthy are taxed at significantly higher levels than the less wealthy;[55]
- the use of tax policy, credit policy, and other policy mechanisms

---

49. *CV* 22, 36.

50. *CV* 41.

51. For example, Paul VI states: "The rule of free trade, taken by itself, is no longer able to govern international relations. . . . Prices which are 'freely' set in the market can produce unfair results. . . . An economy of exchange can no longer be based solely on the law of free competition, a law which, in its turn, too often creates an economic dictatorship. Freedom of trade is fair only if it is subject to the demands of social justice"; *PP* 58–59.

52. Pope John Paul II, "It is not right to demand or expect repayment when the effect would be the imposition of political choices leading to hunger and despair for entire peoples. It cannot be expected that the debts which have been contracted should be paid at the price of unbearable sacrifice," *CA* 35. "Provision must also be made for the rapid, total and unconditional cancellation of the external debt of the Heavily Indebted Poor Countries (HIPCs) and of the Least Developed Countries (LDCs)." See Pope Benedict XVI, "Letter to German Chancellor Angela Merkel," December 16, 2006, http://w2.vatican.va.

53. *PP* 35, 51, 53, and many other CST statements.

54. Pope Francis, "I know that some of you are calling for agrarian reform [i.e. land redistribution] in order to solve some of these problems, and let me tell you that in some countries — and here I cite the *Compendium of the Social Doctrine of the Church* — 'agrarian reform is, besides a political necessity, a moral obligation.'" See Pope Francis, "Address to First World Meeting of Popular Movements." Also see Pope Paul VI, *PP* 24; Vatican Council II, *GS* 71.

55. See Pope John XXIII, *MM* 102.

to provide preferential support to worker-owned businesses and smaller businesses and farms, with decreased subsidization and tax breaks for large corporations and the wealthy;[56]

- measures to prevent capital flight and to regulate potentially destabilizing speculative finance;[57]
- protective measures for developing Third World industries;[58]
- a strong role for the state in development planning;[59]
- a call to the world's wealthy to accept the need for simpler lifestyles and a deemphasis on economic growth, allowing more ecological space for the world's poorest to meet their basic needs in a sustainable way;[60]
- recognition of the "ecological debt" owed by the wealthy nations (who have been responsible for the vast majority of the world's greenhouse gas emissions) to the world's poorer nations, to be paid in part by providing funds to the poorer nations to invest in green technologies;[61]
- a rapid transition away from fossil fuels to alternative, renewable energy sources;[62] and
- the need for greater coordination and regulation at the regional and global levels, including a strengthening (and further democratizing) of international bodies such as the United Nations.[63]

---

56. For discussion of the importance of supporting cooperatives, see the documents cited in n. 46 above.

57. Pope Paul VI, *PP* 24

58. Pope Paul VI, *PP* 61.

59. Pope Paul VI, "Individual initiative alone and the mere free play of competition could never assure successful development. One must avoid the risk of increasing still more the wealth of the rich and the dominion of the strong, while leaving the poor in their misery and adding to the servitude of the oppressed. . . . It pertains to the public authorities to choose, even to lay down the objectives to be pursued, the ends to be achieved, and the means for attaining these, and it is for them to stimulate all the forces engaged in this common activity"; *PP* 33.

60. Pope John Paul II, "Another name for peace is development. . . . Creating such conditions calls for a concerted worldwide effort . . . an effort which also involves sacrificing the positions of income and of power enjoyed by the more developed economies. . . . This may mean making important changes in established lifestyles, in order to limit the waste of environmental and human resources, thus enabling every individual and all the peoples of the earth to have a sufficient share of those resources"; *CA* 52.

61. See Pope Francis, *LS* 51–52.

62. *LS* 26.

63. Pope Benedict XVI, "To manage the global economy; to revive economies hit by the crisis; to avoid any deterioration of the present crisis and the greater imbalances that would result; to bring about integral and timely disarmament,

These policy measures are to be complemented by the fostering of spiritualities of solidarity and of ecological conversion,[64] enabling us to hear both "the cry of the earth" and "the cry of the poor,"[65] and to find the commitment and courage to take constructive action in response.

ENHANCING CATHOLIC SOCIAL TEACHING

In further developing and seeking to implement these visions of economic democracy and of "integral ecology" (to use Pope Francis's terminology[66]), much can be learned from others who are similarly working to envision and build alternatives. Two important authors/ practitioners who have much to offer to CST are James Gustave Speth and Gar Alperovitz. James Speth, former director of the United Nations Development Programme, is the author of works such as *America the Possible: Manifesto for a New Economy* and *The Bridge at the Edge of the World: Capitalism, the Environment, and Crossing from Crisis to Sustainability.*[67] Gar Alperovitz is the author of *America beyond Capitalism: Reclaiming Our Wealth, Our Liberty, and Our Democracy* and *What Then Must We Do? Straight Talk about the Next American Revolution: Democratizing Wealth and Building a Community-Sustaining Economy from the Ground Up.*[68] Speth and Alperovitz are attentive to the seeds of alter-

---

food security and peace; to guarantee the protection of the environment and to regulate migration: for all this, there is urgent need of a true world political authority, as my predecessor Blessed John XXIII indicated some years ago. Such an authority would need to be regulated by law, to observe consistently the principles of subsidiarity and solidarity, to seek to establish the common good"; *CV* 67. This call for the strengthening of international institutions on behalf of the common good is reiterated by Pope Francis in *LS* 175. Also see Pope Paul VI, *PP* 51, 52, 78.

64. For Pope Francis's discussion of the urgent need for ecological conversion, see *LS* 216–21.

65. For discussion of responding to the cries of the earth and of the poor, see *LS* 59.

66. For Pope Francis's discussion of "integral ecology," which highlights the deep connections between social justice and ecology, see *LS* 137–42.

67. James Gustave Speth, *America the Possible: Manifesto for a New Economy* (New Haven, CT: Yale University Press, 2012); and *The Bridge at the Edge of the World: Capitalism, the Environment, and Crossing from Crisis to Sustainability* (New Haven, CT: Yale University Press, 2009).

68. Gar Alperovitz, *America beyond Capitalism: Reclaiming Our Wealth, Our Liberty, and Our Democracy*, 2nd ed. (Takoma Park, MD: Democracy Collaborative Press, 2011); and *What Then Must We Do? Straight Talk about the Next American Revolution: Democratizing Wealth and Building a Community-Sustaining Economy from*

natives that are already being built in the United States and globally and make helpful suggestions for policy measures to strengthen the growth of these alternatives. Speth and Alperovitz are also co-founders of The Next System Project (www.thenextsystem.org), an important new organization devoted to exploring the types of structural transformations that Pope Francis calls for.

Another crucial dialogue partner for CST is Vandana Shiva. An inspiring activist and social critic from India, Shiva is the author of works such as *Earth Democracy, Staying Alive: Women, Ecology, and Development,* and numerous others. She is a very insightful critic of current forms of economic globalization and a leading voice for grass-roots alternatives.[69]

Numerous other authors and activists could be added to this list of valuable dialogue partners for CST. A few include Juliet Schor, Naomi Klein, Joseph Stiglitz, Herman Daly, and David Schweikart.[70]

IMPLEMENTING ALTERNATIVES

A fundamental question that remains, of course, concerns how major structural reforms, such as those suggested above, can be realistically brought about. This problem of implementation has always plagued CST. One of the most important contributions of Pope Francis to CST is his emphasis on grass-roots organizing and social movement-building as the primary mechanism for social change. Breaking from much of past tradition in CST, which relied more on a top-down model of social change in which the church was understood primarily to provide moral formation for the economic and political elites so that they would act more justly, Francis instead stresses the active agency of marginalized people.[71] Significantly, Francis calls the Catholic Church

---

the Ground Up (White River Junction, VT: Chelsea Green Publishing, 2013).

69. For discussion of Vandana Shiva's work in relation to CST, see John Sniegocki, *Catholic Social Teaching and Economic Globalization: The Quest for Alternatives* (Milwaukee, WI: Marquette University Press, 2009), 195–217.

70. See, for example, Juliet Schor, *True Wealth* (New York: Penguin, 2011); Naomi Klein, *This Changes Everything: Capitalism vs. the Climate* (New York: Simon & Schuster, 2014); Joseph Stiglitz, *Making Globalization Work* (New York: W. W. Norton, 2006); Herman Daly, *Ecological Economics*, 2nd ed. (Washington, DC: Island Press, 2011); David Schweikart, *After Capitalism*, 2nd ed. (Lanham, MD: Rowman & Littlefield, 2011).

71. For discussion of the mechanisms of social change in CST, see John Sniegocki, "Implementing Catholic Social Teaching," in *Faith in Public Life*, ed. William Collinge; College Theology Society Annual 53 (Maryknoll, NY: Orbis Books, 2008), 39–61.

to enter actively into solidarity with grass-roots movements (such as those that have played major roles in ending military dictatorships and challenging neoliberal capitalist economic policies in his home region of Latin America) and views this solidarity as a primary indicator of the church's faithfulness in our time. Francis's talks to the various global gatherings of grass-roots movements, cited frequently throughout this chapter, are some of the most powerful documents in CST. It seems fitting, therefore, to conclude with two quotes from Pope Francis on the importance of grass-roots action:

> You, the lowly, the exploited, the poor and underprivileged, can do, and are doing, a lot. I would even say that the future of humanity is in great measure in your own hands . . . the future of humanity does not lie solely in the hands of great leaders, the great powers and the elites. It is fundamentally in the hands of peoples and in their ability to organize.[72]

> You, the popular movements, are sowers of change, promoters of a process involving millions of actions, great and small, creatively intertwined like words in a poem; that is why I wanted to call you "social poets." . . . I congratulate you, I accompany you and I ask you to continue to blaze trails and to keep fighting.[73]

In this chapter, we have demonstrated how the critiques of capitalist economic policies have a long history in CST and continue to be of utmost relevance. These critiques have been well articulated and further developed and deepened by Pope Francis. Facing a world of growing inequality and ecological destruction, the need for alternatives is dire. Pope Francis's challenge to the church is to truly incarnate CST, in collaboration with grass-roots movements around the world, and in so doing to help create a more just, democratic, and ecologically sustainable future for God's creatures on this planet.

---

72. Pope Francis, "Address to Second World Meeting of Popular Movements."
73. Pope Francis, "Address to Third World Meeting of Popular Movements."

16

A Bioethical Vision

Jason T. Eberl

Unlike his predecessors, particularly Sts. John Paul II[1] and Paul VI,[2] Pope Francis has not put himself at the forefront of tendentious issues in bioethics, noting that the Catholic Church's position on abortion, human embryonic stem-cell research, cloning, contraception, and euthanasia are well known. Some commentators have construed Pope Francis's deemphasis of such issues to signal a potential change of authoritative Catholic teaching. A careful review of various addresses, as well as assertions made in authoritative magisterial documents such as *Evangelii gaudium* (2013) and *Laudato si'* (2015), however, makes clear that Pope Francis affirms the church's teaching on these issues as defined by his predecessors. Nevertheless, he has proffered an additional moral lens through which to view such issues, namely, how they factor into the culture of waste that informs global society's "sin of indifference" to both environmental degradation and these associated life issues. In this regard, Pope Francis is recovering the "consistent ethic of life" popularized by the late Joseph Cardinal Bernardin.[3] The moral conclusions Pope Francis draws, far from advancing any sort of departure from previous Catholic teaching, instead provide an even stronger foundation for supporting a culture of life that crosses con-

---

1. See especially Pope John Paul II, *Evangelium vitae* (1995).
2. See especially Pope Paul VI, *Humanae vitae* (1968).
3. See Joseph Bernardin, *Consistent Ethic of Life*, ed. Thomas G. Feuchtmann (New York: Sheed & Ward, 1988); and Joseph Bernardin, *The Seamless Garment: Writings on a Consistent Ethic of Life*, ed. Thomas A. Nairn (Maryknoll, NY: Orbis Books, 2008).

servative and liberal political boundaries. In this chapter, we examine the continuity and development of the Catholic bioethical vision as evident in Pope Francis's writings, interviews, and addresses, as well as the implications thereof for the issues of abortion and euthanasia.

THE CULTURE OF LIFE VS. THE CULTURE OF DEATH

Within the first year of his papacy, Pope Francis gave an extensive interview in which he called for a tonal shift in how the Catholic Church should approach bioethical and related social issues that have predominated Catholic moral teaching for over four decades:

> We cannot insist only on issues related to abortion, gay marriage and the use of contraceptive methods. This is not possible. I have not spoken much about these things, and I was reprimanded for that. But when we speak about these issues, we have to talk about them in a context. The teaching of the church, for that matter, is clear and I am a son of the church, but it is not necessary to talk about these issues all the time.[4]

Some commentators found this shift in emphasis away from traditional life issues an unwelcome change that constitutes, or at least gives the appearance of, a surrender to secular values:

> By refraining from giving salient emphasis to condemnations of abortion and homosexual acts and instead by emphasizing populist themes in social justice, Francis has invited Roman Catholic bioethics to step away from issues of sexuality, reproduction, and abortion, and likely also from end-of-life decision-making. He is actively avoiding the topics that collide with the contemporary dominant secular culture, forever changing the face of Roman Catholic bioethics.[5]

---

4. Antonio Spadaro, "A Big Heart Open to God: An Interview with Pope Francis," *America*, September 30, 2013, 14–38, at 26.

5. Joseph Huneycutt, "Rejoice, for the Kingdom of Heaven Is at Hand! A Deconstruction of the Inaugural Message in the Words of Pope Francis," *Christian Bioethics* 21, no. 1 (2015): 73–83, at 74. For another critique, see Maurizio Mori, "An Address to Doctors by Pope Francis (November 15, 2014): A Doctrinal Mistake and a Lot of Common Sense Presented with Savoir-Faire," *Christian Bioethics* 21, no. 1 (2015): 109–29.

At best, critics charge, "Pope Francis is causing confusion among the faithful";[6] at worst, he is flirting with, or outright propagating, doctrinal heresy.[7]

Pope Francis anticipates and repudiates such criticisms by contending that the *joy* of the gospel—the title of his first apostolic exhortation, *Evangelii gaudium*—must constitute the church's primary proclamation, from which her moral teachings follow:

> The dogmatic and moral teachings of the church are not all equivalent. The church's pastoral ministry cannot be obsessed with the transmission of a disjointed multitude of doctrines to be imposed insistently. Proclamation in a missionary style focuses on the essentials, on the necessary things: this is also what fascinates and attracts more, what makes the heart burn, as it did for the disciples at Emmaus. We have to find a new balance; otherwise even the moral edifice of the church is likely to fall like a house of cards, losing the freshness and fragrance of the Gospel. The proposal of the Gospel must be more simple, profound, radiant. It is from this proposition that the moral consequences then flow.[8]

Grounding the church's moral teaching in the attractively joyful message of the gospel does not entail that Pope Francis has ceased altogether to discuss traditional bioethical issues or to invoke the enframing language of his predecessors: St. John Paul II's vision of a "culture of life" embattled with a "culture of death"[9] and Pope Benedict XVI's warning of a "dictatorship of relativism."[10] In fact, Pope Francis has explicitly included references to each in various addresses and magisterial documents, for instance:

> Pope Francis said that the [UN] should work towards goals which include providing "appropriate protection for the family, which is

---

6. Huneycutt, "Rejoice, for the Kingdom of Heaven is at Hand!," 74.

7. This is most evident in the *dubia* submitted by four cardinals calling for Pope Francis to clarify his stance on the indissolubility of marriage and the intrinsic wrongness of divorce after the promulgation of *Amoris laetitia* (2016): http://www.ncregister.com/blog/edward-pentin/full-text-and-explanatory-notes-of-cardinals-questions-on-amoris-laetitia; as well as a letter of "filial correction" signed by numerous Catholic scholars and clergy: http://www.correctiofilialis.org/wp-content/uploads/2017/08/Correctio-filialis_English_1.pdf.

8. Spadaro, "A Big Heart Open to God," 26.

9. See, for example, *EV* 21.

10. See Joseph Ratzinger, "Homily of the Mass *Pro Eligendo Romano Pontifice*," April 18, 2005, http://www.vatican.va.

an essential element in sustainable human development. Specifically, this involves challenging all forms of injustice and resisting the "economy of exclusion," the "throw-away culture" and the "culture of death" which nowadays sadly risk become passively accepted.[11]

Every life is sacred! Let us go forward with the culture of life to counter the logic of waste and the declining birth rate; let us be close and together let us pray for the babies who are threatened by the termination of pregnancy, as well as for the people who are at the end of life—every life is sacred!—so that no one may be left alone and that love may defend the meaning of life.[12]

A mandate: *be witnesses and diffusers of the "culture of life."* Your being Catholic entails a greater responsibility . . . to contemporary culture, by contributing to recognizing the transcendent dimension of human life, the imprint of God's creative work, from the first moment of its conception. . . . The Lord is counting on you to spread the "gospel of life."[13]

Realities are greater than ideas. This calls for rejecting the various means of masking reality: angelic forms of purity, dictatorships of relativism, empty rhetoric, objectives more ideal than real, brands of ahistorical fundamentalism, ethical systems bereft of kindness, intellectual discourse bereft of wisdom.[14]

Most significantly, Pope Francis explicitly links the "culture of relativism" with the "culture of waste" that impacts various social and bioethical issues:

---

11. Kerri Lenartowick, "Pope Urges UN Leadership to Resist 'Culture of Death,'" *Catholic News Agency*, May 9, 2014, https://www.catholicnewsagency.com. Pope Francis also cites approvingly St. John Paul II's affirmation of the family as the initial locus of education in the "culture of life" against the "culture of death" in *LS* 213.

12. Pope Francis, "Angelus," February 5, 2017, http://w2.vatican.va.

13. Pope Francis, "Address to Participants in the Meeting Organized by the International Federation of Catholic Medical Associations," 3, https://w2.vatican.va.

14. *EG* 231. Other instances where Pope Francis warns against the dangers of various forms of relativism include *EG* 61, 64, 80, 167; *Lumen fidei* (2013), no. 25; *LS* 122–23; *AL* 307; and his "Address to the Italian National Committee for Bioethics," January 28, 2016, https://zenit.org. See also John L. Allen Jr., "Francis Vows to Press Benedict's Fight vs. 'Dictatorship of Relativism,'" *National Catholic Reporter*, March 22, 2013, https://www.ncronline.org.

The culture of relativism is the same disorder which drives one person to take advantage of another, to treat others as mere objects, imposing forced labor on them or enslaving them to pay their debts. The same kind of thinking leads to the sexual exploitation of children and abandonment of the elderly who no longer serve our interests. . . . In the absence of objective truths or sound principles other than the satisfaction of our own desires and immediate needs, what limits can be placed on human trafficking, organized crime, the drug trade, commerce in blood diamonds and the fur of endangered species? Is it not the same relativistic logic which justifies buying the organs of the poor for resale or use in experimentation, or eliminating children because they are not what their parents wanted? This same "use and throw away" logic generates so much waste, because of the disordered desire to consume more than what is really necessary.[15]

Far from rejecting the moral frameworks through which St. John Paul II and Pope Benedict XVI evaluate various bioethical issues, Pope Francis adopts a complementary lens which views problems such as abortion, euthanasia, and environmental degradation "as emerging from consumerism and a throwaway culture, as well as a set of social circumstances in which inequality begets inequality."[16]

THE CULTURE OF WASTE AND
THE "SEAMLESS GARMENT"

In 1970, Van Rensselaer Potter coined the term "bioethics" to refer to the integration of scientific and normative reasoning to address issues of medical and ecological concern, understanding both arenas to have a direct impact on human health and survival.[17] Since then, the term has come to refer almost exclusively to the study of issues in the

---

15. *LS* 123.

16. Christopher Tollefsen, "Pope Francis and Abortion," *Christian Bioethics* 21, no. 1 (2015): 56–68, at 59. See also Ana S. Iltis, "Whither the Future? Pope Francis and Roman Catholic Bioethics," *Christian Bioethics* 21, no. 1 (2015): 1–10.

17. See Van Rensselaer Potter, "Bioethics: The Science of Survival," *Perspectives in Biology and Medicine* 14, no. 1 (1970): 127–53; Van Rensselaer Potter, *Bioethics: Bridge to the Future* (Englewood Cliffs, NJ: Prentice-Hall, 1971). See also Henk A. M. J. ten Have, "Potter's Notion of Bioethics," *Kennedy Institute of Ethics Journal* 22, no. 1 (2012): 59–82; Cory Andrew Labrecque, "Catholic Bioethics in the Anthropocene: Integrating Ecology, Religion, and Human Health," *National Catholic Bioethics Quarterly* 1, no. 4 (2015): 665–71, esp. 669.

biomedical arena, with *environmental ethics* becoming a distinct field of scholarship, activism, and policy making.[18] Today, therefore, bioethics has an almost exclusively *anthropocentric* focus—excepting the ethics of experimentation on nonhuman animals. A similar anthropocentrism can be found in the Catholic approach to bioethics as well, with the primary concern being issues that directly involve the medical care of, research upon, or manipulation of human life, from St. Paul VI's *Humanae vitae* to the Congregation for the Doctrine of the Faith's [CDF] *Declaration on Procured Abortion* (1974), *Declaration on Euthanasia* (1980), *Donum vitae* (1987), and *Dignitas personae* (2008), as well as St. John Paul II's *Evangelium vitae*. It was not until Pope Benedict XVI that ecological concerns began to be explicitly highlighted by the papal magisterium:

> In nature, the believer recognizes the wonderful result of God's creative activity, which we may use responsibly to satisfy our legitimate needs, material or otherwise, while respecting the intrinsic balance of creation. If this vision is lost, we end up either considering nature an untouchable taboo or, on the contrary, abusing it. Neither attitude is consonant with the Christian vision of nature as the fruit of God's creation. . . . Nature is at our disposal not as "a heap of scattered refuse," but as a gift of the Creator who has given it an inbuilt order, enabling man to draw from it the principles needed in order "to till it and keep it" (Gen 2:15) . . . it is a wondrous work of the Creator containing a "grammar" which sets forth ends and criteria for its wise use, not its reckless exploitation.[19]

It took Pope Francis's *Laudato si'*, however, to bring Catholic bioethics full-circle to Potter's original vision by explicitly linking ethical concerns regarding the *bio*sphere with those regarding human *bio*logy and broader social justice issues.[20]

Pope Francis diagnoses the source of environmental degradation, marginalization, and exploitation of the poor, and various offenses against human life as comprising a set of beliefs, values, and practices that characterize a culture of waste—or throwaway culture.[21] While

---

18. This narrowing of focus prompted Potter to publish a follow-up book entitled *Global Bioethics: Building on the Leopold Legacy* (East Lansing: Michigan State University Press, 1988).

19. *CV* 48.

20. See Daniel R. DiLeo, "Care for Persons, Care for Planet," *Health Progress* 95, no. 5 (2014): 35–37.

21. Pope Francis is not the first Catholic authority to invoke this concept. The U.S. Catholic bishops utilize similar language in their *Economic Justice for*

the impact of wastefulness on the environment is clearly evident, the same mindset that generates material waste "affects the excluded just as it quickly reduces things to rubbish."[22] This engrained cultural mentality leads to the exclusion of the poor from just moral consideration, often resulting in their being "treated merely as collateral damage"[23] for the sake of promoting industrialization.[24] The same sin of indifference also

> asks for the elimination of human beings, especially if they are physically or socially weaker. Our response to this mentality is a decisive and unreserved "yes" to life. . . . Things have a price and can be sold, but people have a dignity; they are worth more than things and are above price. So often we find ourselves in situations where we see that what is valued the least is life. That is why the concern for human life in its totality has become in recent years a real priority for the Church's Magisterium, especially for the most defenseless; i.e., the disabled, the sick, the newborn,[25] children, the elderly, those whose lives are most defenseless.[26]

All (1986), no. 334: "Together we must reflect on our own personal and family decisions and curb unnecessary wants in order to meet the needs of others. There are many questions we must keep asking ourselves: Are we becoming ever more wasteful in a 'throw-away' society? Are we able to distinguish between our true needs and those thrust on us by advertising and a society that values consumption more than saving?"

22. *LS* 22.

23. *LS* 49.

24. Pope Francis's thesis here is supported by statistics demonstrating the increased rate of diseases born by the poor, not only in economically developing countries, but even within economically prosperous nations. The American Lung Association, for instance, notes that "Studies have linked air pollution to heart disease, cancer, asthma, other illnesses, and even death. Communities of color are especially vulnerable as both African Americans and Hispanics have been found to be more likely than Caucasians to live in areas with high levels of air toxics and that are disproportionately located near freeways and other areas with heavy traffic" (*State of Lung Disease in Diverse Communities* [2010], 6, http://action.lung. org/site/DocServer/state-of-lung-disease-in-diverse-communities-2010.pdf? docID=8744).

25. Elizabeth Ramage notes that the original Italian of Pope Francis's address has "the unborn child" in place of "the newborn," the latter being used in the official Vatican English translation quoted here. See Elizabeth Ramage, "Pope Francis on Health Care: A Missionary among Us," *National Catholic Bioethics Quarterly* 14, no. 3 (2014): 421–28, at 424n26.

26. Pope Francis, "Address to Participants in the Meeting Organized by the International Federation of Catholic Medical Associations," 2, https://w2.vatican. va.

Pope Francis repeatedly invokes those impacted by the culture of waste: "The victims of this culture are precisely the weakest and most fragile human beings—the unborn, the poorest, the sick and elderly, the seriously handicapped, et al.—who are in danger of being 'thrown away,' expelled from a system that must be efficient at all costs."[27] He calls upon bioethics to "confront, through critical effort, the reasons and conditions required by the dignity of the human person with the developments of the sciences and of the biological and medical technologies, which, in their accelerated rhythm, risk losing every reference that is not useful and profitable."[28] He further emphasizes that "in a society inclined to competition, to the acceleration of progress," bioethics must rise to "the challenge of opposing the throwaway culture, which has so many expressions today, among which is treating human embryos as disposable material, and also sick and elderly persons approaching death."[29]

This thesis is supported by classical virtue theory, in which engrained habits of thought and action characterize one's moral attitudes and behaviors.[30] Saint Thomas Aquinas, for instance, argues that at least one of the reasons human beings should show pity to suffering animals is that it renders us more disposed toward feeling compassion for other human beings:

> But if man's affection be one of passion, then it is moved also in regard to other animals: for since the passion of pity is caused by the afflictions of others; and since it happens that even irrational animals are sensible to pain, it is possible for the affection of pity to arise in a man with regard to the sufferings of animals. Now it is evident that if a man practice a pitiful affection for animals, he is all the more disposed to take pity on his fellow-men.[31]

Echoing this congruence of moral feeling and action, Pope Francis concludes:

> It follows that our indifference or cruelty towards fellow creatures of this world sooner or later affects the treatment we mete

---

27. Pope Francis, "Address to a Delegation from the *Dignitatis Humanae* Institute," December 7, 2013, https://w2.vatican.va.

28. Pope Francis, "Address to the Italian National Committee for Bioethics."

29. Ibid.

30. See Aristotle, *Nicomachean Ethics*, 2nd ed., trans. Terence Irwin (Indianapolis, IN: Hackett, 1999); Thomas Aquinas, *Summa Theologiae*, trans. English Dominican Fathers (New York: Benziger, 1948), Ia-IIae, qq. 49–67.

31. Aquinas, *Summa Theologiae*, Ia-IIae, q. 102, a. 6 *ad* 8.

out to other human beings. We have only one heart, and the same wretchedness which leads us to mistreat an animal will not be long in showing itself in our relationships with other people.[32]

Pope Francis is widening the fabric of the "seamless garment" of integrally related life issues.[33] This image was popularized by Cardinal Bernardin to describe a "consistent ethic of life," which recognizes that a singular moral vision should inform one's assessment of any social issue in which the survival and well-being of human life is implicated, including abortion, euthanasia, biomedical research, access to health care, poverty, the death penalty, and warfare. Pope Francis has augmented this unified moral vision with ecological concerns insofar as they are inherently integrated with these other social issues. Pope Francis is not a unique magisterial voice in this regard, as Pope Benedict XVI also recognizes that engrained moral attitudes toward certain life issues inform individual or social attitudes toward other related issues:

> If personal and social sensitivity towards the acceptance of new life is lost, then other forms of acceptance that are valuable for society also wither away. The acceptance of life strengthens moral fibre and makes people capable of mutual help. By cultivating openness to life, wealthy peoples can better understand the needs of poor ones, they can avoid employing huge economic and intellectual resources to satisfy the selfish desires of their own citizens, and instead, they can promote virtuous action within the perspective of production that is morally sound and marked by solidarity, respecting the fundamental right to life of every people and every individual.[34]

In sum, there is a mutual feedback loop between individual and societal attitudes, behaviors, and policies with respect to human persons at the margins of life, the poor and vulnerable, as well as other animals and the environment. Moral concern, practical action, and just policy-making with respect to these issues cannot be compartmentalized into standard liberal and conservative political camps insofar as representative parties often do not adequately engage all of these interconnected issues in a consistent, morally justifiable fash-

---

32. *LS* 92.
33. See James F. Keenan, "The Francis Effect on Health Care: A Consistent Ethic of Life in a Throwaway Culture," *America*, May 28, 2018, 19–23.
34. *CV* 28.

ion. As Pope Francis affirms once again in his apostolic exhortation *Gaudete et exsultate* (2018):

> Our defence of the innocent unborn . . . needs to be clear, firm and passionate, for at stake is the dignity of a human life, which is always sacred and demands love for each person, regardless of his or her stage of development. Equally sacred, however, are the lives of the poor, those already born, the destitute, the abandoned and the underprivileged, the vulnerable infirm and elderly exposed to covert euthanasia, the victims of human trafficking, new forms of slavery, and every form of rejection.[35]

Referring to the particular politically charged issue of migrants and refugees, Pope Francis distinguishes political rhetoric from the moral obligation of Christian disciples:

> Some Catholics consider [the situation of migrants] a secondary issue compared to the "grave" bioethical questions. That a politician looking for votes might say such a thing is understandable, but not a Christian, for whom the only proper attitude is to stand in the shoes of those brothers and sisters of ours who risk their lives to offer a future to their children.[36]

The all-encompassing moral precept needed to inform adequate engagement with these varied issues is *inclusive justice*.[37] This precept, while it should inform both individual choices and social policy-making, does not dictate any particular political or economic system. As Joseph Boyle contends, "equality of human dignity does not underwrite political egalitarianism"; nevertheless, "inequalities in wealth are often morally significant because they reflect the inability of some people to develop capacities and access resources for a decent human life."[38] Having elucidated Pope Francis's comprehensive bio-

---

35. *GE* 101.

36. *GE* 102.

37. See Larry Snyder, "Changing the Conversation," *Health Progress* 95, no. 5 (2014): 13–15. For further analysis of how inclusive justice should inform Catholic bioethics, see Lisa Sowle Cahill, *Theological Bioethics: Participation, Justice, and Change* (Washington, DC: Georgetown University Press, 2005).

38. Joseph Boyle, "Franciscan Compassion and Catholic Bioethical Engagement," *Christian Bioethics* 21, no. 1 (2015): 35–55, at 49. For further discussion of the concept of justice as fostering human capabilities, see Martha Nussbaum, *Creating Capabilities: The Human Development Approach* (Cambridge, MA: Harvard University Press, 2011).

ethical vision, let us now consider some implications thereof that he has explicitly discussed and the continuity of his teaching with that of his predecessors.

BIOETHICAL IMPLICATIONS OF POPE FRANCIS'S VISION

Abortion and Support for Women

Pope Francis has made clear that he has not altered the church's moral condemnation of the act of directly intended abortion:

> Among the vulnerable for whom the Church wishes to care with particular love and concern are unborn children, the most defenceless and innocent among us . . . defence of unborn life is closely linked to the defence of each and every other human right. . . . Human beings are ends in themselves and never a means of resolving other problems . . . the Church cannot be expected to change her position on this question. I want to be completely honest in this regard. This is not something subject to alleged reforms or "modernizations." It is not "progressive" to try to resolve problems by eliminating a human life.[39]

As noted earlier, Pope Francis explicitly cites abortion as endemic to the "throwaway culture" that sees embryonic and fetal life as disposable for the sake of economic convenience or to avoid other associated burdens of pregnancy and child rearing. He has, however, emphasized the essential role of *mercy* in approaching women who have faced the difficult choice of whether to abort, often in the light of pressures from those—including and especially the child's father—who fail to offer emotional and material support, ranging from condemnatory families who ostracize such women to societies that neglect to provide opportunities for both her and her child to flourish educationally and economically: "We have done little to adequately accompany women in very difficult situations, where abortion appears as a quick solution to their profound anguish, especially when the life developing within them is the result of rape or a situation of extreme poverty. Who can remain unmoved before such painful situations?"[40] Thus, while maintaining that directly intended abortion is a grave sin and those who intentionally procure

---

39. *EG* 213–14.
40. *EG* 214.

an abortion are automatically excommunicated from the church,[41] Pope Francis nevertheless allows priests—initially during the Jubilee Year of Mercy in 2016 but then extending it indefinitely—to forgive women who confess "with contrite heart" to having procured an abortion and lift their canonical excommunication.[42]

As Nicanor Austriaco notes, mercy "is a virtue that not only moves us to feel compassion for someone who is suffering but also moves us to do something about it."[43] For Pope Francis, the church is called to take action not only by extending the sacrament of Reconciliation, but also by providing other forms of emotional and material support for women, ameliorating the pressure many feel to make the choice to abort, as well as providing healing to women who have chosen to abort or others whose lives have been impacted by such a choice.[44]

Pope Francis is not adding something novel to the church's teaching but is reemphasizing a concern for the plight of women voiced previously by St. John Paul II:

> As well as the mother, there are often other people too who decide upon the death of the child in the womb. In the first place, the father of the child may be to blame, not only when he directly pressures the woman to have an abortion, but also when he indirectly encourages such a decision on her part by leaving her alone to face the problems of pregnancy: in this way the family is thus mortally wounded and profaned in its nature as a community of love and in its vocation to be the "sanctuary of life."[45]

He also refers to the Gospel story of the woman caught in adultery and Christ's statement to the men present that her sin is a confirmation of their own sin (John 8:3–11). Relating this story to the issue of unwed pregnancies, St. John Paul II recognizes that women are often

---

41. See *Code of Canon Law* (1983), §1398: "a person who procures a completed abortion incurs a *latae sententiae* [i.e., automatic] excommunication."

42. See Pope Francis, *Misericordia et misera* (2016), no. 12; "Letter according to Which an Indulgence Is Granted to the Faithful on the Occasion of the Extraordinary Jubilee of Mercy," September 1, 2015, https://w2.vatican.va.

43. Nicanor Pier Giorgio Austriaco, "Preaching Catholic Bioethics with Joy and Mercy," *National Catholic Bioethics Quarterly* 14, no. 2 (2014): 217–26, at 225; citing Aquinas, *Summa Theologiae*, IIa-IIae, q. 30, a. 1.

44. A prime example of this type of healing ministry is Catholic Charities' "Project Rachel"; see http://hopeafterabortion.com. For further discussion of Pope Francis's call for *merciful accompaniment* of women facing, or who have made, the choice to abort, see Tollefsen, "Pope Francis and Abortion," 64–65.

45. *EV* 59.

left alone to confront this particular consequence of illicit sexual union due to the men involved disavowing any responsibility:

> A woman is left alone, exposed to public opinion with "her sin," while behind "her" sin there lurks a man—a sinner, guilty "of the other's sin," indeed equally responsible for it. And yet his sin escapes notice, it is passed over in silence: he does not appear to be responsible for "the other's sin"! Sometimes, forgetting his own sin, he even makes himself the accuser, as in the case described. How often, in a similar way, the woman pays for her own sin . . . she alone pays and she pays all alone! How often is she abandoned with her pregnancy, when the man, the child's father, is unwilling to accept responsibility for it? And besides the many "unwed mothers" in our society, we also must consider all those who, as a result of various pressures, even on the part of the guilty man, very often "get rid of" the child before it is born. "They get rid of it": but at what price?[46]

An injustice is done to women who are abandoned to face an unintended pregnancy alone. Those who choose to keep and raise the child often endure social and economic burdens; those who choose to give their child up for adoption face significant emotional hardship; and those who choose to abort may suffer severe physical and emotional scars, as well as the scorn of those who consider their action morally reprehensible. Such is the price women often must pay alone.[47]

Euthanasia and Care of the Dying

Another group identified by Pope Francis as paradigmatic victims of the culture of waste are the elderly, the disabled, and the terminally ill, for whom euthanasia or physician-assisted suicide is sometimes offered as a means to alleviate physical and existential suffering. Neither denying nor downplaying the reality of intense suffering such individuals may experience, Pope Francis nevertheless notes that suffering often results from *neglect*, another aspect of the sin of indifference that infects many modern cultures. As an antidote, he calls for *authentic compassion* and *accompaniment* of those confronting their vulnerability and mortality:

---

46. Pope John Paul II, *Mulieris dignitatem* (1988), no. 14.

47. For further discussion, see Jason T. Eberl, "Cultivating the Virtue of Acknowledged Responsibility," *Proceedings of the American Catholic Philosophical Association* 82 (2008): 39–51.

Compassion does not mean pity, it means "suffering with.". . . True compassion does not marginalize anyone, nor does it humiliate and exclude—much less considers the disappearance of a person as a good thing. You are well aware of the meaning of the triumph of selfishness, of this "throwaway culture" that rejects and dismisses those who do not comply with certain canons of health, beauty and utility. . . . Therefore, we must not give in to the functionalist temptation to apply rapid and drastic solutions, moved by false compassion or by mere criteria of efficiency or cost-effectiveness. The dignity of human life is at stake.[48]

Warning of a "logic of usefulness [that] takes precedence over that of solidarity and gratuitousness, even within the family,"[49] Pope Francis invokes a concept he utilizes in *Laudato si'* to ground our duty to future inhabitants of this planet: *intergenerational solidarity*.[50] In this case, though, he reverses the order to affirm what is owed to those who came before us:

The objective of palliative care is to alleviate suffering in the final stages of illness and at the same time to ensure the patient appropriate human accompaniment. It is important support especially for the elderly, who, because of their age, receive increasingly less attention from curative medicine and are often abandoned. Abandonment is the most serious "illness" of the elderly and also the greatest injustice they can be submitted to: those who have helped us grow must not be abandoned when they are in need of our help, our love, and our tenderness.[51]

Pope Francis is emphasizing a culture of encounter in opposition to the culture of waste in which we compassionately confront our own fragility and mortality by caring for those for whom the inherent limits of human life in this world have become manifest. Emphasizing the essential importance of *interpersonal encounter*, he again echoes St. John Paul II:

Here we are faced with one of the more alarming symptoms of the "culture of death" . . . marked by an attitude of excessive

---

48. Pope Francis, "Address to the Medical Orders of Spain and Latin America," June 9, 2016, https://press.vatican.va.

49. Pope Francis, "Address to the Pontifical Academy for Life," *National Catholic Bioethics Quarterly* 15, no. 3 (2015): 549–51, at 550.

50. *LS* 159.

51. Pope Francis, "Address to the Pontifical Academy for Life," 550.

preoccupation with efficiency and which sees the growing number of elderly and disabled people as intolerable and too burdensome. These people are very often isolated by their families and by society, which are organized almost exclusively on the basis of criteria of productive efficiency, according to which a hopelessly impaired life no longer has any value.[52]

The request which arises from the human heart in the supreme confrontation with suffering and death, especially when faced with the temptation to give up in utter desperation, is above all a request for companionship, sympathy and support in the time of trial. It is a plea for help to keep on hoping when all human hopes fail.[53]

Note that accompanying the dying does not require that every measure be taken to sustain life indefinitely. Warning against "overzealous treatment,"[54] Pope Francis aligns with the teaching of Venerable Pius XII[55] and the CDF's call for "due proportion in the use of remedies," which informs the CDF's conclusion that "it is permitted in conscience to take the decision to refuse forms of treatment that would only secure a precarious and burdensome prolongation of life."[56]

CONCLUSION

Although we have emphasized the continuity of Pope Francis's bioethical teachings with his predecessors, he has advocated for and exemplified an apparent shift in the church's approach to bioethical issues, changing the tone from mere condemnation to an emphasis on *mercy* and *joy*: "proclaiming Christ means showing that to believe in and to follow him is not only something right and true, but also something beautiful, capable of filling life with new splendor and profound

---

52. *EV* 64.

53. *EV* 67. For further discussion, see Jason T. Eberl, "I Am My Brother's Keeper: Communitarian Obligations to the Dying Person," *Christian Bioethics* 24, no. 1 (2018): 38–58.

54. Claire Giangravè, "Pope Francis Calls European Physicians to Morally Withdraw from 'Overzealous Treatment,'" *CRUX*, November 16, 2017, https://cruxnow.com.

55. Pope Pius XII, "Address to the IXth Congress of the Italian Anaesthesiological Society," February 24, 1957: AAS 49 (1957), 147.

56. Congregation for the Doctrine of the Faith, *Declaration on Euthanasia* (1980), §IV.

joy, even in the midst of difficulties."[57] This shift may be more a matter of perception than reality, however, insofar as Pope John Paul II made mercy the central theme of his second encyclical, *Dives in misericordia* (1980), and a renewed emphasis on witnessing to the joyfulness of Christian discipleship and human life in general can be traced back to Vatican II's *Gaudium et spes* (1965).[58] Nevertheless, Pope Francis has reoriented Catholic teaching from a narrow focus on particular issues to the wider context in which such issues arise and must be addressed *systemically*.[59] He further challenges us to confront these issues within the health care context, to "take on the 'smell of the sheep'"[60] and create a "culture of encounter and peace, where the experience of illness and suffering, along with professional and fraternal assistance, helps to overcome every limitation and division."[61]

---

57. *EG* 167. Pope Francis's views on divine mercy can be found in his conversation with Andrea Tornielli, *The Name of God Is Mercy* (New York: Random House, 2016); and on how mercy should inform the church's mission in his *The Church of Mercy* (Chicago: Loyola University Press, 2014). A significant influence on Pope Francis's thinking in this regard is Walter Kasper's *Mercy: The Essence of the Gospel and the Key to Christian Life* (New York: Paulist Press, 2014).

58. My thanks to Gregory Beabout for calling my attention to this point.

59. As John Gallagher notes, Pope Francis's challenge is primarily aimed at *institutions* that support practices that foster these concerns; see John Gallagher, "Pope Francis's Potential Impact on American Bioethics," *Christian Bioethics* 21, no. 1 (2015): 11–34, esp. 29–32. For further elaboration of the role of institutions in the cultivation of virtuous or vicious practices, see Alasdair MacIntyre, *After Virtue: A Study in Moral Theory*, 3rd ed. (Notre Dame, IN: University of Notre Dame Press, 2007), chap. 14, esp. 194–95.

60. *EG* 24. See Ron Hamel, "The Vision of Pope Francis: A 'Disruptor' for Catholic Health Care and Ethics?," *Health Progress* 95, no. 5 (2014): 70–72.

61. Pope Francis, "'Service to the Sick': Message for the Twenty-Fourth World Day of the Sick," *National Catholic Bioethics Quarterly* 16, no. 1 (2016): 135–38, at 137. For some examples of how Pope Francis's teachings are being operationalized within Catholic health care, see Eileen L. Barsi, "'Come and See!' Living the Teachings of Pope Francis," *Health Progress* 95, no. 5 (2014): 64–65.

I am grateful for helpful feedback on drafts of this paper from audiences at "Pope Francis, A Voice Crying Out in the World: Mercy, Justice, Love and Care for the Earth," sponsored by Villanova University, the 73rd Annual Convention of the Catholic Theological Society of America, the Saint Louis University Bicentennial Health and Social Justice Conference, and the Catholic Medical Association's 87th Annual Educational Conference.

Contributors

Margaret S. Archer is past president of the Pontifical Academy of Social Sciences, and professor of sociology and director of the Center for Social Ontology at the University of Warwick, Coventry, England. She is one of the most influential theorists in the critical realist tradition. At the 12th World Congress of Sociology, she was elected as the first woman president of the International Sociological Association. She is a founding member of both the Pontifical Academy of Social Sciences and the Academy of Learned Societies in the Social Sciences. She is also a trustee of the Centre for Critical Realism.

Jason T. Eberl is a professor of health care ethics at Saint Louis University. He has authored three books: *Contemporary Controversies in Catholic Bioethics*; *The Routledge Guidebook to Aquinas' Summa Theologiae*; and *Thomistic Principles and Bioethics*. His articles have appeared in, among others, *Linacre Quarterly*, *Journal of Medicine and Philosophy*, *Theoretical Medicine and Bioethics*, and *National Catholic Bioethics Quarterly*.

Massimo Faggioli is a professor of theology and religious studies at Villanova University. Since 2014, he has been a columnist for *La Croix International*; he also writes for *Commonweal* magazine. Selected books include *The Legacy of Vatican II* (edited with Andrea Vicini, SJ); *The Rising Laity: Ecclesial Movements since Vatican II*; and *Catholicism and Citizenship: Political Cultures of the Church in the 21st Century*.

Austen Ivereigh is a writer, journalist, and cofounder of Catholic Voices. He is author of the biography *The Great Reformer: Francis and the Making of a Radical Pope*; *Faithful Citizens: A Practical Guide to Catholic Social Teaching and Community Organising*; and *Catholicism and Politics in Argentina 1810–1960*. He was formerly deputy editor of *The Tablet* and director for Public Affairs for the former archbishop of Westminster, Cardinal Cormac Murphy-O'Connor.

Óscar Andrés Cardinal Rodríguez Maradiaga is archbishop of Tegucigulpa, Honduras. He was president of the Latin American Episcopal Conference (CELAM) from 1995 to 1999 and of the Episcopal Conference of Honduras from 1996 to 2016, and served as president of Caritas Internationalis from 2007 to 2015. He coordinates the group of cardinals

271

advising Pope Francis on the reform of the Roman Curia, and he is a member of the 14th Ordinary Council of the Secretary-General of the Synod of Bishops and of the Pontifical Academy of Theology.

Thomas J. Massaro, SJ, is a professor of moral theology at Fordham University. His nine books—including *Living Justice: Catholic Social Teaching in Action*—and more than one hundred published articles are devoted to Catholic social teaching and its recommendations for public policies oriented to social justice, peace, worker rights, and poverty alleviation. His most recent book, *Mercy in Action*, analyzes Pope Francis's social teachings.

Marcus Mescher is an assistant professor of theology at Xavier University in Cincinnati, Ohio. He specializes in Catholic social teaching and moral formation, and he has contributed articles to the *Journal of Catholic Social Thought* and the *Journal of Moral Theology*, as well as chapters in several edited volumes. He is currently working on his forthcoming book, *The Ethics of Encounter: Christian Neighbor Love as a Practice of Solidarity*.

Christophère Ngolele, SJ, is studying sociocultural anthropology at KU Leuven in Belgium. A Jesuit priest and native of the Republic of Congo, he is interested in environmental ethics in relation to African culture, and he has developed a theory based on recognition and sacred care. He was a member of the steering committee of the Ignatian Family Teach-In for Justice, and is now a member of Catholic Theological Ethics in the World Church.

John O'Malley, SJ, is University Professor of the department of theology at Georgetown University. He is a prolific scholar and an expert on the Second Vatican Council, and has earned international acclaim for such books as *The First Jesuits* (which received both the Jacques Barzun Prize for Cultural History from the American Philosophical Society and the Philip Scaff Prize from the American Society for Church History); *Four Cultures of the West*; *What Happened at Vatican II*; and *Trent: What Happened at the Council*.

Agbonkhianmeghe E. Orobator, SJ, is president of the Conference of Major Superiors of Africa and Madagascar (JESAM). He is a member of the Eastern Africa Province of the Society of Jesus and comes originally from Nigeria. He currently serves as principal of Hekima University College and Institute of Peace Studies and International Relations in Nairobi, Kenya, a campus college of the Catholic University of Eastern Africa. His research focuses on theological ethics and ecclesiology of the Global South. He is the author of *The Church We*

Want: African Catholics Look to Vatican III and *Religion and Faith in Africa: Confessions of an Animist*. He is also a contributor to *Thinking Faith*, the online journal of the Jesuits in Britain.

Anna Rowlands is St. Hilda Associate Professor of Catholic Social Thought and Practice in the department of theology and religion at Durham University, UK. Her work focuses on theological ethics, asylum and migration, and the political theology of the common good. She works with a wide range of public organizations, including CAFOD, CSAN, Citizens UK, and the Jesuit Refugee Service. She is the author and co-author, respectively, of two forthcoming books, *Catholic Social Teaching: A Guide for the Perplexed* and the *T&T Clark Reader in Political Theology*. She writes occasionally for *The Tablet* and the ABC Religion & Ethics blog.

Annie Selak is a doctoral candidate in systematic theology at Boston College. Her research is in ecclesiology, focusing on issues of power and authority in the Roman Catholic Church. She integrates feminist theology, practical theology, and theological ethics in her approach, grounding her research questions in lived experience and pressing issues.

John Sniegocki is an associate professor of theology and Christian ethics at Xavier University in Cincinnati, Ohio. He is author of *Catholic Social Teaching and Economic Globalization: The Quest for Alternatives*, which draws from the fields of political economy, ecology, and theological ethics.

Antonio Spadaro, SJ, is the editor of *La Civiltà Cattolica*, a Jesuit periodical based in Rome. He published an exclusive interview in September 2013 with Pope Francis in which the pope offered some of his first public thoughts on the state of the church and his priorities. He also edited the first book about the pope for children, *Dear Pope Francis: The Pope Answers Letters from Children around the World*. He has published or edited about thirty volumes on theology and contemporary culture, including *Cybertheology: Thinking Christianity in the Era of the Internet*.

Joseph W. Cardinal Tobin, CSsR, is archbishop of Newark, NJ. In 2010, Pope Benedict XVI named him to the Roman Curia post of Secretary of the Congregation for Institutes of Consecrated Life and Societies of Apostolic Life, and titular Archbishop of Obba. In 2012, Pope Benedict appointed him to serve as the sixth archbishop of Indianapolis, and in 2016, Pope Francis named him to the College of Cardinals and assigned him to lead the Archdiocese of Newark, NJ.

Barbara E. Wall is vice president for mission and ministry and associate professor of philosophy at Villanova University. Since 2000, she has been overseeing the office responsible for ensuring that Villanova's Catholic, Augustinian mission and identity are integrated throughout the university. She founded the *Journal for Catholic Social Thought*, of which she also is the editor; and the *Journal for Peace and Justice Studies*, serving as co-editor for the first thirteen volumes. She is the author of *Love and Death in the Philosophy of Gabriel Marcel* and co-editor, with Kevin Hart, of *The Experience of God: A Postmodern Response*.

Index